A User's Guide to SSADM

Version 4

G Longworth

NCC Blackwell
MANCHESTER • OXFORD

British Library Cataloguing in Publication Data

G Longworth
A User's Guide to SSADM Version 4
I. Title
658.40380285421

ISBN 1-85554-136-X

First published in 1992 by:

NCC Blackwell Limited, 108 Cowley Road, Oxford OX4 1JF, England.

Editorial Office: The National Computing Centre Limited, Oxford Road, Manchester M1 7ED, England.

Typeset in 11pt Times Roman by M Wilson, The National Computing Centre Limited, Oxford Road, Manchester M1 7ED; and printed by Hobbs the Printers of Southampton.

ISBN 1-85554-136-X

Acknowledgements

SSADM, the Structured Systems Analysis and Design Method, was developed for the Central Computer and Telecommunications Agency (CCTA) in 1980. It is the standard method for IT projects in Central Government, and surveys show it to be the most widely-used method in the UK private sector. NCC and the CCTA collaborate on the development, support and promotion of SSADM.

I am indebted to the following people for the time they spent reviewing the draft. I am appreciative of the fact that they are all very busy people, but there is a saying that if you want something doing you should give it to a busy person. Their perceptive comments have been a great help, and the book is a better one for their involvement.

Steve Bouchier	Prinsys Limited
Alan Chard	Zodiac Computer Services Limited
Mr K F Horton	Crewe and Nantwich Borough Council
Dr G R Hudson	Handforth Health Centre, Cheshire
Phil Lomax	Model Systems
Michael McCann	Independent Consultant
Dr Ian Procter	Omnis IT Consultants Limited
Brian West	The National Computing Centre Limited
Chris Williams	Kingsley Enterprises

I should also like to acknowledge permission from CCTA to include the Reference Manual stage diagrams in Chapters 15–21.

Preface

SSADM, the Structured Systems Analysis and Design Method, has been in existence since 1980. It is a method to assist systems analysts and designers with their work, but it also requires the active participation of users if systems development is to be successful.

This book is meant for users of computer systems – 'end users' as they are often known to the technical people who are responsible for the actual computerisation of a project.

A 'user' is a person within a business who will be supplying information to a system or getting something from it. Users may therefore fulfil many different functions. for example, they may be:

- People who fill in forms which provide input to the system, eg salesmen on the road.

- Those who will be working at terminals, eg taking and entering orders.

- Staff who must do something with computer output, eg, people in warehouses who pick goods from the shelves.

- Departmental management, whose staff will be using a system, and who will thus be looking for an effective and efficient operation. They may also be responsible for higher level facilities within the system, such as authorising fulfilment of orders where there is a doubt about a customer's credit worthiness.

- Higher management, who will want to have systems that are effective ones for their company, and who may wish to obtain information from the system to help with the decision making processes and corporate strategy.

All of these are involved in some way with the resulting system. For it to be their system and not a technical one imposed by the developers from a partial understanding of requirements, requires their involvement throughout. Rather than write impersonally about 'users', it has been assumed that the reader will be a user with some degree of involvement in a computerisation project, and so the more personal reference to 'you' has often been used. 'You' means yourself and other users.

SSADM provides for just such a degree of involvement:

- in specifying requirements;
- in ensuring that the developers have understood your requirements;
- in ensuring that the emerging system will meet your requirements.

You need an understanding of SSADM in order to fulfil your duties and exercise your rights as a customer (including *caveat emptor!*). The aim of this book is to explain the nature of your involvement:

- where and when you will be involved;
- what you will see;
- what will be asked of you in an SSADM development environment;
- what decisions you must make.

This book updates *Getting the System You Want: A User's Guide to SSADM* It is in four parts:

Part 1 explains why it is necessary to use a method (a systematic and structured approach to the development of computer systems) for systems analysis and design, and how SSADM meets these needs. An overview of SSADM is given, and of the need for your involvement. The critical importance of setting objectives for the system is then discussed. Finally in this part, the elements of a system are considered to discover the information that must be established during systems analysis. Then what is done in SSADM will be seen to follow a logical and necessary pattern.

Part 2 looks at those techniques used in SSADM which will require your greatest involvement. It describes what directly affects you – what you will see, what you have to do, and how it all relates to the essential elements of systems. After an introduction about the diagrammatic approach, the three diagramming techniques of Data Flow Modelling, Logical Data Modelling and Entity-Event Modelling are described at the level of detail needed for you to understand them, and how they complement each other to give a three dimensional view of a system. This part is completed by a chapter on the heavily user-oriented

Requirements Catalogue. As its name implies, this Catalogue provides the opportunity for you to note what is wrong or lacking with the facilities you have at present, so that their inclusion in the new system can be considered.

Part 3 is devoted to the activities carried out in SSADM; described as stages, steps and tasks. This is the framework that the investigation follows, and on which the facts are hung as they are found. It can be regarded as prescriptive guidelines: prescriptive in that it sets out all the things that should be considered; guidelines in that it does require the employment of common sense and sound management, rather than blind faith that by doing everyting without thought or limit will somehow be an effective way of producing a system.

Part 4 introduces management implications. Whilst SSADM provides the tools and approach that aid the development of effective systems, it doesn't stop people from making mistakes and losing control. Quality control and project management are also required, and are catered for within the method. Practical aspects of these two subjects are dealt with, and a chapter is devoted to the tasks that will need to be considered when the method is brought into use in an organisation.

The final chapter is a general one about practical systems development. The topics covered range from the high level one of developing the right projects, continue with an introduction to development strategies, and conclude by considering the testing and implementation of your systems.

SSADM has undergone a number of enhancements since it was first introduced, and the commitment has been made to review it regularly in the light of research, experience, and comments received from its many users. The current version is Version 4, introduced in 1990, and is the one described here.

This book is one of a series produced by NCC Blackwell in support of SSADM. The others in the series are:

- *SSADM Manual Version 4.*
- *Introducing SSADM Version 4.*
- *SSADM: Models and Methods*

Version 3 of the method continues to be used by many organisations and is described in the following books, also available from The National Computing Centre Limited (NCC):

- *Introducing SSADM*
- *SSADM Manual*
- *SSADM Developer's Handbook*
- *Getting the System You Want: A User's Guide to SSADM.*

Contents

PART 3 SSADM ACTIVITIES

Part 1

SSADM and Users

1

Introduction

System development is not easy. One of the best descriptions of the task was given by Lawrence J Peters, in a thought-provoking consideration of the subject (*Peters, 1981*). He put into words what many developers had, to their cost, found but not defined or perhaps even realised before. Among his conclusions were:

- the solution of any difficulty can reveal even more serious difficulties;
- specifications are never complete: there is always something more that could be added;
- there is no single, correct solution to a problem: there is always the possibility that a better solution could be found given more time;
- there are no right or wrong solutions: only good or bad ones;
- neither the number of possible solutions nor the means of obtaining them is limited.

Development will take time, cost money and require management commitment, but in themselves these do not guarantee the perfect system. It must be accepted that perfection, in the shape of a system that will do everything that everyone wants, that will never fail, and will never need to be changed, is impossible. What *is* possible is to build effective systems that can achieve those objectives that have been precisely specified. This can be done given four provisos:

- The computer department must be technically competent and capable of delivering good systems - SSADM is an aid to competence.
- The opportunity must be offered to you as a user to be actively involved in the development process – and SSADM requires this.
- The design must be capable of coping with the changes that are inevitable in a dynamic business environment – and SSADM aims to provide simple data structures that are capable of change at minimum cost.

- The documentation produced by the developers must be understandable by you – and a prodigiously thick English narrative specification is rarely understandable and is also usually ambiguous. If there is any ambiguity, it is a safe bet that you will read it one way and that other people during the further development of the system will read it in a different way. SSADM avoids this with documentation that, being diagrammatic, is neither ambiguous nor difficult to understand.

The 'Them and Us' situation is regrettably common in many aspects of human relationships – Catholics and Protestants, East and West, home and away teams, men and women, management and unions and, in computer terms, users and developers. In other words there are two sides, and when anything goes wrong, each blames the other. "You never *told* me that," says the analyst. "You never *asked* me that," responds the user.

SSADM gives the opportunity to get away from all that. Development becomes a team effort involving management, users and practitioners. If you don't take the opportunities offered by SSADM, then you mustn't be too surprised if the computer system leaves much to be desired. If you abdicate all responsibility to the developers, you will most certainly get the system you deserve – but it may not be a good one. You may not like it very much. It is likely to do what the developers *thought* that you would want, and this could be a long way from your real requirements. So you and the developers must communicate effectively with each other, and to do so you need to understand something of methods in general, and SSADM in particular.

It is a responsibility of corporate management to ensure that:

- the systems being developed are the right ones for the company;
- the expense and time involved are justifiable and will help the company to meet its objectives;
- the development is proceeding according to plan.

It is a responsibility of user management to ensure that both they and their staff:

- co-operate with the developers in preparing a project plan;
- agree the user content of the plan;
- know what is expected of them during development;
- commit adequate resources to the project.

It is a responsibility of systems development management to ensure that technical resources with the necessary levels of:

- SSADM expertise;

– business experience;

– project management skills;

are all available as and when required, and that any divergence from the plan has been accepted by management before it is implemented.

SSADM is designed to involve users from the start of systems analysis. So you will be involved in:

– supplying information about what you do now (the current system);

– thinking about what could be done better, and what need not be done at all (current inefficiencies);

– specifying what the new system should do (additional requirements);

– specifying in measurable terms how well the new system is to perform (quality objectives);

– specifying in measurable terms the time and cost limits on development and operation of the new system (resource objectives);

– ensuring that your requirements are met (informally by helping with the checking and preparation of diagrams, and formally by participation in quality control).

There is no need for alarm. The level of knowledge of SSADM that you will require is much different for you than it is for the development staff. For example, you do not require the skills necessary to construct the various diagrams, but you must be able to understand the information presented on the diagrams produced by the developers. (It is worth noting that although it is not required, nevertheless many users do become involved in the construction of diagrams, and are quite likely to draw their own. You may well find yourself doing the same before long).

What will be required of you though, is the willingness to consider all the odd little quirks that have developed in your systems over the years, and to decide what you really require. Many of your procedures are likely to have been built up around departments and people. A computer system may well cut across existing boundaries within your company if it is to work effectively for you rather than merely duplicate what happens now. This is not the fault of the developers. What they should produce is the system that you would develop yourself if you were to ignore history and individuals, concentrating only on the most effective way of achieving your objectives. You would then in all probability find that you needed a different organisation, ie the changes are needed not because of the introduction of the computer, but because your existing organisation is lacking in a number of ways. Within the system the computer should be doing the things that a computer is good at, leaving the people to do the things that people are good at – managing, making decisions, resolving problems, and smoothing the ruffled feathers of customers when something has gone wrong.

With SSADM, and given your active involvement, effective high quality systems are within your reach.

2
Why a method is necessary

The first commercial data processing system went live in 1954 (payroll on a LEO computer). Yet, after nearly 40 years of data processing, system developments still often tend to be more of an art than a science; to be more closely related to anarchy than to discipline. Developments commonly overrun budgets on both time and cost, and fail to produce systems that meet the real needs of their users.

A survey (*PA Computers and Telecommunications, 1985*) showed that of the projects covered by their study:

- 66 percent stated a timescale overrun;
- 55 percent stated that effort was over budget;
- 58 percent were affected by a major unexpected problem.

Anyone reading the computer press will see reports almost every week of major projects that have gone off the rails. Things don't appear to have improved a great deal since 1985. Clearly a betting man would get good odds against work being completed to schedule.

It is instructive to consider what happens if a method is not used for system development. Without a method, every project is developed in a different way. (Projects developed in the same way each time *are* using a method.) Without a method, the chances are that the system is likely to be late, will probably cost more than was expected, and may well not do what the user expects or wants.

If systems are never developed in the same way twice, then there is no bank of expertise on which to draw – so there are major management and technical problems with:

- *Estimates.* Without comparable past experience, there is no firm foundation on which future estimates can be based. There are very severe problems in attempting to work to an over-optimistic estimate, particularly for anyone working to a fixed price contract. If the system is delivered on time, in these circumstances, then corners have probably been cut, often on testing, and such systems tend to be unreliable.

- *Control.* Control is notoriously inaccurate when based on estimates of how long it will take to finish a task. (Development staff are notoriously over-optimistic.) Effective control is only possible from the existence of completed work in the form of documentation *end products*) produced at the end of each task. The project manager must be able to establish the precise stage that the project has reached (by end products completed), and how far there is still to go (by tasks remaining).

- *Completeness.* Without some sort of checklist of activities, people cannot be sure that they have remembered to do everything. Anything that is missed or not done in the best sequence is going to cost more later on. The developers must try to do things at the best time. Pay now, or pay more later.

In the absence of a method, what exists is an uncontrollable, incomplete, free-for-all. Ad hoc approaches to development have a long history of not producing the goods. It is not the way to go about developing systems. As the free-for-all peters out, those involved in the project come to their final task – that of apportioning blame. A high staff turnover helps. Then the blame can be attributed to someone who has left.

Over the years a number of techniques has been found to improve specific areas of system development. The integration of techniques in a prescribed way constitutes a development method. Standardising on a method permits developments to be done in the same way each time, and thus provides a basis for estimation, management, control, and subsequent maintenance. It also ensures that the required skills can be defined and developed.

The *1987 NCC Members Survey* indicated that software development methods were used by only 32 percent of those who responded, and they tended to be the big organisations employing in excess of 10,000 people. Yet clearly the use of methods was worthwhile. Among the percentage improvements reported were:

- quality of product 33 percent;
- productivity of staff 22 percent;
- timeliness of delivery 17 percent;
- system life cycle costs 28 percent.

Perhaps yours is a much smaller business. Will the method work in your organisation? The answer is an unqualified YES. It is difficult to envisage any system that would take more than a handful of man days to develop, that would not benefit from the *intelligent* application of SSADM.

Successful organisations and staff are constantly striving to improve their performance. The question for them to ask should not be "Should our organisation be using a method?" but rather:

"Can it afford not to use a method?"

3 What SSADM has to offer

INTRODUCTION

In claiming a method as being the best, the question must arise, "Best for what?" No one method could hope to be perfect for:

- every type of system development;
- every level of complexity;
- every size of installation;
- all levels of experience;
- all sizes of teams;
- all cost and time constraints;
- all languages or development environments in which a system may be implemented.

With literally hundreds of methods, techniques and approaches from which to choose, and with existing methods themselves undergoing constant development, it would be rash indeed to claim SSADM as the best. What can be claimed for SSADM is that it is a good, well tried method, and that it works well in the area of development at which it is aimed – the analysis and design of commercial data processing and information systems.

However, SSADM does have many attributes. It is worth recounting reasons why it was chosen by, and developed with, the Central Computer and Telecommunications Agency (CCTA – the UK government department with overall responsibility for information technology in the civil service), and why it was subsequently chosen as the method to be supported by The National Computing Centre Limited. Many of these considerations will also apply within your own organisation.

HISTORY

Civil Service computing departments, in common with many in the private sector, suffer from a high staff turnover and the consequent lack of a sufficient number of experienced people. They required a way of working that would enable inexperienced people to make an effective contribution quickly, and this was seen as being a method that:

- was already in existence (1980) and close to being what they wanted;
- could be taught easily;
- would dovetail with their standard method of program design; essentially Jackson Structured Programming, or JSP (*Jackson 1975, Ingevaldsson 1980*);
- would dovetail with project control;
- was capable of support by software tools (ie computer programs to help the analyst with his work).

CCTA considered many methods before eventually choosing the one which, after further development, became SSADM.

In 1984, as part of a study sponsored by the Commission of the European Communities and the United Kingdom Government, NCC undertook to establish the ideal attributes for a method and then to review some of those which were then currently available, to see how they matched this 'ideal'. Meanwhile, work on developing a method elsewhere within NCC was temporarily suspended.

The investigation in due course resulted in the derivation of a checklist of 44 attributes against which methods could be compared. SSADM was found to be a very close match to this 'ideal', and was also remarkably similar to the development within NCC. In view of the existing user base for SSADM (almost all UK government computing) it was decided that NCC should collaborate with the CCTA in promoting the use of SSADM in the private sector.

ATTRIBUTES

The benefits of SSADM come not only from the engineering rigour of a method but also, and perhaps even more importantly, from the fact that it offers protection of company investment in systems and in people, and a broad base of supply and support. Its attributes can be summarised into the following categories.

Theoretical:

- it closely matches the carefully researched 'ideal';
- it contains the generally accepted best current techniques.

The method itself:

- SSADM is tried and tested, is widely used, and it works;
- it is available free of licence fees;
- it is well documented, with documentation that is publicly available;
- it is a stable product that will only change in a controlled and considered way in the light of experience, and of new technological developments;
- it provides a national, non-proprietary, *de facto* standard;
- users will not be locked-in to a single supplier – training and consultancy are available from many organisations;
- software support for the method is available, again from many organisations.

The system:

- three independent but cross-checking viewpoints ensure that the delivered system will be closer to the ultimate one, ie there will be fewer of the inadvertent omissions that would otherwise turn up as modifications or enhancements during maintenance;
- the emphasis on data, which is normally more stable than processes, helps to produce a sound, flexible design;
- the system will be described in an unambiguous specification;
- easier and better validation can be carried out on the analysis and design;
- early identification of possible problems is provided;
- a logical design is produced that is independent of equipment (hardware) and implementation language (software); this design can then be implemented (given its physical form) within any computing environment.

Project management and control:

- the structural framework of the method helps in planning, defining what tasks should be carried out, and when they should be done;

- the standard approach permits the collection of statistics and, therefore, better future estimates based on actual experience in the installation;
- completed products compared with the checklist of tasks show how much has been done, and what work still remains;
- end products of each step permit project control by actual achievements rather than by estimates of progress;
- the products can be used to link SSADM with other methods.

Technical staff:

- SSADM makes effective use of both experienced and inexperienced people;
- communication between team members is more effective;
- the team is more resilient to the loss of key staff;
- because of the stability of the method, the cost of training represents an investment rather than an expense;
- new staff are quite likely to know the method;
- trained staff can join a project and make an immediate contribution.

Users:

- users are closely involved with the work right from the start, and their contribution is critical to the success of the project;
- better communication between users and developers causes fewer misunderstandings and consequent rework.

Contractors:

- The method provides known standards for them to work to;
- SSADM is likely to be known to them already.

Maintenance

There are significant savings on maintenance:

- thorough analysis ensures that from the start there are fewer accidental omissions and logic errors;

- integral documentation, created throughout development, gives a thorough, detailed picture of the system, which aids understanding and helps to make clear the consequences of proposed changes;

- more effective use of resources is achieved during maintenance itself because the systems are well structured, both for data and processes, and so changes are easier to implement.

Quality

- the thoroughness of the analysis, effectiveness of communication between developers and users, consideration of different ways of implementing systems, and formal checking throughout, ensure that a quality solution is attained;

- the procedural approach can be used to show conformance to national and international quality standards. (There is more on this in Chapter 23).

4
An outline of SSADM

SSADM IN CONTEXT

The development of computer systems entails many activities. Together, these activities are known as phases in the system life cycle. The life cycle can be drawn in many ways in an attempt to show what really happens during system development.

Figure 4.1 is the simplest version of a life cycle and shows nothing of the iterative nature of the work that takes place within and between phases. Its only purpose is to indicate where SSADM fits within the total of all the development activities.

The first column in Figure 4.1 shows the sequence of activities, starting with the high level planning studies. The strategic study should establish corporate objectives, and the sequence in which systems will be developed. The business study takes the selected project and defines the scope of the systems work, and the objectives and constraints of the system. It produces the Project Initiation Document, which provides the starting point for SSADM.

The next five boxes show the modules which comprise SSADM. The second column shows how the seven stages of the method (numbered from 0 to 6) match the modules.

Within each stage, a number of documents are produced. At the end of the stage the documents are assembled into a composite report or specification, as shown in the last column.

The work after SSADM is for the actual physical construction of the system.

Systems analysis and design, as encompassed by SSADM, are critically important phases in the systems development process. Errors and omissions during these phases, that are not discovered until after coding or later, can be

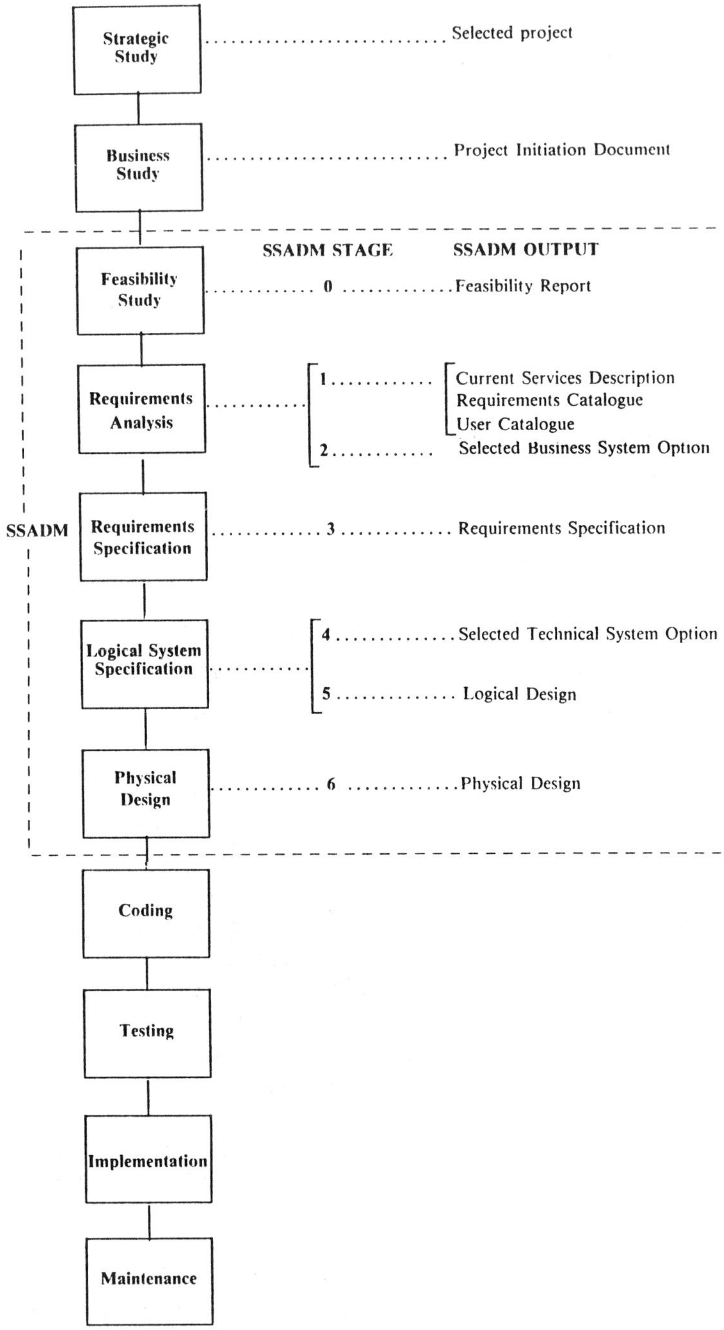

Figure 4.1 SSADM in a system development life cycle

much more costly to resolve than if they were picked up shortly after they were made. (Some surveys have shown that the cost can be 100 times as high).

SSADM is a formalised method that addresses much of this critical work.

COMPONENTS AND CONTROL

Figure 4.2 shows what goes into SSADM, the components of the method, and how the components are related to the control techniques. The control techniques, although not a part of SSADM itself, are essential to the successful development of *any* project. They are discussed in Chapters 23 and 24.

The Project Initiation Document

The Project Initiation Document is the input to SSADM as provided by management. It gives the first definition of the area of study, and the aims and objectives of the system. It is known by many other names, depending on the organisation. Some of these are:

- Analysis Requirements;
- Analysis Startup Document;
- Terms of Reference.

Activities

The activities describe *what* is to be done, and *when* it should be done. (Whilst SSADM sets out the activities to be considered, these are more in the nature of guidelines rather than a strict set of rules that must be followed blindly in all circumstances.) The activities are described in Part 3.

Techniques

SSADM employs 13 techniques which say *how* the work is to be done. Your organisation may already use and have standards for some of this work, in which case the descriptions given may in practice be modified slightly within your installation. The principal techniques, so far as you will be concerned, are described in Part 2. The other techniques are mentioned briefly in Part 3 where the activities require their use.

Documents

The documents are *where* the information gathered about the system is to be recorded. (Some of these may be replaced by software that assists with the application of the method. Such software is known as CASE (Computer Aided

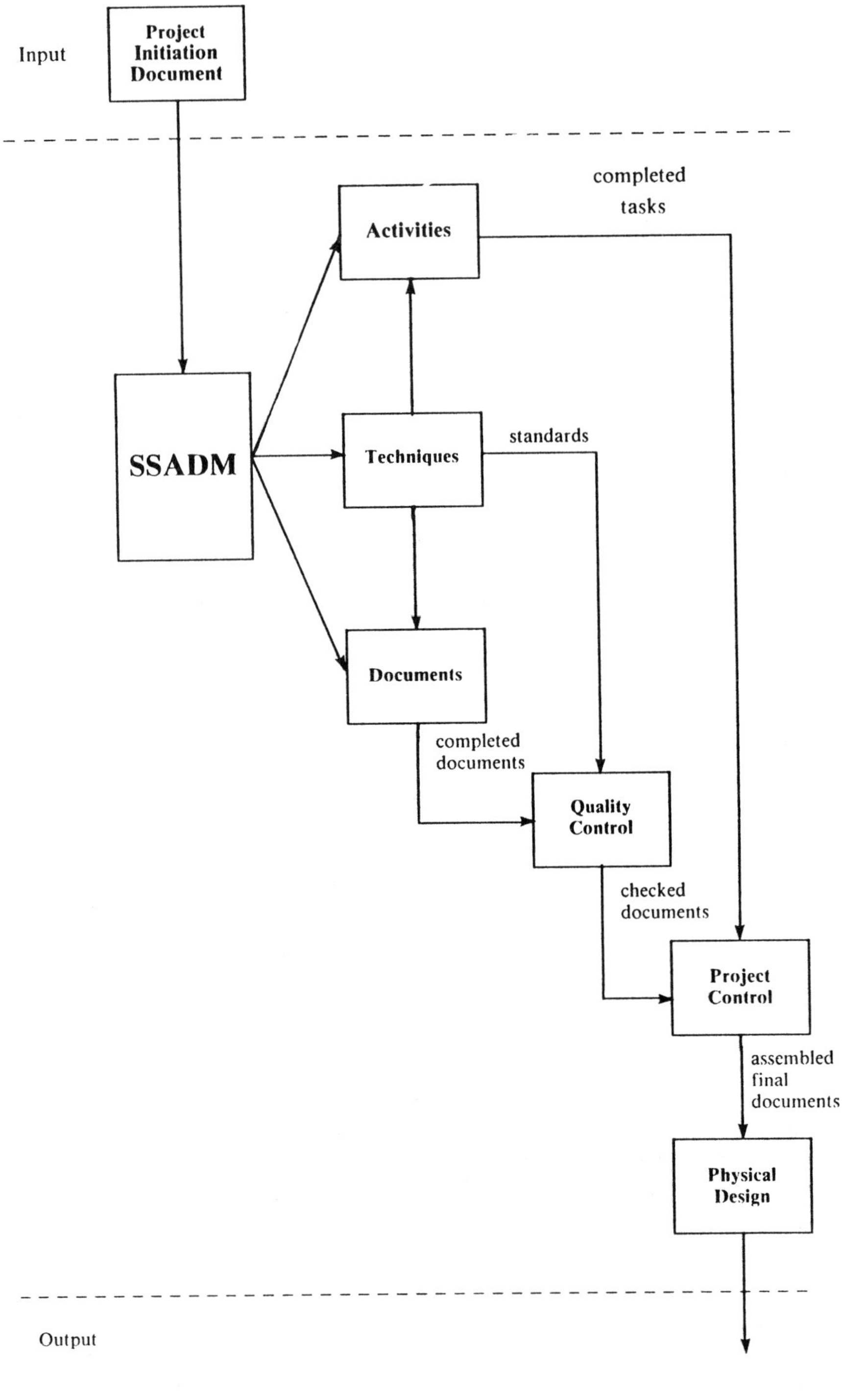

Figure 4.2 The components and control of SSADM

Software Engineering). Samples of the documents mentioned in the text are included in Appendix 2. Organisations may, of course, design their own forms.

Quality Control

Quality control is the formal checking to ensure that the work has been carried out thoroughly and correctly. This is done by confirming that all the documents that should have been produced are, in fact, present, that the information they contain is factually correct, and that they have been completed to the required standard.

Project Control

Visible evidence that a task has been completed is provided by the availability of completed, quality assured, documents. The management of the project is achieved by monitoring the completion of tasks against the agreed plans, estimating the remaining workload, and allocating resources accordingly.

Physical Design

The final activity in SSADM is to put together the documents which fully define the required system. This collection of documents is known as the Physical Design. It goes forward to the next phase in the system development cycle.

SCOPE

SSADM, whilst complementing other development activities, does not encompass them all. For instance, it does not itself cover what may be regarded as the basic skills of the analyst, which include such tasks as interviewing, writing reports, making presentations, forms design, screen design, etc. The interfaces of SSADM with other aspects of development are shown in Figure 4.3.

ACTIVITY STRUCTURE AND CONTROL

Figure 4.4 shows the stucture and control of SSADM.

The work to be done in SSADM is split into five modules. Each of the modules consists of one or two stages. The stages are further subdivided into steps. Each step has a three digit number. The first digit indicates the stage. For example, Stage 0 consists of Steps 010, 020, 030 and 040. The steps themselves consist of a number of tasks, each describing an activity that can be subject to control, both of quality and of progress.

The seven stages of systems analysis and design are described in Part 3, Chapters 15 to 21.

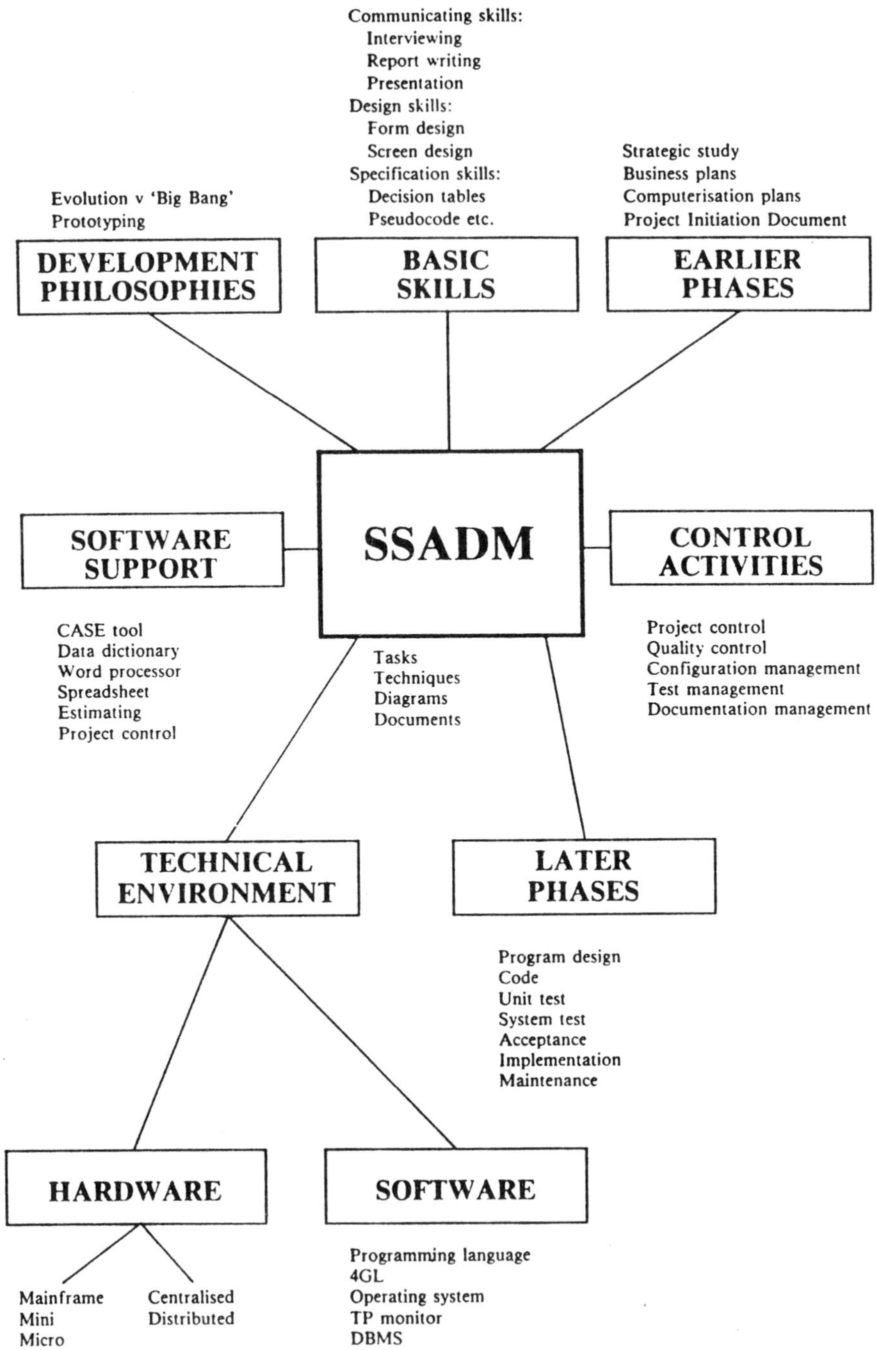

Figure 4.3 SSADM interfaces with other skills

SSADM consists of

5 modules:
- Feasibility Study
- Requirements Analysis
- Requirements Specification
- Logical System Specification
- Physical Design

The Modules are broken down into 7 stages:
- 1 in Feasibility Study
- 2 in Requirements Analysis
- 1 in Requirements Specification
- 2 in Logical System Specification
- 1 in Physical Design

Each of the 7 stages is broken down into steps. There are 33 steps in all.

Each step is further sub-divided into tasks, of which there are 149 in all.

Each task has an end product

SSADM products are subject to control

Each end product is subject to a quality control review

Project control is done by checking that all work on the specified end products, both development and quality review, has been completed.

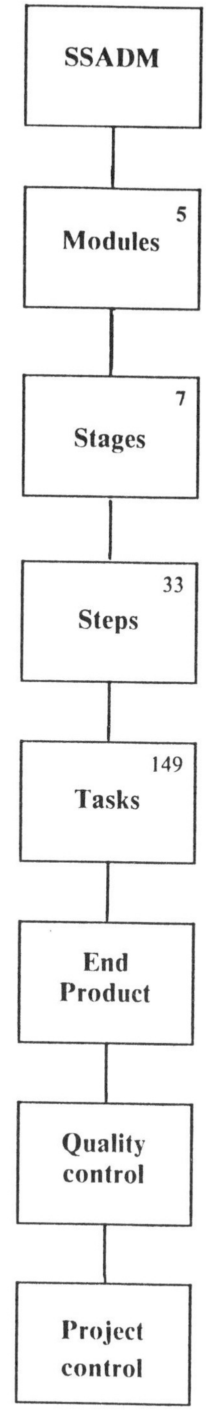

Figure 4.4 The activity structure and control of SSADM

5

Why you are involved

INTRODUCTION

The use of SSADM needs your involvement in the project – and this means both opportunities and responsibilities. The likelihood of success at the end of the development will be directly related to the degree of your concern and involvement.

If the system is to provide new facilities, or to perform operations not previously carried out, you are the only person who can think through the requirements. To change a computer system after it has been implemented is likely to be many times more expensive than getting the design right in the first place. It is essential that you consider in detail the way you will work and how the system is going to help you.

Consider some of the things that only you and other users can do.

You must establish:

- WHAT THE SYSTEM IS TO DO
- HOW WELL IT MUST DO IT
- HAVE THE DEVELOPERS UNDERSTOOD?
- YOUR CHOICE OF THE FINAL SOLUTION

WHAT THE SYSTEM IS TO DO

You are the best person to say:

- what you do;
- what your problems are;
- what you need of the new system.

An invoicing system that failed to produce invoices would not meet requirements no matter how elegantly it was written or what other features it provided. This may seem an extreme example, but regrettably the horror stories of computerisation projects that have gone wrong include the most appalling failures to do what was required.

HOW WELL IT MUST DO IT

A clear and precise quantification of requirements is needed, for example:

- How much can you afford (money, time, etc)?
- How many are there (records, transactions, enquiries, etc)?
- How fast should it operate, eg when do you need the report; how long can you wait for a response at the terminal?
- How well must it carry out its complete range of tasks?

How well it must do the work is vitally important, and is considered in detail in Chapter 13. Your satisfaction with the system should be paramount. At its simplest, it must be able to handle a normal day's work in a normal day. At least one big system is known that failed to do this.

This information (what, when, how much and how well) must be clearly established before any attempt is made to design the system.

HAVE THE DEVELOPERS UNDERSTOOD?

The traditional situation is that the developers and users speak different languages, with enough familiar sounding words for communication to have apparently taken place, but not for understanding to have been achieved. SSADM aims to help both communication and understanding by the use of diagramming techniques.

- How long you are prepared to wait, for example, do you want a robust, effective system, or do you want it next Thursday? There must be some limits on development time, and some target for qualities, but demanding delivery for a totally unrealistic date is likely to bring you more grief than you would want to handle.

6
System objectives

INTRODUCTION

System objectives are critically important and are your responsibility. The developers cannot define your objectives for you, nor can they deliver systems that will meet your requirements unless you make those requirements clear. This needs much careful thought on your part, but if your requirements are vague, then your system is likely to reflect this, and to be unsatisfactory on first implementation. Maintenance costs and total system costs will then be unnecessarily high.

TYPES OF OBJECTIVES

There are two types of objectives:

- the overall, high level justification for needing to consider a system at all;
- the lower level aims of the system itself.

Valid high level management objectives when considering the use of a computer include:

- to do the work faster;
- to do the work more cheaply, reliably or accurately than by existing methods;
- to use fewer people (it is perhaps optimistic for senior management to expect total commitment from those users whose jobs may be at risk after computerisation);
- to open up new business opportunities;

- to increase market share;
- to stay competitive;
- to improve cash flow;
- to give a better service, either within the company or to customers;
- to relieve high grade staff of routine tasks;
- to control access to information more effectively;
- to give a greater degree of control;
- to allow more informed decisions to be made;
- to reduce stock levels;
- to cope with increased volumes and higher peak loads;
- because there is no other way of doing it, for example because sufficient people of the type required are not available, or because they could not do the work within the time needed;
- because of the potential breakdown of the existing system (but do remember that there will also be breakdowns of a computer system).

Depending on the choice of these or similar objectives it is then possible to define your sub-objectives, ie:

- what the system is to do;
- how well it is to do it.

MEASURABLE OBJECTIVES

The diagramming techniques in SSADM help to establish the 'what'. The 'how well' (or 'how much') is equally important. You must define in measurable terms all the quality and resource objectives that are important to you. Unless you can (and do) say precisely what you require, you have no yardstick to measure whether the delivered system is meeting your needs. Also, precise requirements are essential for design. Then:

- The designer knows the quality levels at which he must aim.
- He must *know* whether these levels are achievable and how it can be done. Hoping for the best can prove to be very expensive and totally unsatisfactory. Impossible or prohibitively costly requirements are best recognised early and renegotiated or abandoned.

- It will be necessary to consider ways of proving that the targets have been reached. It may require the development of additional programs to do the necessary measurement or collection of statistics. This is an overhead on system development, in terms of both time and cost, that you will have to accept if you want proof of performance.

Requirements that all too often appear in specifications are statements such as:

- The system must be user-friendly. (What does that mean? Different users will have different ideas of user-friendliness.)

- The system must be secure. (Against what? Earthquake? Flood? Intruder? Illegal use? How secure? What will management pay?)

- The system must be portable, ie usable on other equipment. (Portable to what? When? Why? At what effort?)

- The response must be reasonable. (What is reasonable? A week? An hour? Five seconds?)

- Access to the system must be controlled. (Why is restriction of access necessary? Restricted to whom? To a terminal or to a person? What parts of the system are to be subject to such controls? Who can see data but not change it?)

You must bring precision to your quality requirements. 'Response in a reasonable time', is not good enough. 'Response within four seconds', is precise. It can be measured. Then there can be no argument about whether the delivered system has met the specification. So what you need are statements such as:

> "Invoices received before 12.00 should be entered into the system ready for cheque production by 14.00. The corresponding accounting information should be available for on-line enquiry by 09.00 on the next working day."

These requirements indicate the need for data entry facilities during a period that is conventionally regarded as lunch time. The update of the accounting system can then be done after the end of the normal working day.

> "Between 08.55 and 09.30 a reply to an order enquiry must be received at the terminal within three seconds of its transmission. For the rest of the day the response must be received within five seconds."

This could mean that the system must be loaded and ready to run by perhaps 08.30 to permit the resolution of early problems. Then for the period to 09.30 the order enquiry system may be the only one on-line. After 09.30 it could run concurrently with other on-line systems.

The possible solutions to the two examples above may indicate that new work patterns have to be established with the staff involved, which in turn would need consultation between management and staff, or their representatives. Deferring the on-line running of other systems until after 09.30 may not be acceptable, which would then require a rethink, perhaps involving the purchase of more equipment or acceptance of a slower response from the system.

As mentioned earlier, without a method, management control is not possible. This also applies to undefined qualities. Something for you to bear in mind is that *if you can't measure it, then you can't control it.*

QUALITY OBJECTIVES

You will want to know what qualities should be addressed in this way. Table 6.1 shows examples of some that should be considered. There will no doubt be many others that are specific to your system.

The bad news is that you will almost certainly find that quantification of your requirements in this way is likely to be rather more demanding than in any terms of reference or system specifications you have been involved in before. (You should note that qualities very often have mutual dependencies, so changes to one may affect others. Improvements in speed of recovery after a failure are likely to have a detrimental effect on response time. Improvements in response time may be at the expense of additional hardware or speed of recovery.)

Below are just a small selection of all the possible questions that could be asked about the particular qualities listed in Table 6.1.

Archiving policy. When can data be moved from on-line (where it is immediately available) to backup off-line (where it will be necessary to retrieve it in some way and there will therefore be some delay before it can be accessed)? Will there be sufficient off-line storage? When can it be removed completely from the system?

Availability. At what times, precisely, must the system be available to you?

Confidentiality. Who can access data, and who can update it?

Correctness. Errors will creep in. Monitoring can check for some of these. How often must these checks be made? What control data is needed from the system? Is some inaccuracy permissible, eg to produce information that management can act on at 10.00, although further updating will not have been completed until 14.00?

Cost of Development. How much are you able or prepared to pay for development?

Cost of Operation. What cost is acceptable per run, or for each transaction?

- **Archiving policy**
- **Availability**
- **Confidentiality**
- **Correctness**
- **Cost – Development**
  Operation
  Maintenance
- **Currentness of data**
- **Delivery date**
- **Downtime**
- **Ease of learning**
- **Ease of use**
- **Interfaces**
- **Longevity**
- **Maintainability**
- **Performance**
- **Performance**
- **Portability**
- **Response time**
- **Security**
- **Throughput**
- **Volume of data**

Table 6.1 Some qualities to consider in system development

Cost of Maintenance. There may be a known maintenance requirement, for example payroll systems need changes for new tax legislation each year. What is economic for you? What are *ad hoc* reports worth to you? Can you accept the cost of correcting any errors that may be found in the system?

Currentness of Data. How up-to-date must the data be? Totally, ie a real time system; as at close of business the previous night; or is some other time interval acceptable?

Delivery Date. When is the system needed? Why has this date been selected? Is it critical? When is the next best date?

Downtime. For how long can you do without the system in the event of failure, and what will you do whilst the system is down? How will you know if anything has been lost?

Ease of Learning. Who will operate it – regulars or casuals? How long can they devote to learning how to use it? What about new employees, arriving individually?

Ease of Use. How easy must it be to operate? This is tied in with ease of learning and security. If unauthorised people can gain physical access to it, and if it is also easy to operate, there will be a greater security risk.

Interfaces. With what other systems must it integrate now? What interfaces could there be in the future?

Longevity. What is the planned life of the system? Is it a stopgap until you replace your computer in two years time, or is it a system being designed for posterity? If it is short term, what comes after it? If it is long term, how is it likely to grow?

Maintainability. How quickly must it be possible to make changes to the system? Does this time factor vary for different types of changes?

Performance. How long can it take from receipt of data to production of results?

Portability. Will the system need to run on more than one type of equipment? If so, what equipment, and when?

Response Time. How long can you wait for a response to each of the various transactions?

Security. What levels of precautions must be taken against unauthorised access to the system? How secure is the equipment against disasters? Where can backup copies of data be stored away from the computer? How much backup material will be required, one or two floppies or 500 magnetic tapes?

Throughput. How many transactions must the system be able to cope with per minute, hour, day etc, normally and at peak times? Now and five years hence?

Volume of data. How much data must be immediately available for urgent enquiries? How much data is to be held in archives for non-urgent requests? What will the position be in five years time? In ten years?

The only way of being sure of getting what you want is to spell it out precisely, in a way that can be checked. This effectively defines your acceptance criteria, and failure to meet these criteria means that you are justified in deferring acceptance, renegotiating terms, or, in extreme cases, rejecting the system.

Provided that you or the designers can conceive a way of measuring it, there can be no argument about whether the delivered system has met the specification.

7
The elements of a system

INTRODUCTION

Before looking at what happens within SSADM, it is as well to have an understanding of what the application of SSADM is trying to achieve. This chapter therefore ignores computers and considers instead the nature of systems. The aim is to establish what facts the analysts must discover before they can properly specify a system.

Consider a purely manual system, with no part of it automated in any way. There may be no written instructions – what needs doing may be held in people's heads. When the lights are switched off at night and everyone goes home, all that is left behind is a heap of data – in filing cabinets, on record cards, on notes and memos. The critical base of the system is:

DATA

The next morning the office is opened up, people come in; and things start to happen – the telephone rings; the mail arrives; people visit; payment of an invoice is authorised; some things are done because it is the first day of the month. These are occurrences of:

EVENTS

Each event causes something to happen – an appointment is made; an invoice is paid; a report is prepared; ie some action is taken; people carry out:

PROCESSES

Systems don't work in isolation. They have an effect on, and are affected by, other systems. A system to order books must interface in some way with systems for cataloguing and for controlling the circulation of books. A system for recording prescriptions given to patients may need to be linked to an appointments system, to a recall system and to statistical systems. A pay system may interface with staff records, estimating systems, superannuation systems, and to the accounting system.

All such communication with the world outside the system being developed is by means of:

INTERFACES

Not only are things done, but if the business is to succeed, then *what* is done is not the only concern. *How well* it is done is likely to be at least as important. It is no good delivering orders randomly - they must be delivered when they are needed. And quality doesn't necessarily mean the highest quality possible; it means the quality needed for the purpose. There are times when you may want a Rolls Royce, but there are other times when a wheelbarrow will suffice. You don't need a Rolls Royce for spreading compost. The design must achieve the required levels of:

QUALITIES

The system probably grew up over a period of time. Someone devised it and explained what to do to those who operate the system. This will have involved people, money, and equipment. It used:

RESOURCES

The development of the new system will also consume resources, and it is essential that these are kept under control. It is up to you decide how much you are willing to pay for development, how long you are prepared to wait for the system to be operational, and what are acceptable running costs.

SUMMARY

The six elements of a system are summarised in Table 7.1.

Systems analysis must establish the facts about each of these system elements. Do remember that:

- The data is *your* data, and the system can only work on what it has got. You can have major systems problems if you find that you want to use data that is not in the system.
- The events are the happenings that matter to *you*.
- The processes are how *you* want the work to be done.
- You will get the biggest payoff from your efforts if the systems can be integrated with each other. It's rather like a jigsaw. When you get the final piece in place, the whole thing is so very much more meaningful.

A system consists of:	
DATA	which is affected by
EVENTS	which trigger
PROCESSES	which have
INTERFACES	with the external world. The work must be done to defined levels of
QUALITIES	and consume agreed levels of
RESOURCES	commensurate with the benefits of the system.

Table 7.1 The six elements of a system

- The qualities establish exactly what levels of performance will make the system acceptable and useful to you.
- You won't be very pleased if it costs twice what you thought it would, and won't run on the equipment that you expected it to run on, and might not be ready until the next visit of Halley's Comet instead of the next financial year or whatever date you had in mind.

Development costs are often closely monitored, whilst running and maintenance costs often tend to have a much lower profile. Maintenance consists of correcting errors and enhancing the system to meet changes in requirements, many of which are caused by external circumstances; new legislation is an example. (Local authorities will be well aware of the effects of changes in the collection of domestic rates in its various guises.) Maintenance over a system life of several years can cost many times more than the original development. It is worth noting that the more that is done correctly in the first place, the less it will cost over the life of the system, taking maintenance into account as well. The subject is considered in more detail in Chapter 26 under *Coping with Change.*

All these system elements are vitally important to you, and somehow or other you must convey all of this information to the analysts.

HOW SSADM HELPS

It is the purpose of SSADM to facilitate the collection of all this information, and this is done with the aid of diagrams (Chapters 9 – 11), the Requirements Catalogue (Chapter 13), and supporting documentation.

The diagrams serve three purposes:

- they provide an extremely effective means of communication;
- they provide a framework in which the information can be captured and recorded as it is found;
- the very task of constructing the diagrams prompts the questions that need to be asked.

The Requirements Catalogue permits the precise specification of:

- functional requirements, ie the processing to be carried out by the new system;
- non-functional requirements, ie the qualitative elements of the system.

Part 2

SSADM Techniques

8
The SSADM techniques

INTRODUCTION

In working through a complete application of SSADM, 13 different techniques are used:

The principal techniques for modelling the system are:

- Data Flow Modelling.
- Logical Data Modelling.
- Entity-Event Modelling.

A picture, they say, is worth a thousand words. These three techniques are diagram-based and they certainly succeed in conveying a lot of information in a simple way. They are considered in Chapters 9 – 11

These techniques, or something very similar, appear in other structured methods. Their effectiveness has been known for many years. Most of your work with the analysts will be in the preparation and checking of these diagrams.

Requirements Definition, entailing completion of the Requirements Catalogue, is dealt with in Chapter 13.

The nine other techniques, and the steps where they are used and briefly described, are shown in Table 8.1.

WHY USE DIAGRAMS?

The problem of communication between yourself and the developers was mentioned earlier, as was the inadequacy of an English narrative specification of a system.

Technique	**Step**				
Dialogue Design	120	310	330	350	510
Relational Data Analysis	140	320	340		
Business System Options	210	220			
Function Definition	330				
Specification Prototyping	350				
Technical System Options	410	420			
Logical Database Process Design	520	530			
Physical Data Design	610	620	640		
Physical Process Specification	610	630	650	660	

Table 8.1 Other SSADM techniques

In SSADM the products of the main techniques,as you will see them, are diagrams rather than narrative. SSADM is a diagram-based method. It aims to help both communication and understanding by using diagramming techniques.

During the investigation the analysts will be talking to you and constructing diagrams to record their understanding of the discussions. The diagrams will be augmented with other information that the analysts find during their study.

These diagrams have been shown to provide an excellent and unambiguous means of communication between users and analysts. The analysts will talk through their diagrams with you as they go about their investigations, and will want you to check that the information they have recorded is correct.

The diagrams, used initially for communication, fact finding, note taking and discussion, evolve as the work progresses to provide the base on which the system will be structured. They are supported by other documents which give more detail, but the correctness of the diagrams is the key to successful systems.

DIAGRAMS AS WORKING DOCUMENTS

It is important to appreciate that the diagrams are working documents. They represent the current understanding of the system *at that point in time*. As such, they are not sacrosanct. You must feel free to make changes to them, and such changes must be regarded as an integral part of the development process, not as the desecration of a work of art. Modifying them is ‘a good thing’ and is to be encouraged, with the proviso that modifications must be for correctness rather than beauty, and must fall within the agreed scope of the project. Much time can be spent fruitlessly 'improving' diagrams rather than advancing knowledge. The diagrams are tools to move the analysis on towards a more complete understanding of, and ultimately to a definition of, the required system.

STANDARDS

In the diagrams and forms that follow, SSADM conventions are used in showing:

- the shape of symbols;
- upper and lower case;
- alphabetic and numeric identifiers.

Your own organisation may have its own conventions for these things. What is important is not that boxes have right-angled or rounded corners (hard boxes and soft boxes), or that an entry is made as alphabetic or numeric, or upper or lower case, but that it is always done in the same standard way. Then everyone knows what the standard is, and quality control must see that the standard is adhered to.

9

Data Flow Modelling – DFM

INTRODUCTION

The elements of a system were considered in Chapter 7. The analyst must elicit *all* this essential information from the user. In SSADM the starting point for the task of information gathering is by data flow modelling, part of which entails the construction of Data Flow Diagrams (DFDs) of the current system.

The objectives of the analyst are threefold:

- to obtain information from the user;
- to record that information;
- to agree the record with the user.

DFDs provide the means of achieving all three of these objectives. The other information in the Data Flow Model amplifies the DFDs.

THE DATA FLOW MODEL

The DFDs are concise, precise and unambiguous. However, they do not stand alone. They are supplemented by several other documents which, together with the DFDs, go to make up the Data Flow Model:

- Elementary Process Descriptions (EPDs), being detailed descriptions of the lowest level processes;
- External Entity Descriptions for each entity on the DFDs;
- I/O (Input/Output) Descriptions showing the contents of data flows which cross the system boundary.

Also, and additional to the Data Flow Model, are the:

- Data Catalogue, holding all the information about each data item in the system;
- Logical Data Store/Entity cross references showing the relationship between data stores on the DFDs and the corresponding entity structures on the Logical Data Model.

WHAT DFDs SHOW

Their simplicity, combined with the fact that (initially) they illustrate the system as it is known to the user, ie the *current physical system*, make DFDs an ideal tool for communication.

DFDs show:

- data, both dynamic as it moves around the system in data flows, and static where data is stored;
- events, by inference from the data flows which trigger the processes;
- processes, ie what is done with the data;
- system boundaries, showing the interfaces with other systems and the outside world, ie where data comes from initially, and goes to after processing.

It can thus be seen that DFDs help to identify four of the six elements of a system (Table 7.1), which gets the analysis off to a good start.

SUPPORTING DIAGRAMS

It is worth noting that because properly drawn DFDs are easy to understand, there is sometimes the tendency to think that they are equally easy to draw. It is certainly true that the technique is easy to apply when some experience has been gained, but there can be much agony in the early days. It is a problem similar to knowing how chess pieces can move, but not knowing how to start the game. For this reason, three additional diagrams may be used to help in obtaining the facts and drawing them on a DFD. They are:

- The Context Diagram, essentially a very high-level DFD, which is illustrated in Figure 9.15.
- Document Flow Diagrams showing the movement of documentation in and out of the system, and between the various departments and people

within the area to be covered by the system. They are an aid to establishing data flows. A Document Flow Diagram is shown in Figure 9.18.

- Resource Flow Diagrams showing the movement of physical objects rather than data. These objects will still exist after the system has been computerised. Examples are deliveries of materials (a load of bricks; a pack of stationery; a book). Each diagram shows the movements of a single resource. As resources are supported by data, again they are an aid to production of data flows. Figure 9.19 shows a Resource Flow Diagram.

One further point to appreciate is that no matter how skilled the analyst may be, early DFDs will be incomplete and inaccurate. This is because:

- The analyst will not initially know all the questions to ask.

- The user will not recall all that he knows of the system.

- The familiarity of the user with his subject may mean that he takes it for granted that the analyst understands elementary things about the system, and consequently these may not be mentioned.

- There will be misunderstandings.

The good news is that DFDs, being an excellent medium for communication, make these shortcomings apparent.

What the designers must ultimately do is to find a way of putting together all the system elements indicated on the DFDs in the 'best' way – whatever 'best' means, and there is no need to worry about that at this stage.

DFD SYMBOLS

DFDs are simple in concept. They consist of just six different symbols, illustrated in Figure 9.1.

External entities are people, organisations, or other systems that send data into the system or receive data from it. An external entity can thus be:

- something in the real world, but outside the organisation, as shown in Figure 9.2.

Other examples are:

- APPLICANT

- BOOK

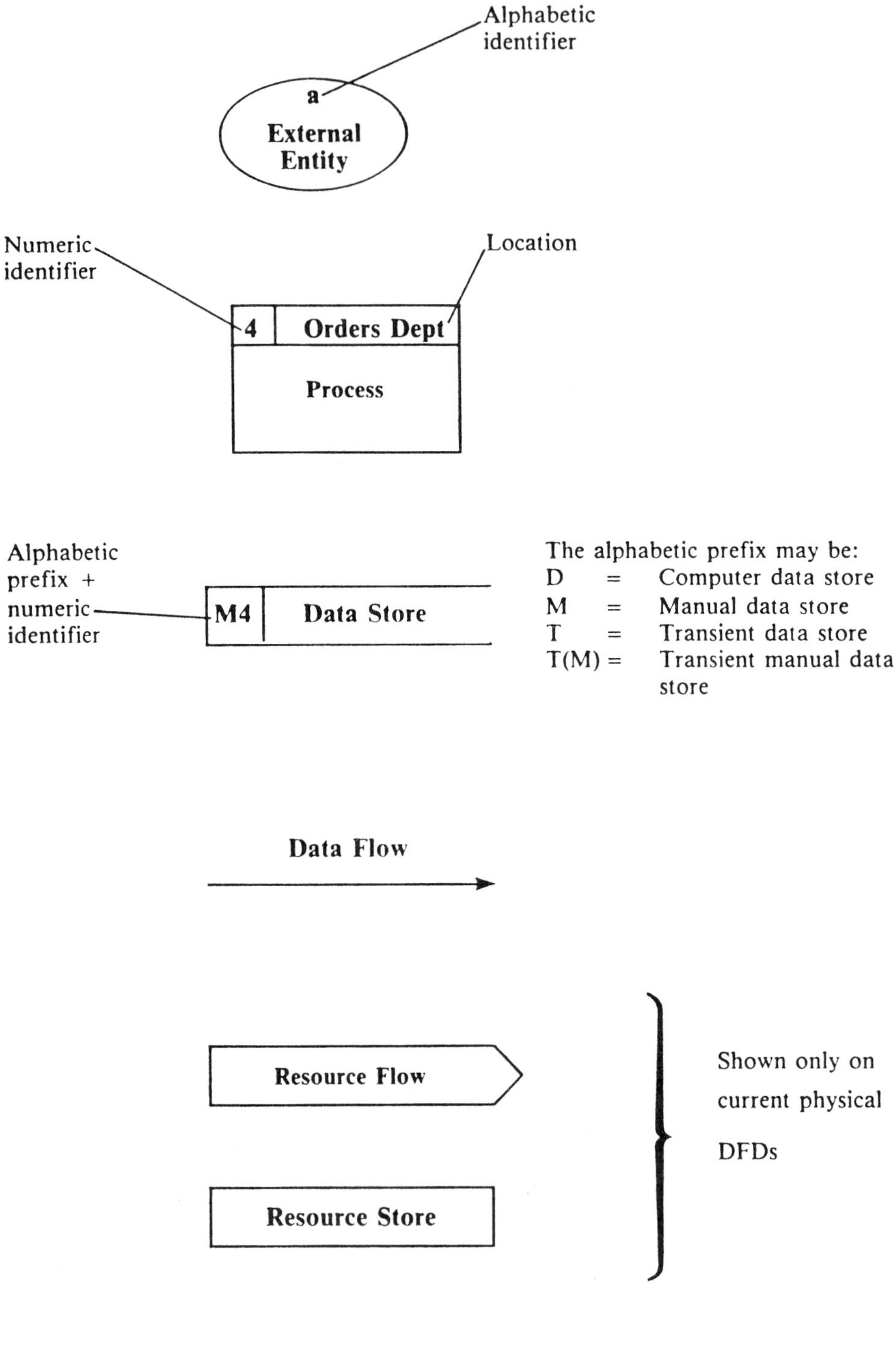

Figure 9.1 DFD symbols

- PATIENT
- READER
- SUPPLIER
- WAREHOUSE
- BANK.

Figure 9.2 External entity (1)

- something within the organisation, but outside the system under consideration, as in Figure 9.3

Other examples are:

- ACCOUNTS DEPARTMENT
- SALESMAN
- STAFF RECORDS SYSTEM.

Figure 9.3 External entity (2)

Note that:

- Each symbol is uniquely identified by a lower case letter at the top of the ellipse (its identifier or ID).
- The same entity can be shown more than once on a diagram, to avoid the use of tenuous or criss-crossing lines, or connectors, and thus to make the

diagram easier to understand. A multiple presence is indicated by the diagonal line within the ellipse, as illustrated in Figure 9.4.

Figure 9.4 External entity (3)

Processes

Processes are actions that are carried out when data is received, for example, prepare a cheque, note details of a new customer, check credit rating, issue invoice. A process does something to or with data, eg it sets it up, retrieves it, or updates it in some way.

The process box, illustrated in Figure 9.5, is divided into three areas:

- a unique numeric ID (which does *not* indicate sequence);
- the location where the process is carried out, eg a business department or an existing computer system;
- a concise, precise, statement of the process, using strong, active verbs.

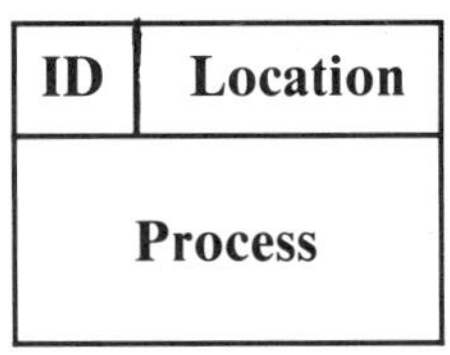

Figure 9.5 A process box (1)

An example of a completed process box is given in Figure 9.6.

Other examples are:

- Authorise credit
- Calculate discount
- Check availability
- Print payslip
- Record issue.

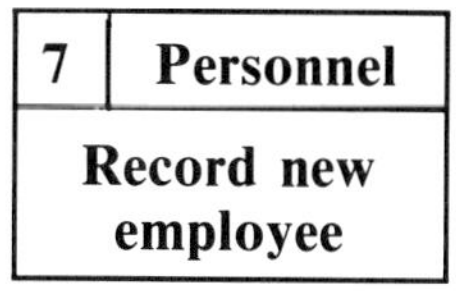

Figure 9.6 A process box (2)

Data Stores

Data stores are groups of data, for example, customer records, paid invoices, personnel records, stock records. They are repositories for data in any form. In the physical system they may hold manually-maintained data, eg files in a filing cabinet, cards in a card index, or documents in a folder. If an existing computer system is involved, they will include computer files, eg employee records.

Many external entities will be represented in some way in a data store in the system, for example the external entity *Customer* may be in a *Customer Name and Address File* or (temporarily, together with other data), in a *New Orders File.*

The data store box, illustrated in Figure 9.7, is in two parts:

- the ID, being the prefix

D	computer data store
M	manual data store
T	transient data store
T(M)	transient manual data store

  followed by a unique number
- the name of the data store, as known to the user.

Figure 9.7 A data store (1)

As with external entities, the same data store may appear in more than one place on a diagram. Where this is done, the multiple presence is indicated by an additional vertical bar at the left-hand edge of the open box, shown in Figure 9.8.

Figure 9.8 A data store (2)

Data Flows

Data flows show the movement of data around the system – between external entities, processes and data stores. Each data flow from outside the system triggers off some processing and can thus been seen as indicating an event which will have an effect on the data held within the system.

Data flows are representations of such things as documents, telephone messages, and information transmitted to and from terminals, workstations and computers. Examples of data flows are new customer details, orders, invoices, statements, reminders, etc. Data flows are shown in Figure 9.9.

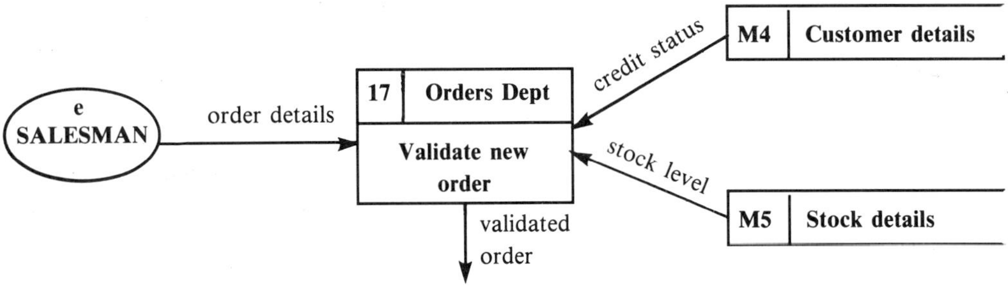

Figure 9.9 Data flows

The direction of flow is indicated on the diagram by the arrowhead. Bi-directional arrows should be avoided, by use of two or more separate arrows, each with its own description of the data.

Physical Resource Flows and Stores

A data processing system moves data, not physical objects, around the system. Physical resource flows and stores are thus irrelevant to establishing the logic of the system. However, this representation exists to overcome the difficulty which sometimes occurs in trying to establish data flows. For example, if a delivery of stationery is left in the reception area, it's unlikely to be a gift from an anonymous philanthropist. It will be accompanied, preceded or followed by some documentation. Figure 9.10 shows this.

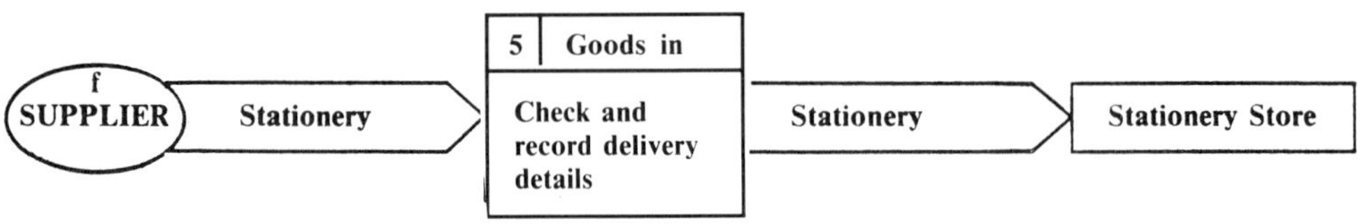

Figure 9.10 Resource flows and stores

If the movement of the stationary is then tracked around the building, it will indicate the need for information to be moving around in a similar way. The physical resource flow, if used, only appears in early current physical system DFDs, and is omitted when it has served its purpose of identifying the related data flows. The resource flows and stores in Figure 9.10 have been converted to data flows and stores in Figure 9.11.

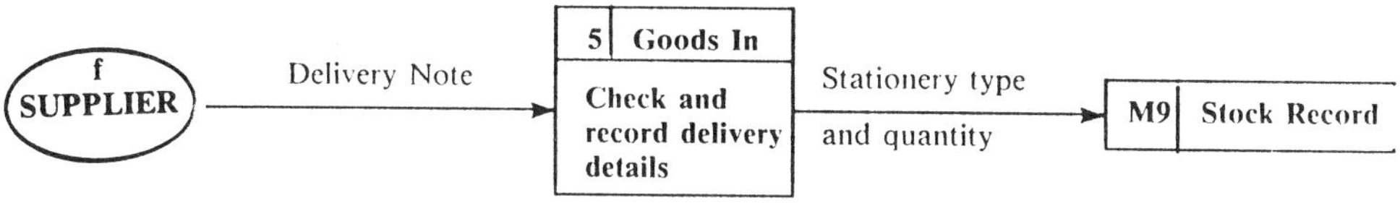

Figure 9.11 Conversion of resource flows and stores

PERMISSIBLE CONNECTIONS

Not all symbols can be connected to each other. All the permissible connections are shown in Figure 9.12.

The rules illustrated are:

- External entities cannot be connected directly to data or resource stores. A process in the system must come between them.

- Resource stores can only be connected to processes, and only by resource flows. Obviously enough, a resource can only get into a resource store by means of a resource flow.

- External entities can be connected to each other, both by data and by resource flows. Although these are outside the system, they are included if they aid understanding.

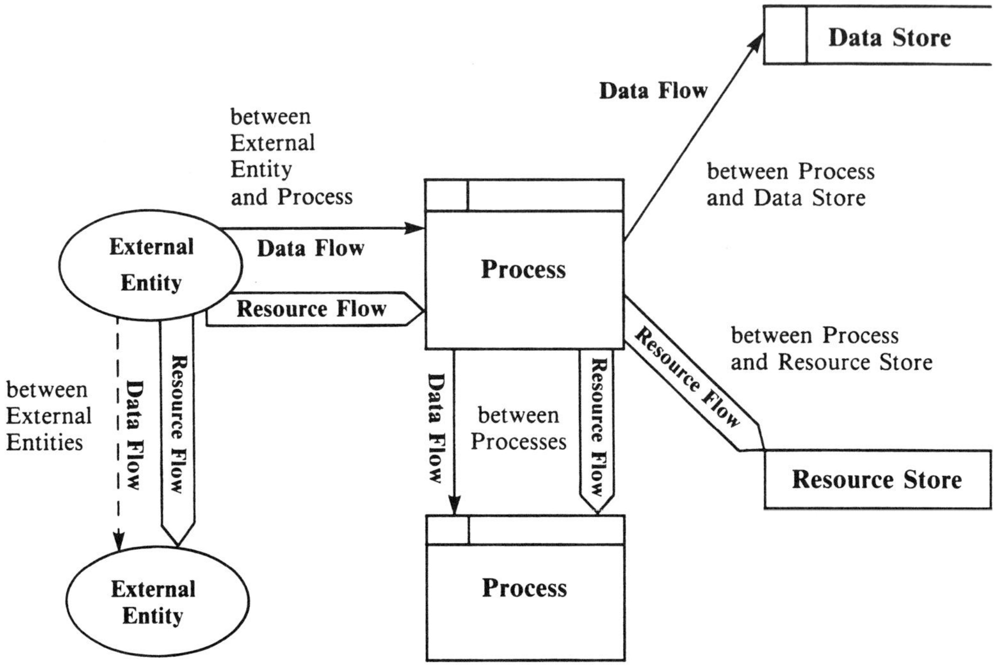

Figure 9.12 Permissible connections (all arrows may point in either direction)

Note that stores may only be connected to processes.

DFD DEVELOPMENT

The early DFDs are of the current physical system (where one exists) and, as mentioned above, are inevitably incomplete.

The further development of DFDs is done in two ways:

- by transformation, progressing from the current system to the required system (*see* Transformation of DFDs);

– by decomposition, starting with a high-level view and then decomposing it into greater levels of detail (*see* Decomposition of DFDs).

TRANSFORMATION OF DFDs

The starting point for SSADM is the current system. This is the system as it physically exists. The aim is to replace it with a new physical system that will solve existing problems and include new requirements. DFDs help to move the analysis on from the old to the new system. This transformation is shown in Figure 9.13.

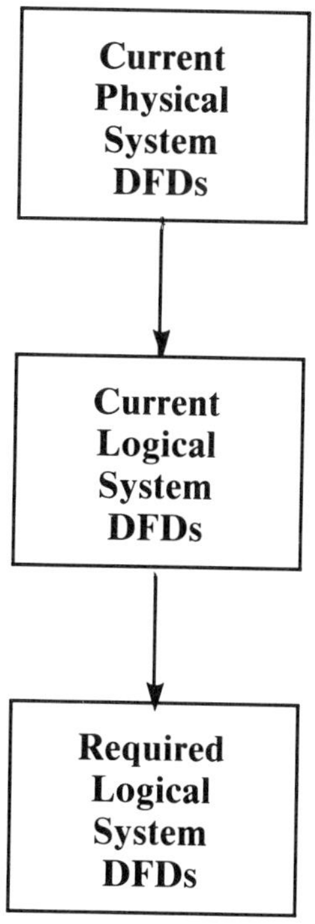

Figure 9.13 Transformation of DFDs

The *current physical system* DFDs record things as they are, complete with all the existing problems and inefficiencies. They show both *what* is done, and also the existing physical aspects of *where* and *how* it is done, and *who* does it. It cannot show *why* it done, but this is essential background knowledge.

(If there is no existing current system it will be necessary to move directly from the Context Diagram to the construction of the logical DFDs. This will show the processes that can be inferred as being necessary to produce the required outputs. The Requirements Catalogue (which shows additional requirements when there is an existing system) will show *all* requirements.)

When all the details of the current system have been investigated and recorded, the DFDs are *logicalised*. This means that the physical aspects of *who, where* and *how* are removed, leaving only *what* is done. Inefficiencies are usually found. Typically DFDs reveal:

- data that is duplicated;
- data that is input to the system but never used;
- processes that are currently carried out but are no longer relevant;
- processes that are carried out separately, which could usefully be combined.

These inefficiencies should be avoided in the new system, and are removed by means of a process known as *logicalisation*. The DFDs are then of the *current logical system.*

The logical system may be implemented in a variety of ways and SSADM requires alternatives to be devised and considered. High level DFDs may be used to represent different Business System Options (BSOs), with variations in:

- the position of the system boundary, showing the processes to be carried out and the data to be stored within the computer part of the system;
- existing problems that will be solved;
- new requirements that will be included;
- quality and resource objectives that will be met.

The selected option may be a hybrid of those considered. The DFDs are amended to include the agreed new requirements, and to take out any processes that are no longer needed. They have then become DFDs of the *required logical system.*

The Data Flow Model is finally used in the derivation of Function Definitions, which provide the base from which the *required system* will be built.

DECOMPOSITION OF DFDs

Even superficially simple systems, when fully documented, are likely to give rise to so much information that it would be difficult to understand if shown in a single diagram. This is remedied by presenting different levels of information in different levels of diagram. This aids understanding of the system because each diagram is simple and compact. The hierarchical structure allows each user to home in on those areas of the system that are of particular interest to him or in which he is an expert.

The levels of diagrams, illustrated in Figure 9.14, are known as:

- Context Diagram.
- Level 1 (high-level diagram).
- Lower level diagrams, consisting of intermediate level diagrams (where three or more levels are necessary), and lowest level diagrams, from which primary business functions (ie complete units of processing as seen by the system user) are identifiable. The objective is to decide *what* has to be done, not *how* it should be done.

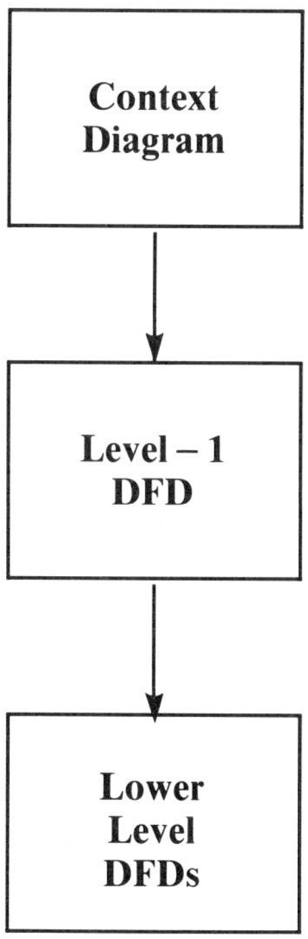

Figure 9.14 Decomposition of DFDs

These levels may (but do not necessarily) exist in the transformations from current physical to current logical, and then to required logical system.

DFDs ILLUSTRATED IN A LIBRARY ORDERS AND ACQUISITIONS SYSTEM

The Context Diagram

This diagram, as its name implies, puts the system in context. It contains only one box, representing the system, surrounded by external entities and the data flows to and from the system. A Context Diagram gives an excellent overview of the system.

Figure 9.15 shows the first attempt to document the items that are acquired by a public library. It was done very quickly and proved to be an excellent way of clarifying initial thoughts about what the system should do.

It resulted in the following decisions:

- Voluntary bodies (g), exhibitors (j), and evening classes (l) being omitted as no records are maintained about them, nor will records be needed in the future. Essentially the library is merely providing publicity and services for these other organisations.
- Music suppliers (c) and video tape suppliers (d) being combined as audio video suppliers. Both types of order are the same, and loans of the material are chargeable.
- Magazine suppliers (e) and newspaper publishers (f) being combined as newsagent, both being obtained by standing order and being reference material in the library.
- Reader recommendations (a) and library management requests (m) being combined as requesters, as both cause the ordering of books.
- Bookseller (b) and business and trade organisations (k) being combined as booksellers, as orders for books are placed with both.
- Other libraries (i), from which books are borrowed and returned rather than added to stock, are regarded as part of the circulation system.

These decisions resulted in the revised Context Diagram at Figure 9.16.

At this point the Context Diagram is incomplete, although it has satisfied its primary purpose of putting the system into context and setting an initial boundary for its scope. Further data flows in and out of the system will be revealed when

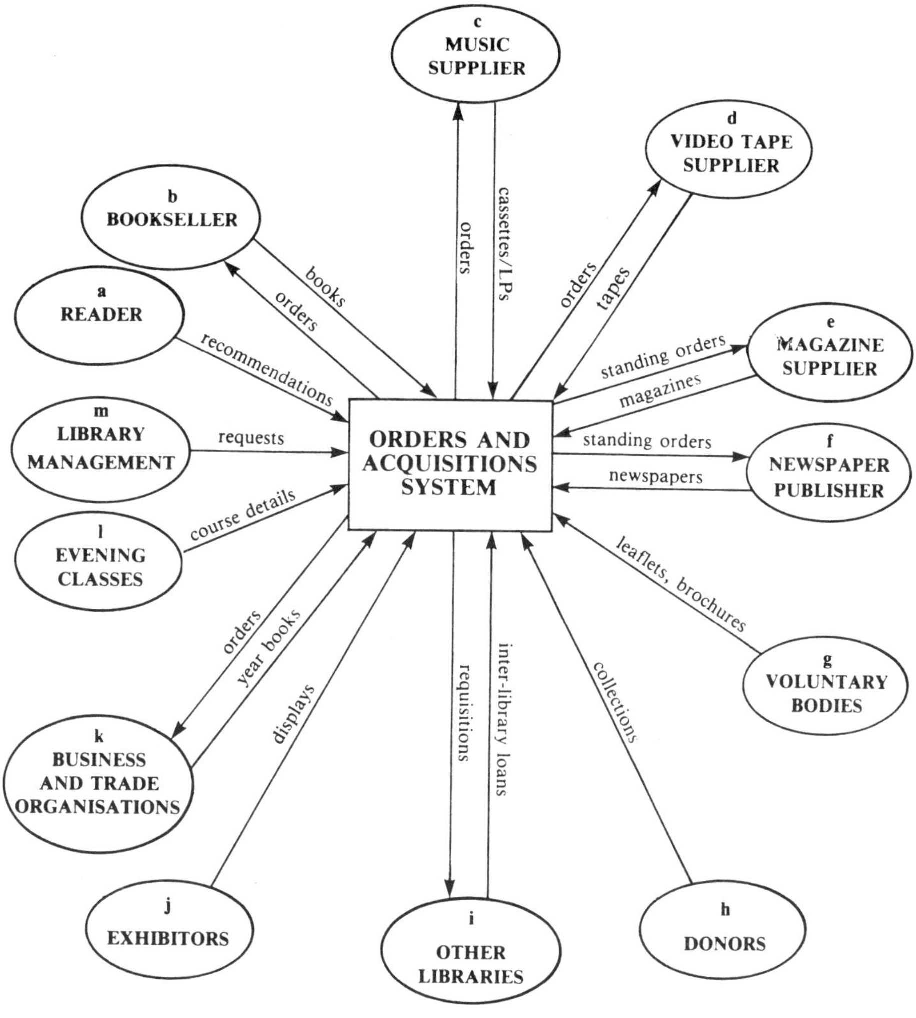

Figure 9.15 Context diagram for a Library Orders and Acquisitions System

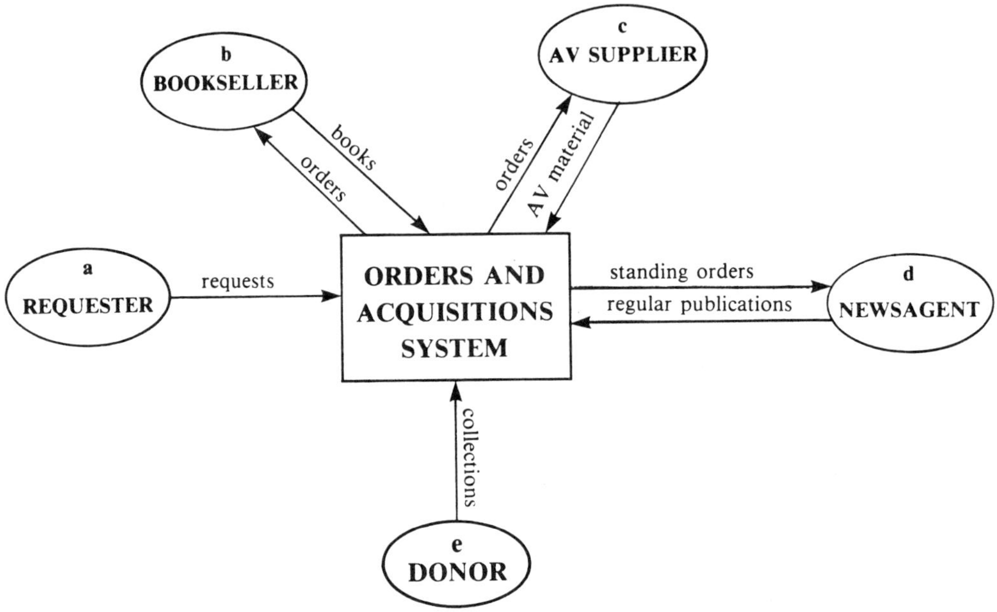

Figure 9.16 Revised context diagram for a Library Orders and Acquisitions System

the Level-1 DFD is constructed. The additional data flows will then be added to the Context Diagram.

Throughout a system development using SSADM, new discoveries will lead to the amplification (or correction) of earlier work.

Level-1 or High-Level Diagram

At this level the first breakdown of a system is provided. The external entities are all present as on the Context Diagram, but the system box is expanded to show the major functions and data flows within the system. The diagram should preferably be limited to showing no more than nine process boxes on each sheet.

The number of boxes per sheet is not a constraint within SSADM, and has no bearing on the ultimate design, but is suggested here as an aid to comprehension. According to the psychologist-mathematician George Miller (Miller 1956), the human mind is capable of coping with only about seven items at a time, the limit being taken as seven, plus or minus two. Also, an A4 sheet will be getting too cluttered if more than about nine processes are shown.

The recommendation is therefore that the complete system should be broken down into no more than nine high level processes, each of which can be shown in more detail on lower level DFDs.

Figure 9.17 shows a Current Physical Level-1 DFD for the Library Orders and Acquisitions System.

Drawing this diagram revealed the following data flows that had been omitted from the Context Diagram at Figure 9.16:

- notification of receipt to the requester;
- reminders to booksellers, reports from them about the order (further stock awaited; out of print and no longer available; now reprinting, etc), and payments for books received;
- reminders to audio video suppliers, reports from them, and payments to them;
- payments to newsagents;
- acknowledgements to donors or their representatives for books given to the library.

Additionally, some of the wording on data flows differed between diagrams and would need to be made the same to avoid any possibility of misunderstandings in the future. (This is a problem that should not arise if the computer department is using a CASE (Computer Aided Software Engineering) tool, as the software should carry the data flow notation down to the different levels of DFDs.)

Updating the Context Diagram to include these additional data flows does not move the development forward, but does make it easier for anyone joining the project to understand the work done so far. It also helps those who will eventually be involved in the maintenance of the system.

Note that this diagram may well be a totally accurate picture of what now happens. However, anyone doing a quality review check on the diagram would be likely to raise several queries:

- Are no reminders sent, or reports received, for orders to newsagents?
- Is there no record of periodicals on order? (In a small library, the record may be in someone's head. This may cause problems when the owner of the head is not present.)
- Are there no recently received lists for AV material or periodicals?

Resolving these queries may reveal omissions from the diagram, or prompt entries for future needs to be made in the Requirements Catalogue. If the diagram is correct, and user management do not consider future requirements to improve the service in these areas to be worth the cost, then these decisions should be documented.

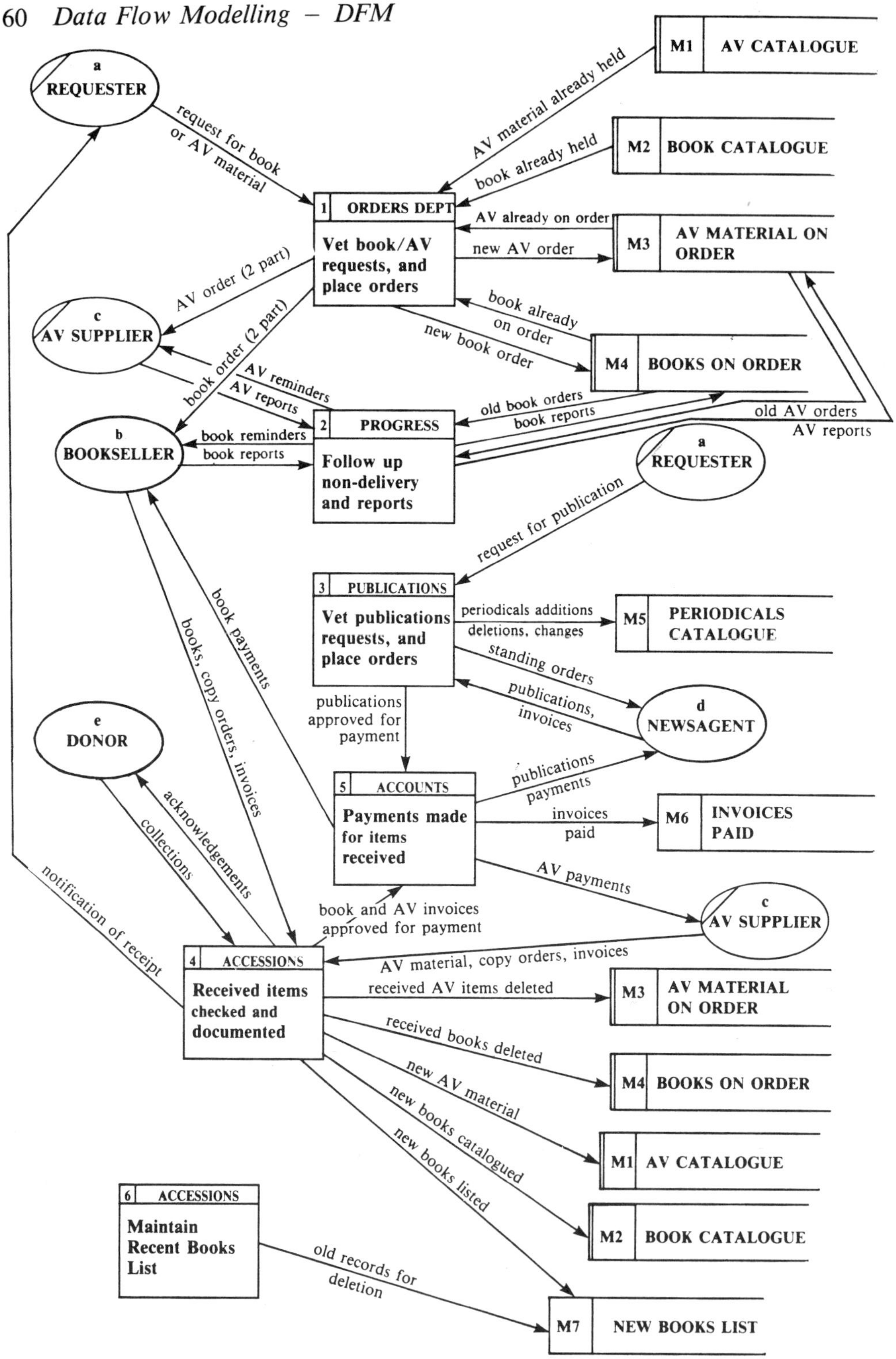

Figure 9.17 Current physical Level – 1 DFD for a Library Orders and Acquisitions System

Note also that the DFD shows neither priority nor sequence. Requests for books do not necessarily come in before requests for publications.

Consideration should also be instigated on how to treat the same text in different media, eg:

- some books are also available on audio cassettes;
- some books have been filmed and can be obtained on video tapes;
- music is available on LPs, compact discs, video tapes, audio cassettes, sheet music, and music compilations.

However, these are perhaps topics for a cataloguing system rather than an orders system.

DOCUMENT FLOW DIAGRAMS

Document Flow Diagrams are constructed for each document flow on the Level – 1 DFD. Their purposes are:

- To validate the DFDs. They may reveal processes, departments or individuals that have been omitted.
- To discover any major documents that may have been missed. This will come about during your discussion of the diagrams with the developers.
- To help in the placement of the system boundary. It should be the same as on the Context Diagram.

Note that if there is difficulty in establishing the facts that are needed for construction of the DFDs, progress may be made by creating some of the Document Flow Diagrams at the same time, starting with the flows into and out of the Context Diagram.

Depending on the complexity of the system under investigation and the number of people available for the work, one diagram may cover the complete system, or separate diagrams drawn for each document and then merged.

The diagram at Figure 9.18 shows the Document Flow Diagram for the various parts of the Library Book Order Form. The system boundary has been drawn on it and the Accounts Department excluded. This will require amendment of the Context Diagram to show the Accounts Department as another external entity. It will also require a corresponding change to the DFD to exclude process box 5 and to replace it with an external entity.

Once more there is the realisation that too much concern over the earlier work is unnecessary. Working through SSADM can be seen as a process of continuous refinement.

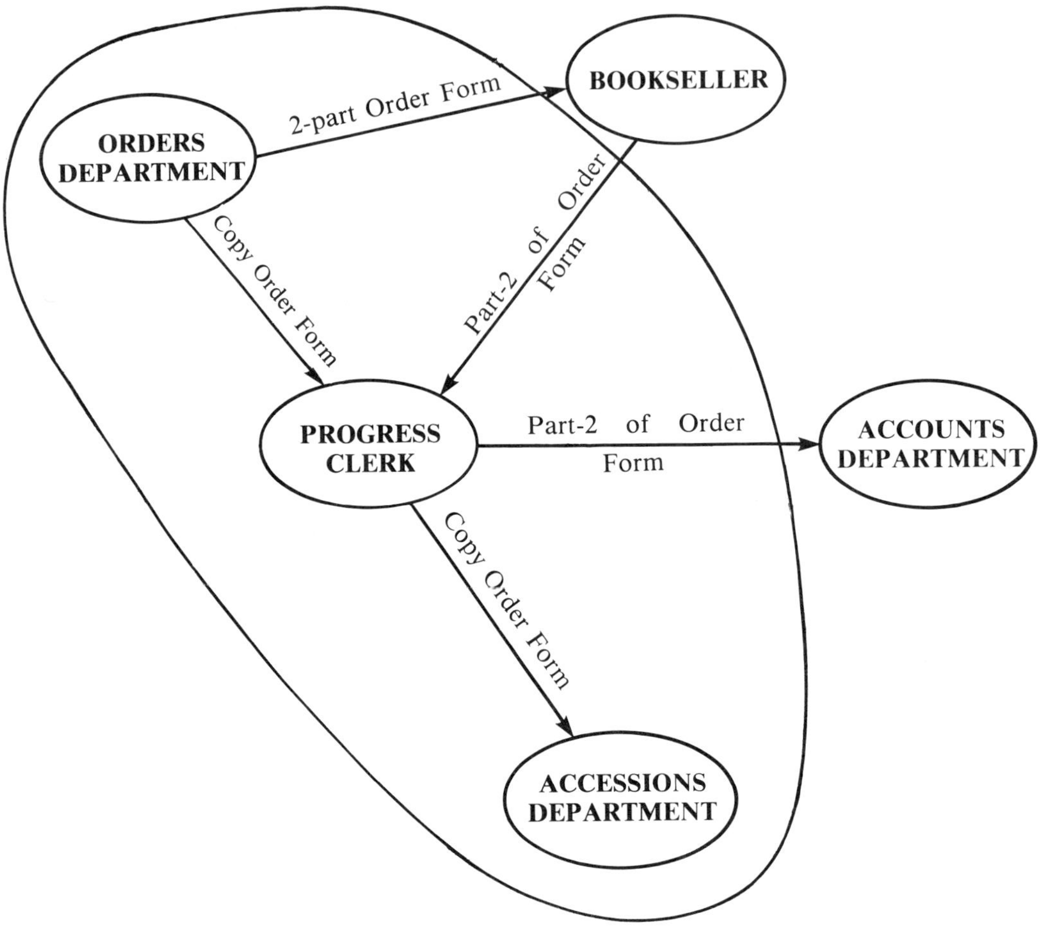

Figure 9.18 A Document Flow Diagram for a Book Order

RESOURCE FLOW DIAGRAMS

Resource Flow Diagrams serve the same purpose as Document Flow Diagrams, ie they are prepared at the same time, and with a view to achieving the completeness and correctness of the DFDs. A separate diagram is drawn for each resource. Figure 9.19 shows the diagram for the resource 'Book'.

In this instance nothing new is revealed. The book, on receipt, should be accompanied by a copy order and an invoice. Although these were already shown on the DFD, they *could* have been missed at the time and then picked up through creation of the Resource Flow Diagram.

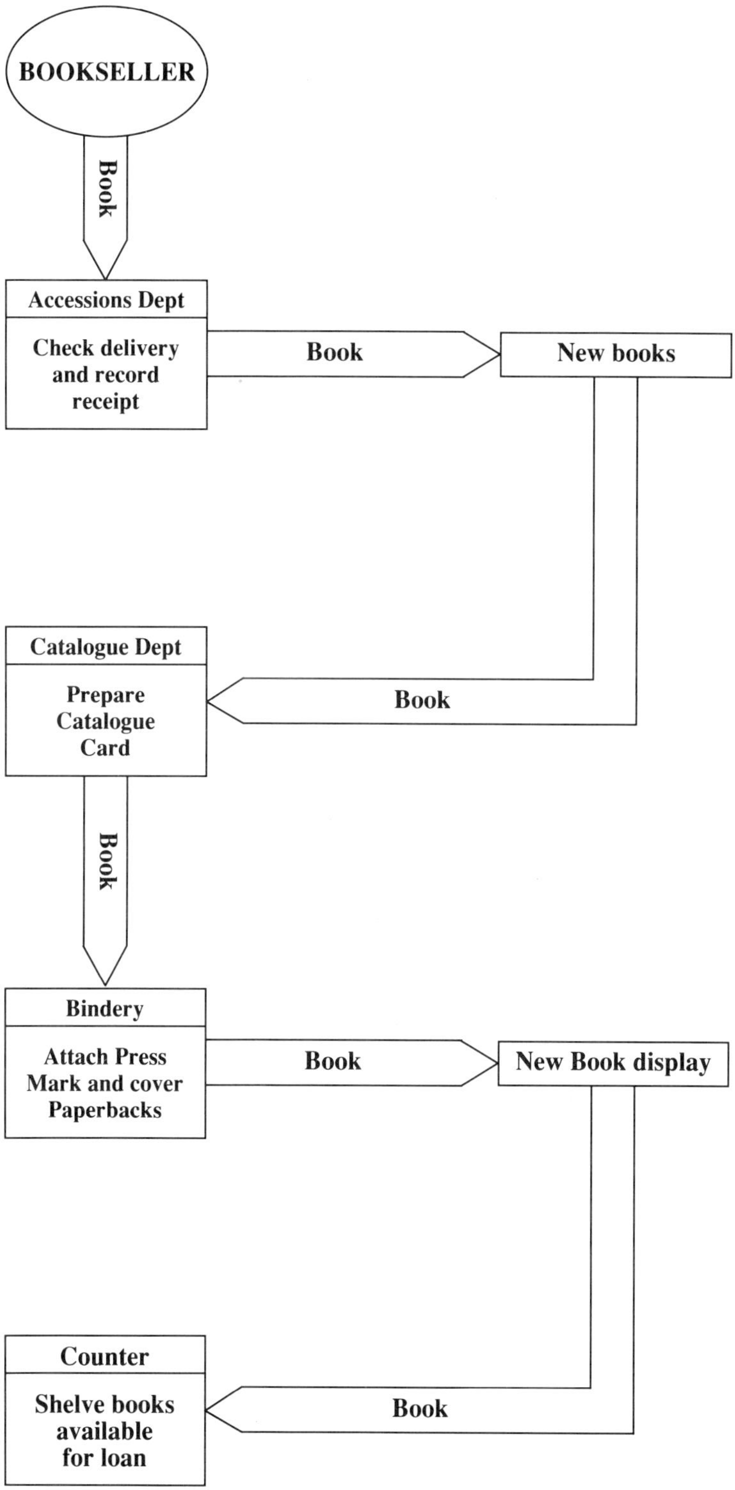

Figure 9.19 Resource Flow Diagram for a book

Note that the diagram indicates other systems with which the Orders System may interface at some time in the future (the Cataloguing System and the Circulation System will both duplicate some of the data available from the book order, ie author, title, publisher, place and date).

Although outside the scope of the Orders System, these other two systems are worth some thought at this stage. It could save a lot of time in future if additional features were to be built into the Orders System to make interfacing a simpler task. (Chapter 26 discusses this topic under *Coping With Change*.) If the other systems are somewhere beyond the current planning horizon, then some high level thought may suffice. If they are to follow on immediately after implementation of the Orders System, then preliminary Feasibility Studies would be worth considering.

LOWER LEVEL DFDs

The boxes on the Level-1 DFD present a high level view of the processes. Each of these high level descriptions can be expanded on a separate sheet into a further set of sub-processes, each of which may itself be subdivided, and so on. Going down to Level-3 and following Miller's recommendation would therefore permit 9 x 9 x 9 = 729 processes to be shown. Of course, not every process would break down into nine parts, and some processes may need to go down to Level-4 or even Level-5. However, Level-3 will usually be found to suffice.

Process box 1 in Figure 9.17 has been taken down to a lower level in Figure 9.20.

The investigation of process 1 reveals that the file of request slips has been omitted from the Level-1 DFD, unless this is the same file as Books on Order. The Accessions Department will need to know who has requested each item if they are to issue a notification of receipt to the requester. This implies that either details of the requester will have to be entered into the system, or the request slips will have to be retained.

WHAT DFDs DON'T SHOW

DFDs can only show what has been discovered. Some information will have been missed, and so the DFDs will be incomplete. The diagrams help in the identification of such instances. For example, data is sometimes shown as being used that has apparently appeared from nowhere. Other omissions may not be so readily apparent. The single viewpoint will rarely reveal all that needs to be known about a system. The complementary techniques of Logical Data Modelling and Entity-Event Modelling give two further viewpoints that will rectify most of the omissions.

Whilst DFDs show processes, they do not show the sequence in which they are carried out. It is not necessary at this stage of analysis. Also it would complicate

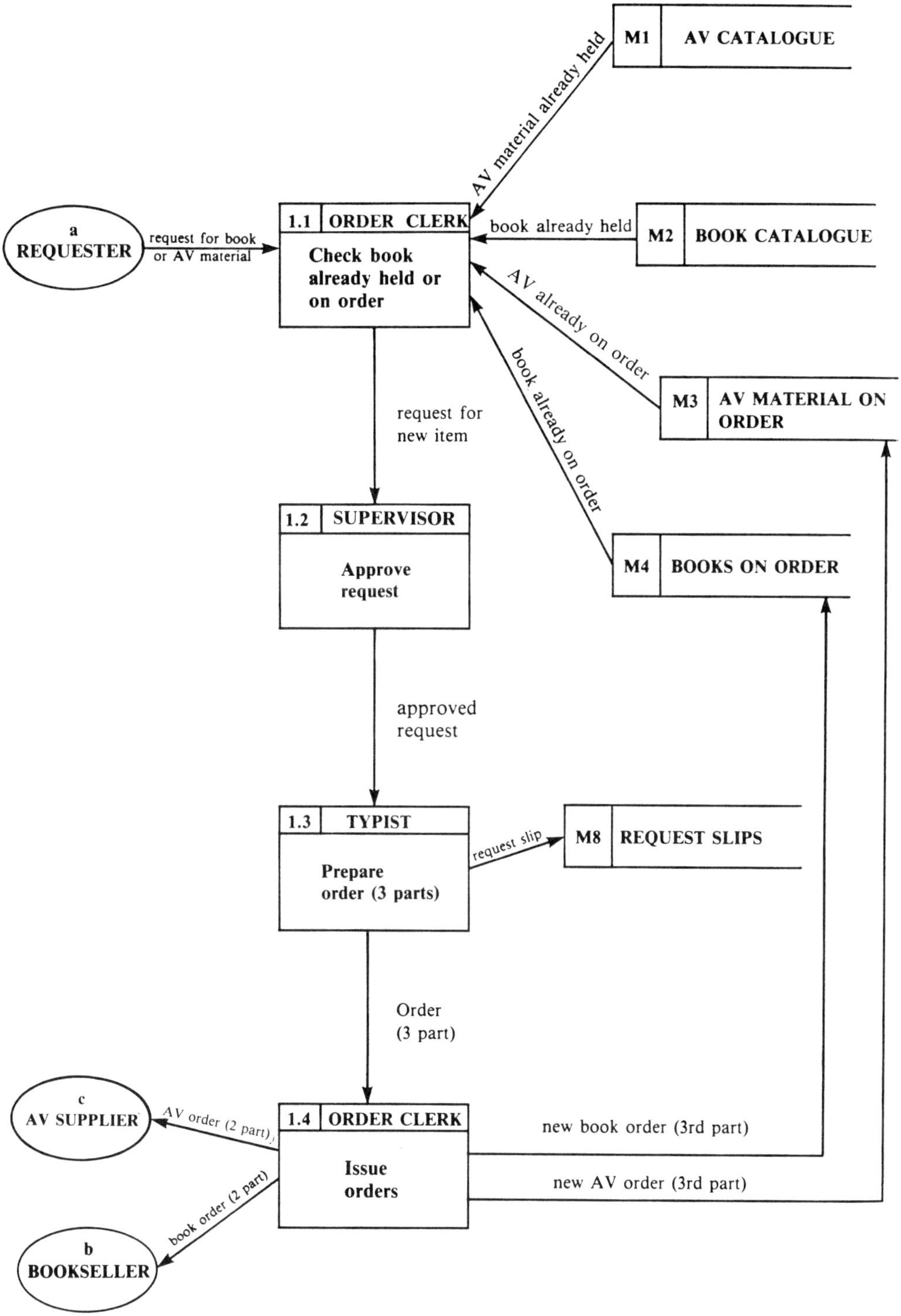

Figure 9.20 Lower level DFD for process 1 in Figure 9.17

the diagrams and thus make them less effective for communication. Sequence and priority, which are essential for design, are established later during the construction of Entity Life Histories (*see* Chapter 11).

The DFDs do not show system qualities and resource usage. These form a part of the Requirements Catalogue (*see* Chapter 13).

As a generalisation the DFDs only show processes that update information held within the system. Processes that merely re-sequence data or present it in reports or as screens of information are recorded in the Requirements Catalogue. DFDs may exceptionally include this type of process if it is critical or sufficiently complex. However, enquiries and reports shown on the early DFDs will normally be removed as part of the logicalisation process (Step 150, Chapter 16), and included instead in the Requirements Catalogue. Eventually they will be defined as enquiry functions at Step 330 (Chapter 18).

PRINCIPAL USES OF THE DFM IN SSADM

The DFM is used throughout the fact finding in SSADM. It is eventually superseded at Step 330 by Function Definitions, which are prepared from the DFM. The Model is a prime source of reference, and is subject to almost constant updating as the investigation proceeds and more and more information is discovered about a system. The steps where information in the Model is created, expanded, significantly changed or used are:

- Step 010 Context Diagram and Current Physical DFD (Level-1) are created.

- Step 020 Level-1 Data Flow Diagram for the required environment is drawn. The Level-1 DFD for the current environment may be extended to Level-2 for processes that are seen as being particularly critical, complex or obscure.

- Step 030 DFDs may be used in support of short listed composite Business System and Technical System Options. The diagrams are amended to show the system after its scope has been agreed.

- Step 110 DFDs from the Feasibility Study are updated to show the current position. In the absence of a Feasibility Study, a Context Diagram and Current Physical Data Flow Diagram (Level-1) will be created during this overview of the full study.

- Step 130 The investigation concentrates on the information contained in the Level-1 DFD and, using Document Flow and Resource Flow Diagrams as an aid to improve the DFD, produces lower level DFDs and the other Data Flow Model documentation: Elementary Process Descriptions, Input/Output Descriptions and External Entity Descriptions.

- Step 140 The Elementary Process Descriptions are used to check that the Logical Data Structure will support the processing.

- Step 150 The DFDs are logicalised to remove the existing physical constraints.

- Step 210 A number of different logical Level-1 DFDs may be created, each showing a different way in which the system could be implemented (Business System Options or BSOs). These will show different boundaries for the system, and the inclusion of different facilities.

- Step 220 The boundary of the system is fixed following selection of a Business System Option.

- Step 310 The DFDs and supporting documentation are amended to whatever level is required to fully define the processing of the selected Business System Option.

- Step 320 The Elementary Process Descriptions are used to check that the Logical Data Structure for the selected Business System Option will support the processing.

- Step 330 Used in preparation of Update Function Definitions.

- Step 360 Used for reference when creating Entity Life Histories.

The DFDs of the required system, as created in Step 310, should continue to be updated throughout development and subsequent maintenance. They will then provide an excellent overview of the system as it finally exists, and so will be an ideal way for someone to learn about the system, either as a user of the system or as one of the computer department with responsibility for maintenance.

USER INVOLVEMENT

Users must check that the information shown on the DFDs and supporting documentation is complete and correct (to the extent that it should be for that stage of development). You will have the opportunity of doing this both informally as the investigation proceeds, and formally during the quality reviews. If the informal checks have been carried out with care there should be no nasty surprises during the formal reviews.

Checklists

Context Diagram (form SSADMv4 3)

Ensure that:

- all of the external entities are shown;
- the data flows correctly indicate the scope of the system.

DFDs (form SSADMv4 4 and 5)

Check that:

- The diagram conforms to SSADM or installation standards;
- all of the external entities are shown, as on the Context Diagram;
- the system boundary is clear and is correctly shown, (unless establishment of boundaries is the task under consideration);
- the main system inputs and outputs are shown, as on the Context Diagram;
- all of the job functions are represented;
- all of the terminology, ie of external entities, data flows, processes and data stores, is meaningful to you;
- the different levels of DFDs are consistent in terms of:
    - external entities;
    - data flows;
    - data stores;
- the only enquiries remaining on the DFDs after logicalisation are major ones;
- all physical aspects of the current system have been removed by logicalisation, unless they are a constraint on the design;
- supporting documentation describes support for functions outside the system boundary, such as the production of reports and the availability of enquiry facilities;
- all current system facilities are included in the required system, or reasons for their exclusion noted.

Document Flow Diagrams (form SSADMv4 12)

The Document Flow Diagram is not an output product at the end of a step. Its purpose is to elicit information that should be on the DFDs, but that may have been missed. Once it has served this purpose it has no further use within the method. However, you will be involved in its production and checking.

Check that:

- all the documents that are currently in use in the system are represented on the diagram(s);
- the data flows that represent the documents show *all* the document's movements, for every copy of each document, from initiation to final filing, to disposal outside the system, or to destruction.

Elementary Process Descriptions (form SSADMv4 14)

These forms amplify the information shown on the lowest level process boxes on the DFDs. One form is used for each lowest level process.

Check that:

- one form is held for each lowest level process;
- the names of the processes are meaningful;
- the description of each process is both correct and complete.

External Entity Descriptions (form SSADMv4 21)

One form is required for each external entity shown on the DFDs. Remember that these comprise real world people/organisations, other systems, and other departments/people within your own organisation who interface with the system.

Check that:

- one form is held for each external entity;
- the descriptions correctly specify the responsibilities or functions of the external entity, and any constraints on how it will interact with the system.

I/O (Input/Output) Descriptions (form SSADMv4 26)

One form is required for each data flow that crosses the system boundary to or from an external entity.

On each form, check that all of the data items contained in the data flow are listed.

Logical Data Store/Entity Cross-reference (form SSADMv4 29)

These forms are created after logicalisation of the DFDs.

Check that:

- all data stores from the logicalised DFDs, and all entities from the LDS are represented;
- the matching of data stores and entities has been done correctly;
- each entity is contained within only one data store (ie no entities are split between two or more data stores);
- each data store consists of one or more related entities on the LDS.

Resource Flow Diagrams (form SSADMv4 43)

The Resource Flow Diagram is similar to, and serves the same purpose as, the Document Flow Diagram. Once it has served this purpose it has no further use within the method. Your involvement is in its production and checking.

Check that:

- the resources that have been documented are correctly represented on the diagram(s);
- the resource flows show *all* of the resource's movements within the system;
- data flows have been added to the diagram where known;
- no data flows will be required in the system where none is shown on the diagram.

10

Logical Data Modelling — LDM

INTRODUCTION

If you go into your office in the morning and find that you have had an overnight visit from one of the light-fingered fraternity you may find papers scattered everywhere. You may have a lot of trouble carrying out your tasks. Scattered data is not a lot of use. It needs to be organised in some way. There are probably many ways in which it *could* be organised. Some will be better than others. What you could do with is knowing the best way to organise it, – a *data structure* that is the best, not just for one task, but for all the tasks you may need to do, including the ones that will be needed some time in the future and which have not yet been considered. (Guidance on thinking about future requirements is given in *Coping with Change* in Chapter 26.)

Minimisation of problems arising from requirements which you totally fail to envisage, is achieved by having a simple data structure. Drawing a Logical Data Structure (LDS) is the first step on the way to achieving such a structure.

Data Flow Diagrams show three aspects of data:

- what is stored;
- where it is used;
- what happens to it in the system.

In computer systems, as in manual systems, all this data will be organised into files (or a database). The task for the analyst/designer is deciding how to do this organisation. He must decide what to store and, if more than one data file will be needed, how to distribute the data between the various files. The aims are:

- to hold each item of data once only, to avoid duplication;
- to refer to the minimum number of records while doing the processing, to minimise disk accessing.

Unfortunately these are conflicting aims, and so some compromises will often be necessary in the final physical design. The software used may also impose some restrictions, for example on the number of files that can be open currently.

THE LOGICAL DATA MODEL

The LDS shows the names of the entities, but not the detail they contain nor their relationships with the DFDs. The LDS is therefore supplemented by other documents to make up the Logical Data Model:

- Entity Descriptions which include details of the data held for each entity, and its relationships with other entities.
- Relationship Descriptions which describe every relationship on the LDS. The documents are completed in pairs, there being one for each end of the relationship.

Also, and additional to the Logical Data Model, are the following:

- Data Catalogue (which was also mentioned as supplementing the Data Flow Model). This contains the:
  - Attribute/Data Item Descriptions (information about each element of data).
  - Grouped Domain Descriptions (for attributes of identical format or with identical validation rules, such as dates. Several different dates may be held within a record, eg date of birth, date employment started, dates of promotions).
- Enquiry Access Paths showing the routes through the LDS to satisfy each of the enquiries.
- Logical Data Store/Entity cross-references showing the correspondence between data stores on the DFDs and entities on the LDS.

TERMINOLOGY

In any system, individual data items are grouped. If information is held about a customer it is likely to show name, address, telephone number, and possibly more information depending on his relationship with the company, typically delivery address, credit status, balance owed and so on. These individual items – name, address, etc are known as *fields* or *attributes* or *data items*, and the collection or group of related attributes is known as an *entity*.

If you wished to look up any information about a customer in a manual system, you would probably use his name. Then, provided that the file of records was in alphabetical order, you would be able to locate the information that you require. You would have used the name as the *key*.

An entity is thus something about which you need to store information, and which has a unique key.

Perhaps the customer might require a car part. His dealer may hold his stock record of car parts in the manufacturer's part number order. Unfortunately the customer is unlikely to know the manufacturer's code for the item he needs. If he wishes to buy a new red ash tray for his Florentini Aspazzio GTi, he is unlikely to know that it is part number FA/1275/86/rh/r, and most likely nor will the person who serves him, as most people will have traded their Florentinis in when the ash trays were full, let alone broken. The assistant will thus need to refer to a parts list which will show:

Ash trays, Aspazzio, 1992– ,	**right hand drive:**
	black: FA/1275/86/rh/b
	red: FA/1275/86/rh/r
	white: FA/1275/86/rh/w

Table 10.1 Parts list

From this he can go to his stock list and check whether he has any in stock. This trail from one record to another related one is called an *access path*. If all the information you need is not in the one place, then you need access paths to navigate you around the various files in which the different pieces of information (attributes) are held.

DATA DESIGN WITH THE LDS

The starting point for data design is the Logical Data Structure. The LDS is SSADM terminology for a diagram that, sometimes with minor variations, is also known as an Entity Relationship Model, or a Bachman Diagram. The technique for constructing it is also known as data modelling or entity modelling.

The LDS is all about establishing the entities you are interested in, and seeing what access paths you need (ie how the entities are related to each other) in order to get to all the information you require.

The initial LDS gives a top down view of the data that will be stored and used by the system. It is top down in that it shows logical groupings of data, without initially looking in detail at the data contents of the groups. It also shows how the groups are related to each other. An alternative view of the data (bottom up) is obtained by Relational Data Analysis (Stage 3, Step 340, Chapter 18). As development proceeds, the LDS is modified and developed into the data structure from which the final physical design will be derived and held within the computer system.

REPRESENTATION

The LDS contains only two elements, illustrated in Figure 10.1.

Figure 10.1 LDS symbols

ENTITIES

In computer jargon, anything about which data is stored is known as an entity. The customer is an entity, and so is an order. Clerks who have held such information in written records may be alarmed to find that they have been filing away entities all this time. Their manual records can be considered as being approximately equivalent to entities.

Each entity is represented in the system as a group of items of data (attributes). Thus the entity *Customer* will be represented by an identifying number (Customer ID), name, address, telephone number, credit limit, etc.

In the system as it is finally developed, it is highly likely that whilst the same data may be held in total, it will be grouped differently to give the *logical entities* as used by the system.

Entities must be uniquely identifiable within the system. Depending upon the type of system, other typical entities are:

- supplier;
- account;

- reader;
- book;
- department.

The unique identifier (key) for each of these is, typically, supplier number, account number, etc.

Entities are drawn on the LDS as soft boxes (ie boxes with rounded corners), as shown in Figure 10.2.

Figure 10.2 LDS representation of an entity

RELATIONSHIPS

The line joining two entities shows that they are directly related. The degree of relationship is also shown. There are three possible degrees of relationship between entities, as shown in Figure 10.3.

The *crow's foot* indicates the *many*. The one-to-one and the many-to-many relationships are the subject of particular scrutiny during analysis, with the objective of converting them to one-to-many relationships.

The *crow's foot* attached to the order in Figure 10.4 indicates many, and drawing this shows that one customer may have one or more orders. The diagram tells the designer that:

- he will need to have two files;
- that to make up an order the system will need to look at both files;
- there must be a cross-reference between them.

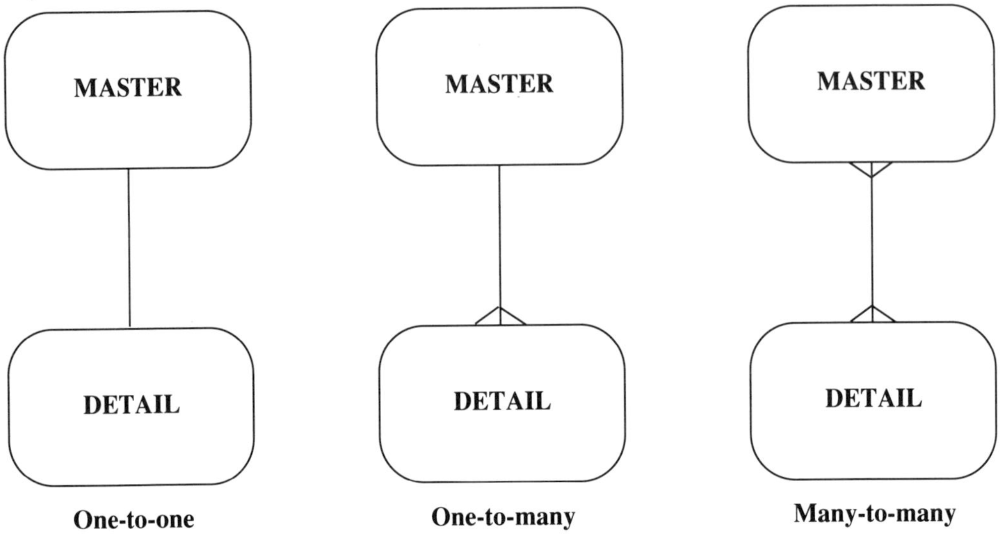

Figure 10.3 Degrees of relationships between entities

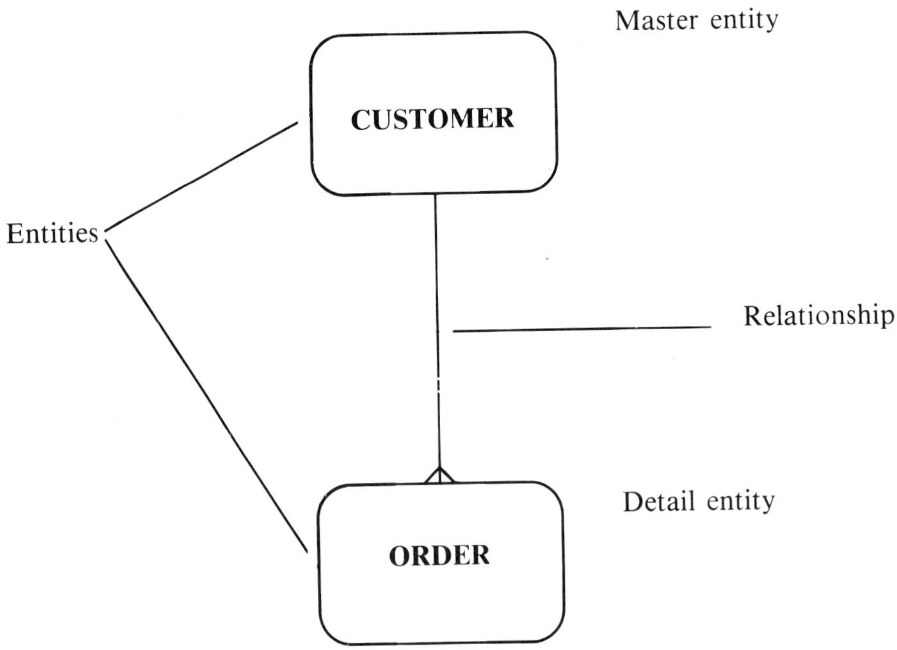

Figure 10.4 The relationship between Customer and Order

The One-to-One Relationship

A university library was planned to have a Short Loan Collection, for books with few copies but in heavy demand for limited periods after certain lectures and before exams. The loan condition was that a student could take out one book, for one hour. This required a one-to-one relationship, shown in Figure 10.5.

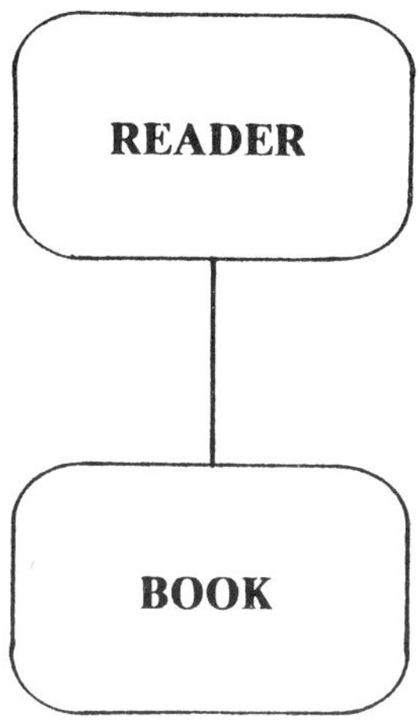

Figure 10.5 A one-to-one relationship

The One-to-Many Relationship

In most libraries each reader can take out several books at a time. This is the conventional one-to-many relationship as in Figure 10.6.

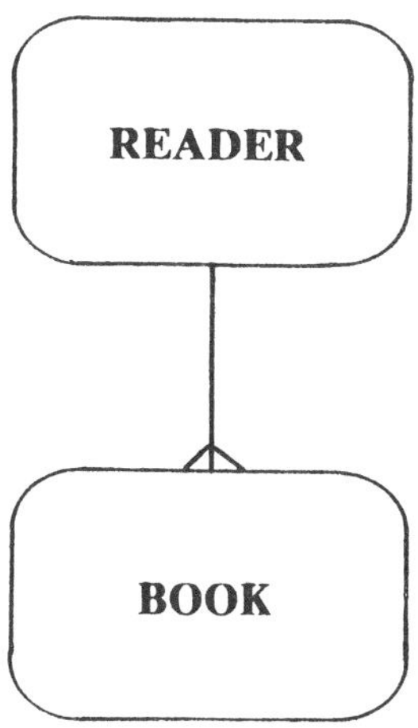

Figure 10.6 A one-to-many relationship

The Many-to-Many Relationship

Most issues of books are one-off affairs: a book is borrowed, read, and then returned. If the library wished to maintain a historical record so that they would know who had borrowed each book, the LDS would show a many-to-many relationship as in Figure 10.7. Anyone planning a pornographic library could find this a useful facility for blackmail purposes.

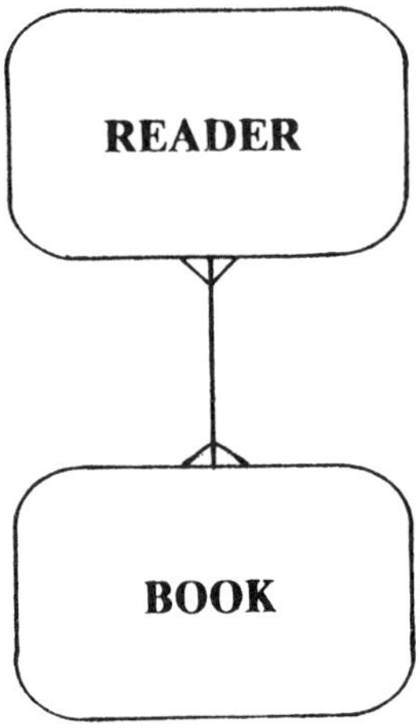

Figure 10.7 A many-to-many relationship

Validity of Relationships

In first constructing an LDS, all three types of relationship may well be shown. Two of the three are, however, suspect. Valid one-to-one relationships, although they can exist, are rather rare. At an early stage in the evolution of the LDS, consideration will be given to removing such relationships and joining the two separate entities together to form a single composite entity. One-to-one relationships are only valid if the two entities have:

- different keys; or

- different lives, for example they come into the system and leave the system through different events, at different times (this is a consideration for Entity Life Histories in the next chapter).

The one-to-one example in Figure 10.5 is a valid relationship in the circumstances described. Nevertheless, in the final diagram it will be shown as a one-to-many relationship, the important concept being that of master to detail rather than the actual degree of the relationship.

The many-to-many relationship is a perfectly valid concept, but is difficult to handle by computer program and is outside the scope of many data base management systems (DBMSs). Because complexity should *always* be avoided if at all possible, the many-to-many relationship is *always* removed in SSADM. This is done by inserting a *link* entity, giving two one-to-many relationships instead. The link entity is an entity in its own right and will often be found to have other attributes. Its absence in the first place is often an omission from the diagram rather than something that did not already exist. The example at Figure 10.7 would therefore be rationalised by the insertion of a *loan record* to give the diagram at Figure 10.8.

Figure 10.8 Insertion of a link entity

The *loan record* would thus contain at least two attributes:

- book number;
- reader number.

One such record would be held for each occasion on which a book was loaned. (The record could, of course, contain more attributes, depending on the requirements of the system.)

Multiple Relationships

A master may be related unconditionally to several detail entities, and a detail may have several masters. This is shown in figure 10.9.

Relationship link phrases

Each relationship is described by a phrase that indicates the nature of the relationship between the two entities. In Figure 10.12, the phrases show that the customer places orders, and that orders are placed by the customer. These phrases are then formalised into relationship statements that specify the relationship in terms that are both precise and unambiguous, eg *Each order must be placed by one and only one customer*. Derivation of these statements is important. If it proves to be difficult it may be due to an incomplete understanding of the data.

Volumetric information

The diagram may also be annotated with volumetric information (how many of each? how often? when? etc). Fully detailed volumetric information is recorded on the Entity Descriptions.

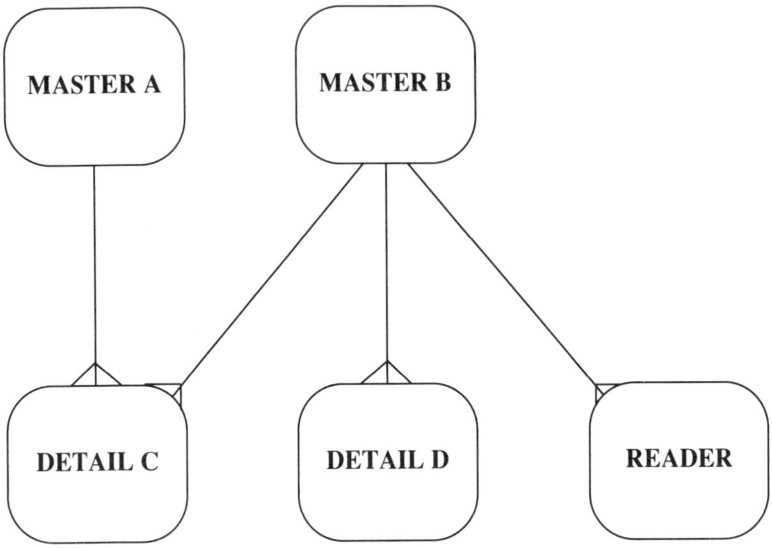

Figure 10.9 Relationships with multiple entities

PROCESSING IN PRACTICE

If a customer places an order, then the supplier will need to hold data on both the customer (name and address) and order (what he wants). A customer may place many orders. To hold the customer's name and address with each order will duplicate the name and address within the system. This is shown in Figure 10.10.

There are four problems with this:

- The customer's name and address will have to be entered each time;
- it will occupy more space;
- what is meant to be the same data may not be identical;
- if the customer changed his address before delivery, there would be n different records to change.

To overcome this, in the computer system the customer data could be held in one file and the order details in another. As it would then be necessary to refer from one to the other a cross-reference would be necessary, and would be achieved by noting the Customer Number on each of the order records. Figure 10.11 illustrates this.

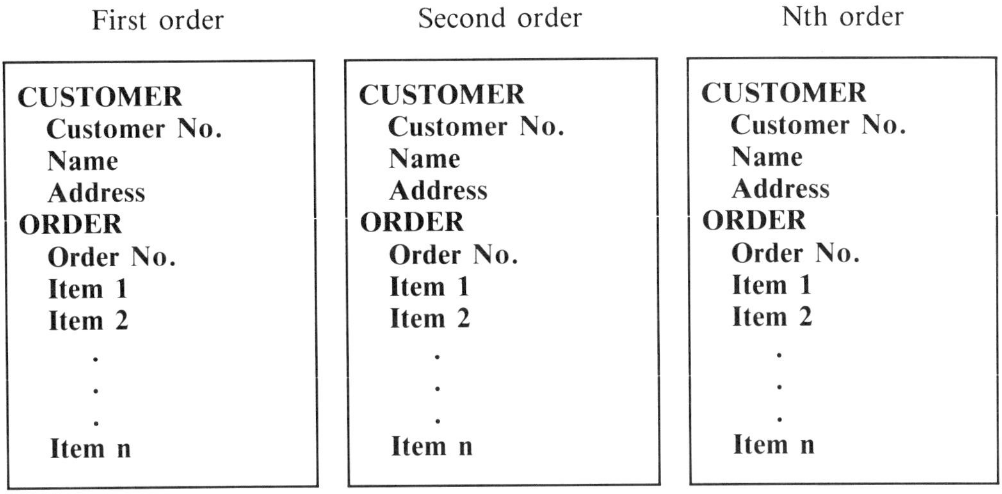

Figure 10.10 Multiple orders for the same customer (1)

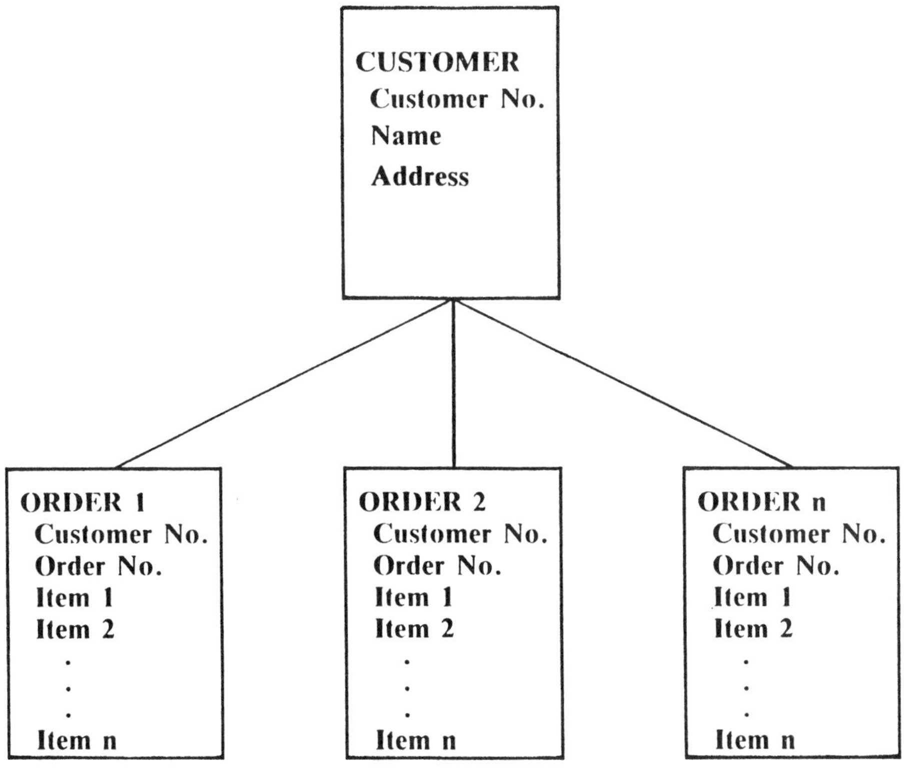

Figure 10.11 Multiple orders for the same customer (2)

To send an order to a customer, the system will need to find the name and address from the customer file and all the orders from the orders file. The two files are thus related. The relationship is shown diagrammatically in Figure 10.12.

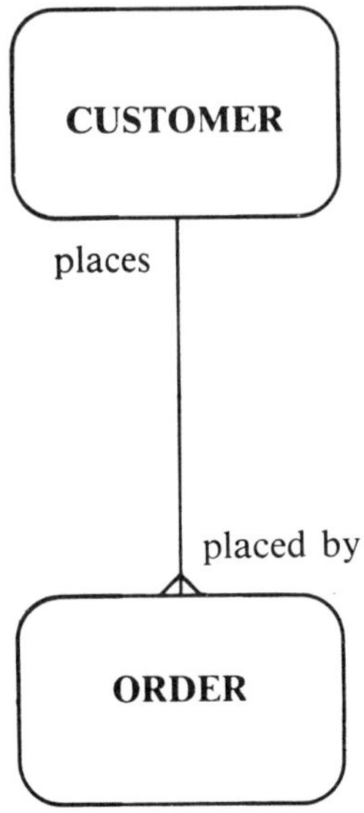

Figure 10.12 Link phrases in the relationship between Customer and Order

THE LDS DEPENDS ON REQUIREMENTS

The relationship between entities will vary depending on the system requirements. Extending Figure 10.12 to include the issue of invoices could result in any of the relationships shown in Figure 10.13, where the different system requirements are:

1. Each order to be completely filled and a separate invoice to be issued for each separate order processed that day. Orders which cannot be completed are to be retained until adequate stocks are available.

2. Each order to be completely filled, but only one invoice to be issued if more than one order is processed that day.

3. Orders may be sent out part filled, with a separate invoice for each part.

4. Orders may be part filled, but only one invoice is to be issued if more than one part order is processed that day.

RELATIONSHIP WITH THE DFDs

The LDS represents a second viewpoint on the system. The cross-checking between DFDs and the LDS can always be expected to reveal information that

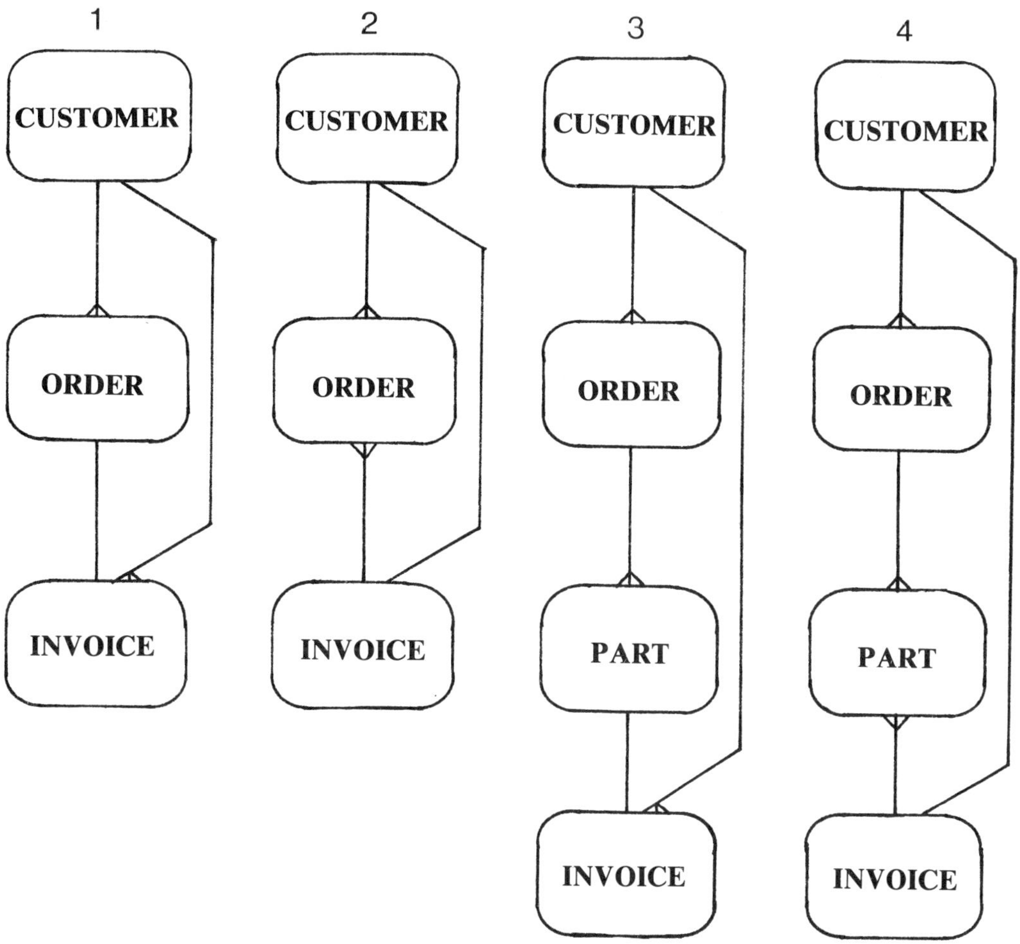

Figure 10.13 Relationships depend on requirements

has initially been missed from each of them. It assists towards a more thorough analysis of the system.

A little thought will show that there is a relationship between entities on the LDS (which represent data) and data stores on DFDs (which also represent data) and this permits (and requires) that cross-checks are made between them. Inevitably in drawing the two separately, a comparison between the two is likely to reveal omissions from both. The DFDs and the LDS must contain the same information in total, and the data structure on the LDS must permit the processing indicated on the DFDs. Thus the two diagrams are complementary, and whilst entities and data stores may not be identical in content, nevertheless there are relationships between them. These relationships are shown on Logical Data Store/Entity Cross-references.

AN LDS FOR A LIBRARY ORDERS AND ACQUISITIONS SYSTEM

Figure 9.17 showed the current physical system Level-1 DFD for a Library Orders and Acquisitions System. The library has decided that every item ordered should be prepared on an individual form. Thus if two copies of the same book are ordered, two separate order forms will be created, even if both are going to the same bookseller. This:

- permits the supplier to send one copy of an order back with each item supplied, which assists in control;
- removes the need to cater for partial orders being supplied;
- permits the orders for two identical items to be placed with different suppliers, so that comparisons can be made between the service provided by each.

(Note that if the library regularly ordered large numbers of identical books, then thc requirements would be different. Separate forms would not be practical and a different solution would be needed.)

When the analyst constructs the LDS it could look something like Figure 10.14.

Comparison of DFDs with the LDS

A comparison of the LDS with the DFDs shows that several LDS entities are not shown as data stores. The possibilities are:

- they have been missed by the analyst who drew up the DFD; or
- they are not entities, and should not be present on the LDS.

Five of the omissions are:

- AV supplier;
- Bookseller;
- Donor;
- Newsagent;
- Requester.

These appear on the DFD as external entities. External entities can be expected to be represented within a system as data stores, and an experienced analyst would have been unlikely to have missed them all. However, not all analysts are

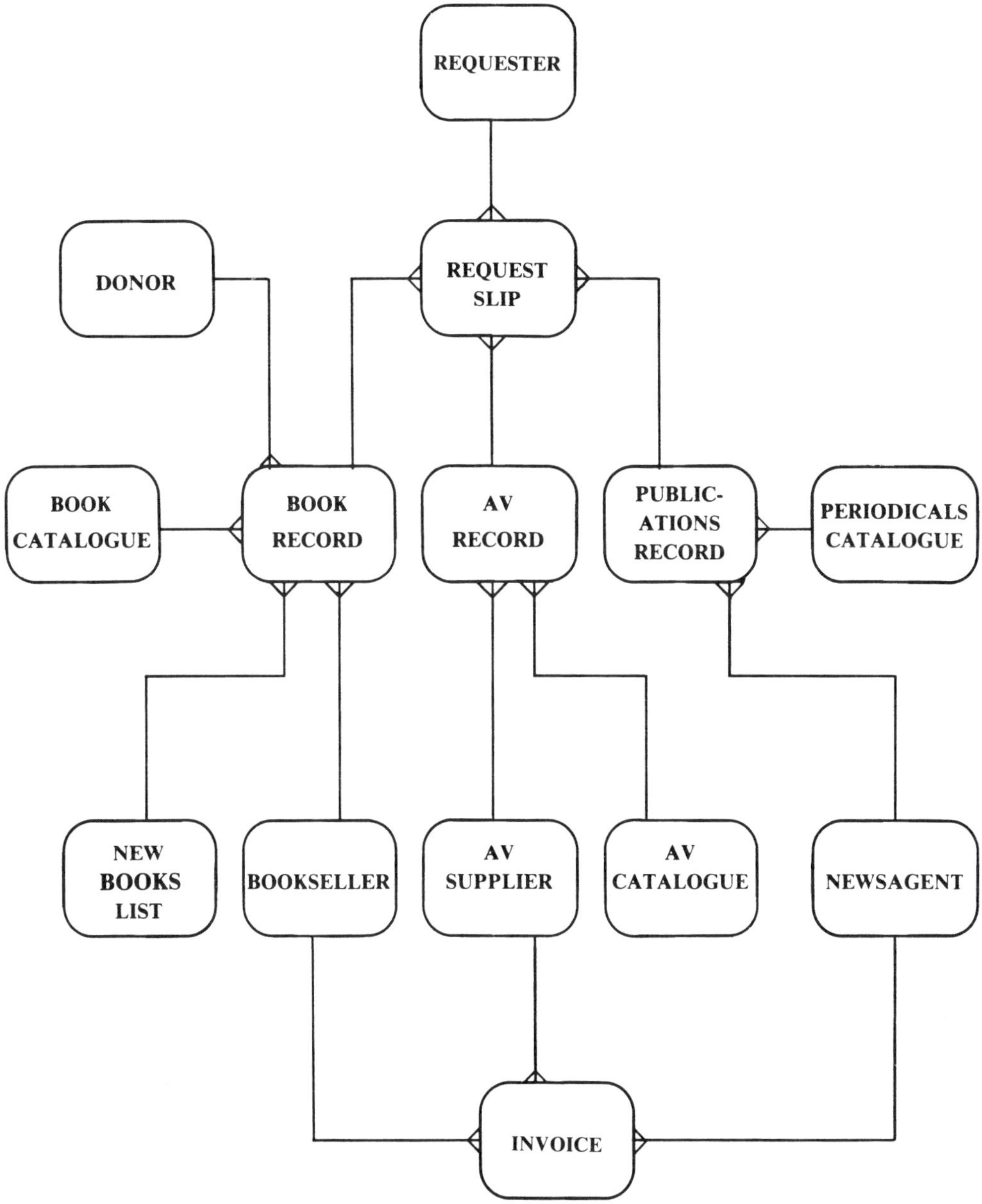

Figure 10.14 LDS for a Library Orders and Acquisitions System

experienced, and this comparison shows that what is missed by one technique can be picked up by another. A revised DFD could conceivably show five more data stores – AV Supplier Records, Bookseller Records, etc. In practice it would be more likely to combine some or all of them; for example the first four could all be classed as Supplier Records.

The other entity shown on the LDS but not on the DFDs is Publications Record. A copy order is held in the library for each publication ordered, and was missed when the DFD was drawn up. Again, a further data store must be added to the DFD.

An important lesson to be learned is that there is no need to strive for absolute perfection in the end product of one technique before going on to the next. Managers must keep a very careful eye open for this excessive pursuit of a technique, and call a halt when the returns no longer justify the effort. Continuing with the analysis techniques will pick up omissions, even from diagrams that were thought to be complete and correct when they were drawn up.

PROCESSING REQUIREMENTS ON THE LDS

The primary purpose of the LDS is to establish the data structure. However, a little thought about relationships will also reveal that some processing requirements can (and must) be indicated.

The examples given in this chapter have necessarily been simple ones to illustrate the technique. The LDS for a real system would be likely to contain many more entities, and more complex relationships between them, which may be:

- mandatory or optional (mandatory relationships must exist, whereas optional relationship may or may not exist);
- exclusive (relationships may be with more than one other entity, but only with one at any one time);
- multiple (more than one relationship between the same two entities);
- recursive (the relationship is with itself), for example a middle manager will manage others, but will also himself be managed.

The conventions for showing these on the diagrams are illustrated below.

Mandatory and Optional Relationships

The relationship line between two entities may be solid, dashed, or a combination of the two.

In Figure 10.15, A cannot exist without B, and B cannot exist without A. The relationship is mandatory. In the example, a book cannot become part of the circulation system until catalogue cards have been prepared.

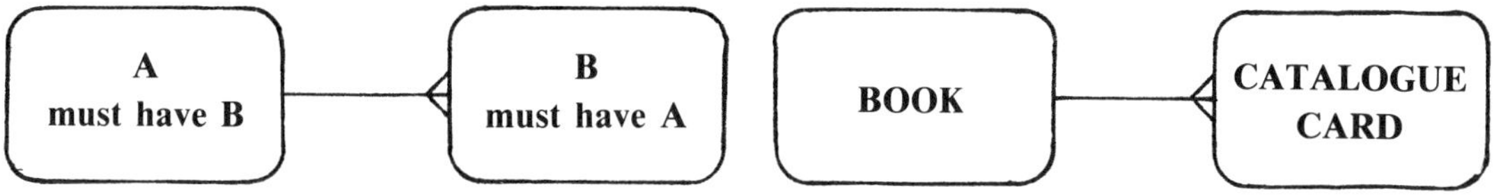

Figure 10.15 A mandatory relationship

In Figure 10.16, neither A nor B is dependent on the other. The relationship is optional. A registered reader may not have any books on loan, and all the books on the shelves are without readers.

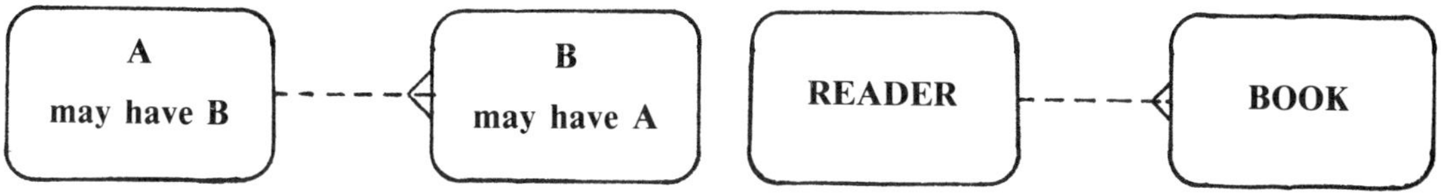

Figure 10.16 An optional relationship

In Figure 10.17, *A* can exist without *B,* but *B* cannot exist without *A*. A reader may make a reservation, but a reservation is impossible without a reader.

Figure 10.18 shows that *A* cannot exist without *B,* but *B* can exist without *A*. If a supervisor leaves the company the assistants will continue to be employed until a new supervisor is appointed. Processing will need to accept that this is a valid condition. It will also have to ensure that access to the detail continues to be available in the absence of the master. (Note that if provision is needed for all the assistants to go, leaving the supervisor with no-one to supervise, then the relationship will be optional as in Figure 10.16.)

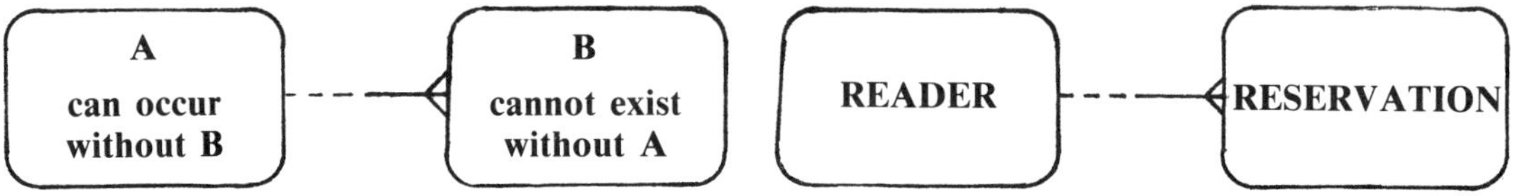

Figure 10.17 A master with optional detail

Exclusive relationships

There are often occasions when entities can be related to perhaps only one of two (or more) possible relationships. This is an either/or situation, and is shown by drawing an arc on the relevant relationship lines. In the example at Figure 10.19, for each separate loan a reader may borrow either a book or an audio cassette (a master with exclusive details).

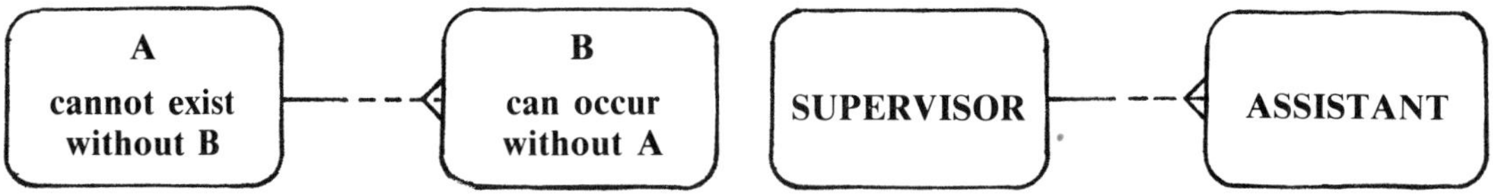

Figure 10.18 A detail with optional master

He could, of course, borrow both items, but this would count as two separate loan transactions.

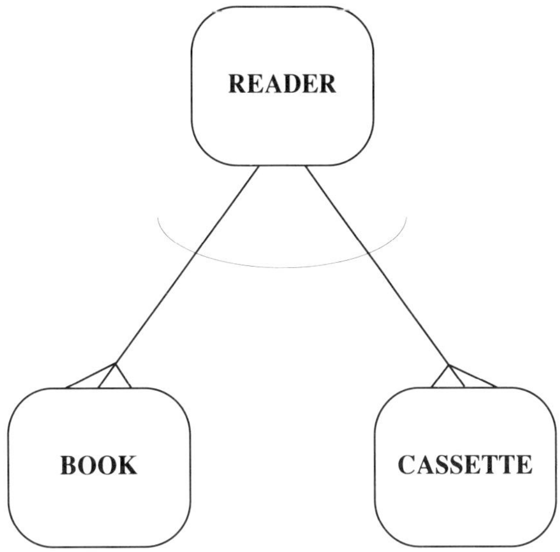

Figure 10.19 A master with exclusive details

A book may be borrowed from the library by one of its registered readers, or may be loaned to another library (an inter-library loan) for one of its readers (a detail with exclusive masters). Figure 10.20 shows this.

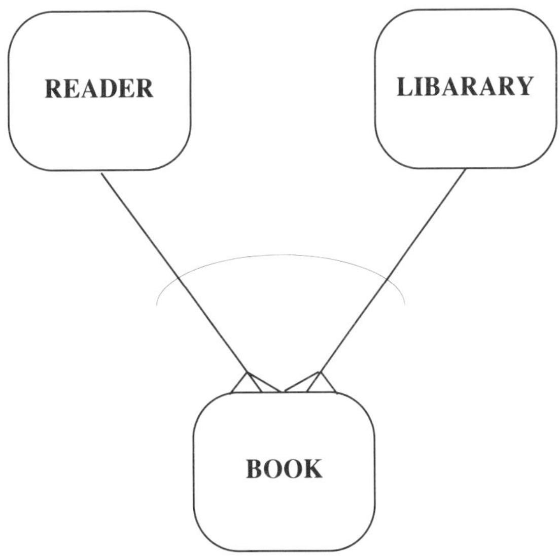

Figure 10.20 A detail with exclusive masters

Such restrictions on relationships are aspects of the system that must be covered by processing logic within the system.

Multiple relationships between the same entities

There may be occasions when entities are related in more than one way. Figure 10.21 shows that a systems analyst may be the creator of a diagram, and may also be responsible for the checking of diagrams prepared by others.

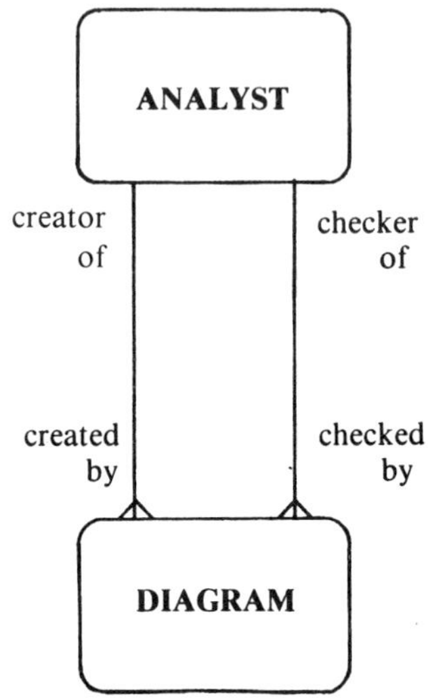

Figure 10.21 Multiple relationships between the same entities

Recursive relationships

The managerial hierarchy in a company may consist of senior managers, middle managers, and junior managers. These could be shown on an LDS as in Figure 10.22.

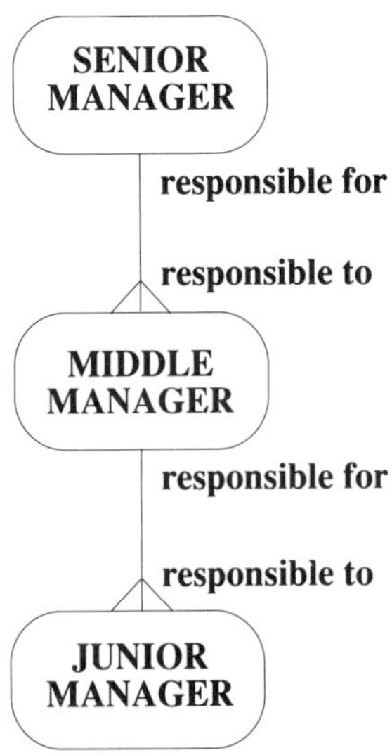

Figure 10.22 A management structure

A shorter way of showing the same type of structure is the recursive relationship notation, or pig's ear as it is usually known. It is illustrated in Figure 10.23.

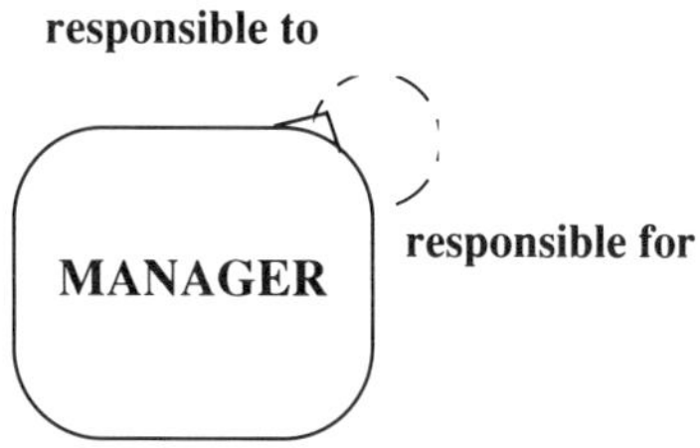

Figure 10.23 Recursive representation of the management structure

Note that both Figures 10.22 and 10.23 would usually allow for optionality. The most senior manager may not be responsible to another manager, and the junior manager would not be responsible for any other managers.

PRINCIPAL USES OF THE LDM IN SSADM

As with DFDs, the LDS is another prime source of reference throughout the Analysis Phase.

The steps in which the LDS (and other documents in the Logical Data Model) are specifically featured are:

- Step 010 Overview LDS created for the required environment
- Step 020 LDS created for the current environment
- Step 030 Used in support of short listed composite Business System and Technical System Options
- Step 110 Overview current system LDS created
- Step 140 LDM created of the data in the current environment, consisting of the updated LDS together with the Data Catalogue items, Entity Descriptions and Relationship Descriptions

- Step 150 Current environment LDM validated against the logicalised DFDs and Logical Data Store/Entity Cross-references prepared
- Step 210 May be used in support of the short listed Business System Options with a different LDS for each different way in which the system could be implemented
- Step 320 Required system LDM created
- Step 340 Relational Data Analysis used to enhance the LDS
- Step 360 Used in the creation of Entity Life Histories (ELHs), which in turn results in the enhancement of the LDM. Enquiry Access Paths are created
- Step 520 State indicators from ELHs added to the Entity Descriptions
- Step 620 Used in the creation of the first-cut Physical Data Design
- Step 640 Data design may be restructured to meet performance criteria
- Step 660 Physical implementation cross-referenced to the Required System LDM.

USER INVOLVEMENT

In order to carry out the processing you require, the system needs to obtain the relevant data which it holds, and this is likely to be contained in several different records (entities). The system must be able to get at this linked group of records. It does this from the relationships that have been expressed in the LDS. Simplicity and speed of processing, and even the ability to do the work at all, are dependent on an efficient data structure and so it is important to establish that all of the relationships have been correctly expressed. Errors in the structure can have a heavy cost later in development and maintenance. It is in your own interests to ensure that the LDM documentation is correct.

Checklists

LDS (form SSADMv4 30)

Check that:

- the diagram conforms to SSADM or installation standards;
- each box represents a meaningful entity and has:
  - a plausible, unique identifier (key);
  - data items associated with it;

- all of the data groups held, or required to be held, by the systems are present;
- the relationships between the entities are *direct* ones;
- the types of relationship, ie mandatory, optional, exclusive, multiple, recursive, are correctly shown;
- all the many-to-many relationships have been satisfactorily modified to one-to-many relationships;
- the LDS structure will support the processing shown on the DFDs and Elementary Process Descriptions.

Entity Description (form SSADMv4 17 and 18)

One must be held for each entity. Check that:

- a plausible identifier (key) has been selected;
- meaningful names have been given to each attribute (data item), and all synonyms are shown;
- initially the major attributes are included, building up to a complete record of all associated attributes by the end of the study;
- the volumetric information is correct (how many occurrences there are, what growth there is in the data, and how often reference is made) so that sufficient room can be allocated for the data within the system, and so that the time taken for processing can be calculated (some of this information is often also entered on the LDS);
- the relationships have been correctly described;
- the user role information is correct;
- the access rights meet with your security requirements;
- the active life of an entity has been considered when defining the archiving and destruction details.

Attribute/Data Item Descriptions (form SSADMv4 1)

One form must be held for each attribute. Check that:

- each document is complete and correct as far as the information for which you are responsible (or have knowledge) is concerned;

- validation information has been provided, so that the system can check that no errors of format have been made when entering the data ie:
  - whether the attribute is numeric, alphabetic, or a mixture of the two (alphanumeric);
  - its length, ie how many characters it contains;
  - what validity checks can be applied to it, eg does it contain numbers within a specified range?
  - whether it can be validated against any other information held within the system, eg if the diagnosis is pregnancy, is the patient female?

Grouped Domain Descriptions (form SSADMv4 25)

These forms are used to show formatting and validation rules that are common to more than one attribute, and are used if it saves time to do so. A frequent use is for 'Dates', which often occur many times within a system (date of birth, date of marriage, date of death, etc). Checks are as for Attribute/Data Item Descriptions.

Relationship Descriptions (form SSADMv4 41)

A pair of forms is held for each relationship. Check that:

- the relationship is a direct one between the two entities;
- mandatory/optional has been correctly identified;
- the volumetric information is correct.

Logical Data Store/Entity Cross-reference (form SSADMv4 29)

It is permissible for a data store to contain more than one entity. It is not permissible for an entity to be split over more than one data store. When investigating the current system, these requirements may not be satisfied. Logicalisation should resolve these anomalies. Checking is facilitated by transference of matching parts of each diagram onto the Data Store/Entity Cross-reference. Check that:

- all data stores from the logicalised DFDs, and all entities from the LDS are represented;
- the matching of data stores and entities has been done correctly;
- each entity is contained within only one data store, ie no entities are split between two or more data stores;
- each data store consists of one or more related entities on the LDS.

Enquiry Access Paths (form SSADMv4 15)

These forms, created at Step 360, are derived from Function Definitions and the Required System Logical Data Model. They are diagrams that show extracts from the LDS. They illustrate the route to be taken through the data structure to process each enquiry. You are unlikely to see them.

11
Entity – Event Modelling – EEM

INTRODUCTION

The Data Flow Diagrams show processes, but give no indication of the sequence in which they are carried out; and data, but not in any sort of structured way.

The LDS puts a structure on the data and cross checks against the DFDs, but does not show how data changes over a period of time.

The third diagrammatic view of a system is provided by Entity Life Histories (ELHs), created during Entity-Event Modelling (EEM). ELHs give a visual picture of each entity, and put a time structure on every event that may affect an entity throughout its existence in the system. Thus they put a sequence on the processes on the DFDs. Where events could be inferred from data flows on DFDs, on ELHs they are made specific.

An ELH therefore relates to the LDS, there being one ELH for each entity on the LDS. Also, events identified during Entity-Event Modelling correspond to the flows on the DFDs. Thus all three of the major diagramming techniques complement each other. Between them they ensure that there is very little of any significance that escapes the very tight analysis net which SSADM casts around the system. Note that there may also be system induced events, triggered by time or by information generated within the system.

THE ENTITY-EVENT MODEL

The Entity-Event Model consists of the ELHs and Effect Correspondence Diagrams.

ELH REPRESENTATION

There is only one symbol on an ELH. A rectangular box, shown in Figure 11.1, is used for all purposes.

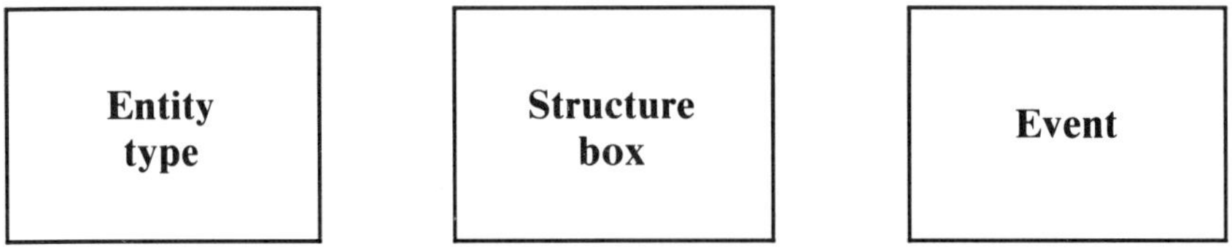

Figure 11.1 The single ELH symbol

AN ENTITY LIFE

Events, when they occur, are not totally at random. If you want to draw some money from your bank account, you can't do it unless you have first opened an account and put sufficient money into it. A life insurance policy would not be paid out until a proposal had been accepted, a premium paid, and the insured person had died. So the sequence of events is important. Things happen over a period of time, and charting this valid sequence gives a *life history.*

So ELHs show events in sequence: the things that happen, which cause the system to do something, which changes the state of the data.

An ELH is constructed for every entity on the LDS. The idea is essentially a simple one. Each event that can affect the entity in any way *during its life in the system* is entered on the diagram, and this is done in the form of a hierarchy (or tree). The idea is really very simple. Events are shown that:

- initially create an entity (its birth);
- occur during its life in the system, set out in the sequence in which they will logically occur;
- finally remove an entity from the system (its death).

So far as the data is concerned, these events equate with additions to the system, amendments and deletions.

The simplest possible representation of an ELH is given at Figure 11.2, which shows the life cycle of an entity, documented diagrammatically as an ELH.

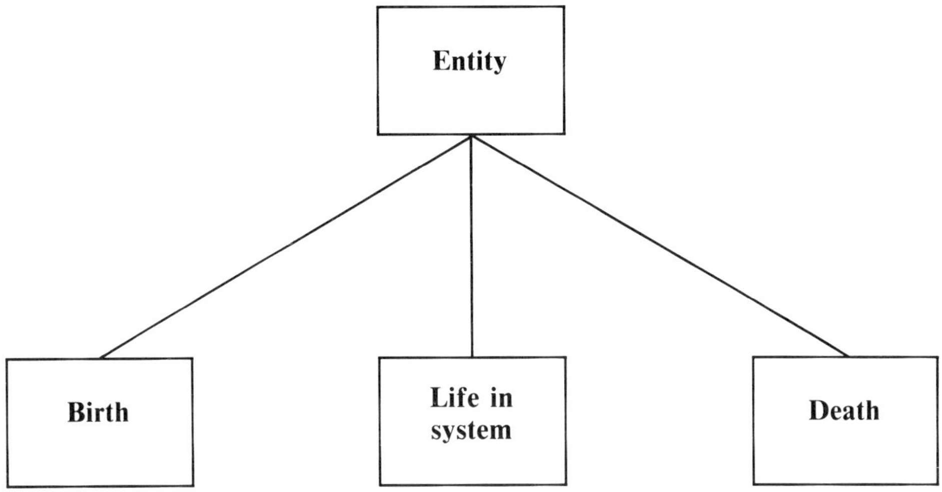

Figure 11.2 An entity life

Whilst most events in a data processing system are initiated in the outside world, it is worth noting that events can also be generated by things other than data coming into a system. Examples are:

– a state of the data causing something to happen, eg:

- the amount owed to a supplier is now greater than the value of credit notes held, and so a cheque must be issued;
- orders for 100 different items have now been received and so someone in the warehouse can be given a list of them (a picking list) so that he can go and take them from the shelves;
- it is four weeks since a book was due for return, so a reminder must now be issued;

– a time, for example:

- the last day of the month and so statements must be sent out;
- 4.00 pm and so cheques are to be printed.

ELH NOTATION

Whilst the notion of sequence is a simple one, needless to say in real life things tend to become rather more complicated. In fact there are seven different constructs which can be shown on an ELH diagram:

- sequence;
- selection;
- structure;
- iteration;
- parallel structures;
- quits and resumes;
- null events.

Sequence

Sequence simply means that all of the events shown on the ELH must occur, one after the other, in the way shown on the diagram, as illustrated in Figure 11.3.

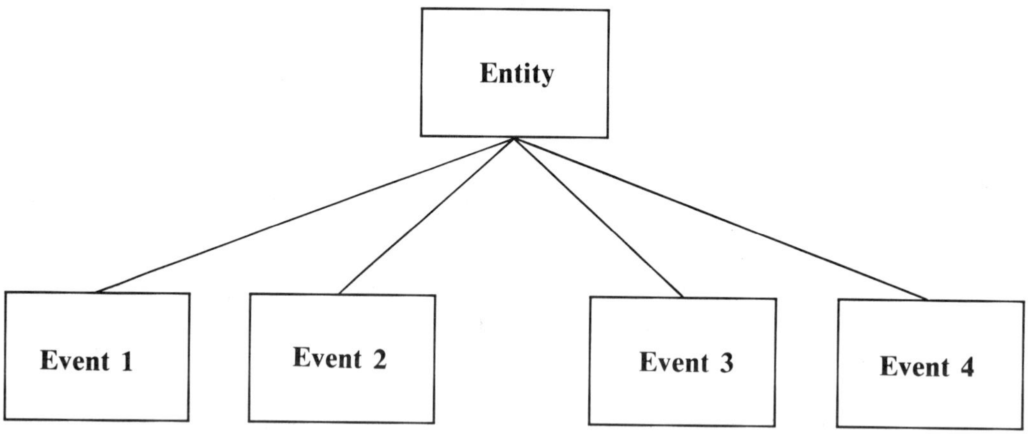

Figure 11.3 A sequence of events

Before considering this example, the difference between *entity type* and *entity occurrence* should be mentioned. These equate to file (a collection of records), and record (a single record from a file) respectively. There can be many different occurrences of an entity type. For the entity type *tree* there will be occurrences of ash, oak, sycamore, chestnut, etc. For the entity type *reader* there will be occurrences of Smith, Jones, Brown, and so on. The word *entity* is often used when *entity occurrence* would strictly be the more accurate term. ELHs are drawn for *entity types.*

Figure 11.3 shows that the first thing that can happen to any occurrence of this particular entity (type) is Event 1. When all the processing invoked by Event 1 has taken place, then Event 2 can occur, followed by Event 3 and finally Event 4. After Event 4, nothing more can happen to this particular occurrence of the entity (other occurrences of the same entity (type) within the system could be at different stages in their lives).

In the simplest ELH, events happen in a strict sequence. Figure 11.4 shows an example from the library system, where the sequence of events is that a book is acquired, is then available for loan, and is finally disposed of.

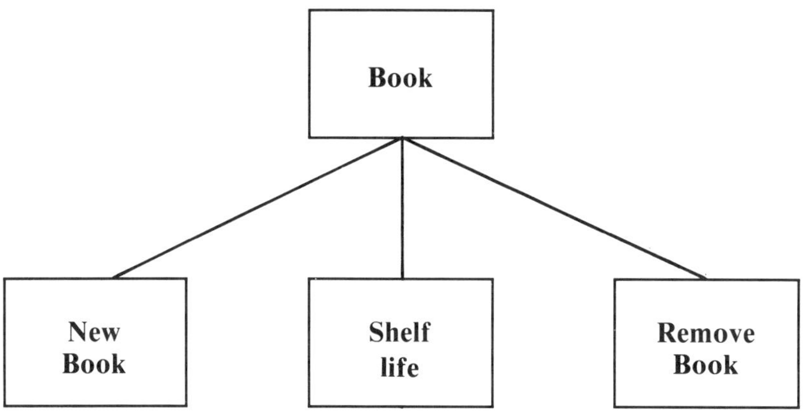

Figure 11.4 A simplistic ELH for the entity Book

Selection

Sometimes there is a choice of events that may affect an entity. This is known as a selection. It is shown by the entry of the symbol ° in the top right hand corner of the box as shown in Figure 11.5.

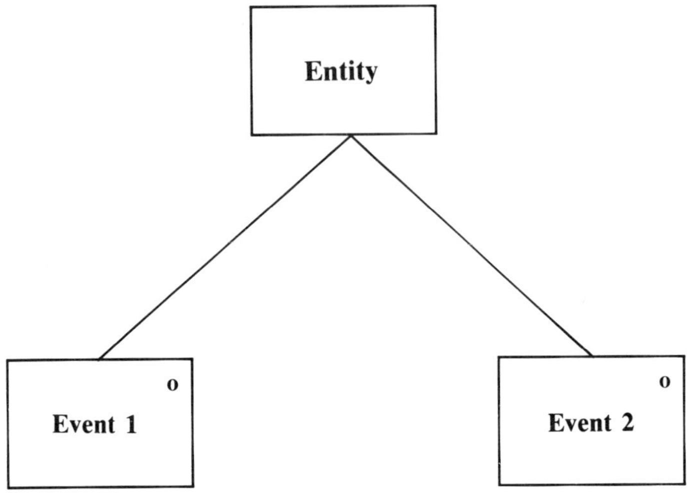

Figure 11.5 A selection: either Event 1 or Event 2

The library example shown in Figure 11.4 is expanded in Figure 11.6 to show selection. In this example, a book may be added to the library by buying it or by being given it as a gift (people sometimes leave collections to libraries). Each represents the birth of one occurrence of the entity type *Book,* but one would require a payment to be made, whilst the other would require preparation of a letter of thanks.

Structure

The original box *New Book* in Figure 11.4 is now regarded as a structure box in Figure 11.6, ie it no longer represents an event. The actual events are at a lower level in the hierarchy, with their place in the structure shown by *New Book.*

It is a rule of ELH construction that all boxes at the same level in a hierarchy must be of the same type. If the higher level box is regarded as the parent, and the lower level box is the child, then all boxes with the same parent must be of the same type (ie sequence, selection or iteration).

Iteration (Repetition)

Sometimes the same event can legitimately occur many times in the life of an entity. This is known as an iteration, and is shown by the inclusion of an asterisk * in the top right hand corner of the box, as in Figure 11.7.

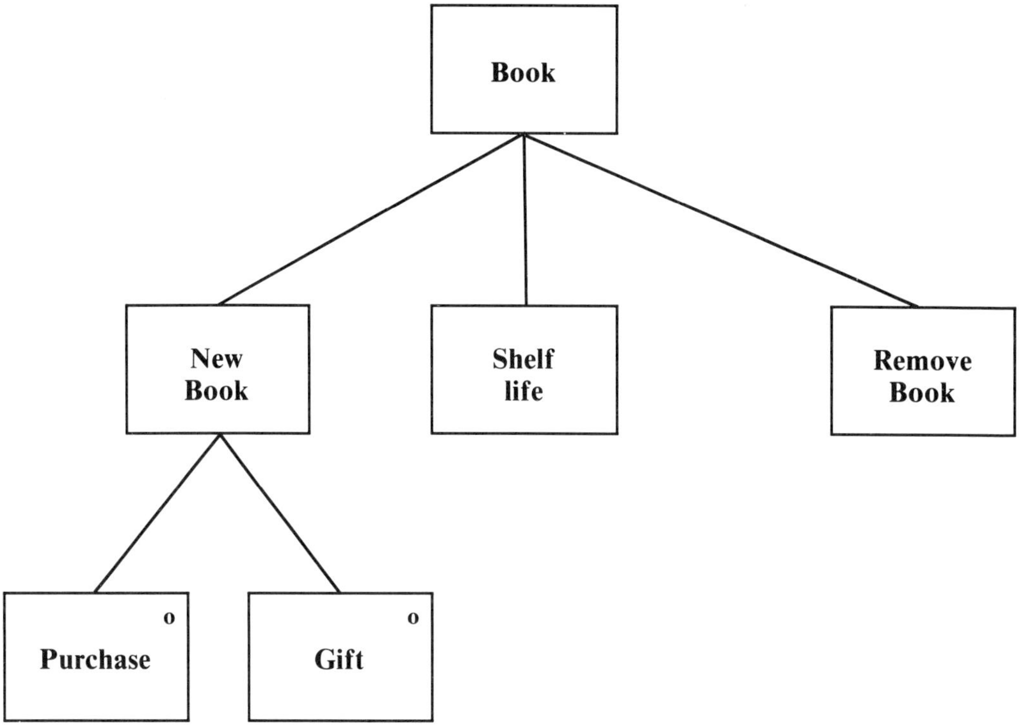

Figure 11.6 Optional ways of acquiring a book

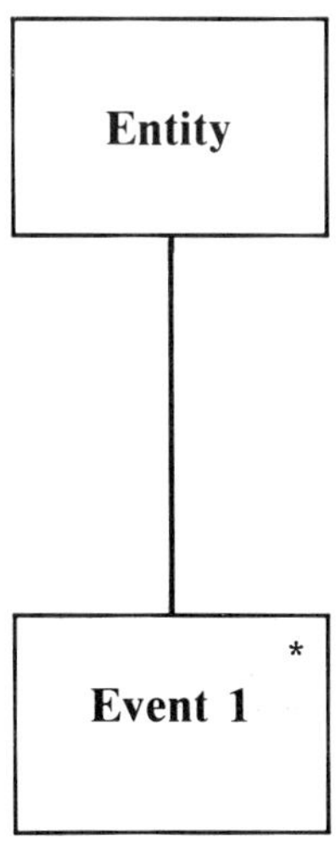

Figure 11.7 ELH representation of an iteration

For instance, the event *Shelf life* in Figure 11.4 may represent many loans of a book. This is shown in Figure 11.8, where a new box *Loan* has been drawn to show the iteration, above two sequential boxes *Issue* and *Return*. (*Shelf life* and *Loan* are now structure boxes. Note that the asterisk was not entered in the box *Shelf life*. If this had been done, then two of the children of *Book* would have indicated sequence and one would have indicated iteration, ie the children boxes would have been of different types.)

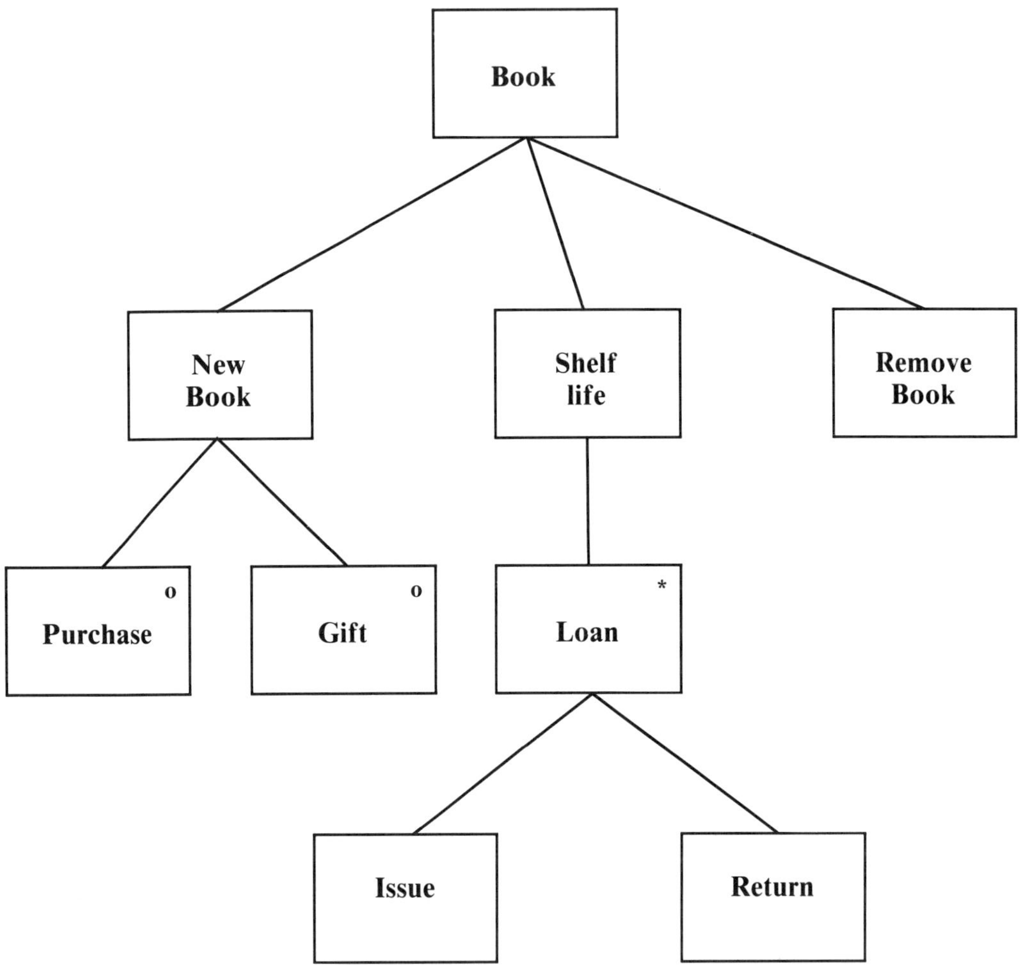

Figure 11.8 An iteration of loans

Parallel structures

All the structures in the examples above show events occurring in a totally predictable way.

Real life is not always like that. There will be occasions when it is impossible to know the sequence in which events will take place.

Events which may take place in an unpredictable order, or even concurrently, are shown by the use of parallel lines. In the structure shown in Figure 11.9, either Event 1 or Event 2 could occur first, or the two may occur together.

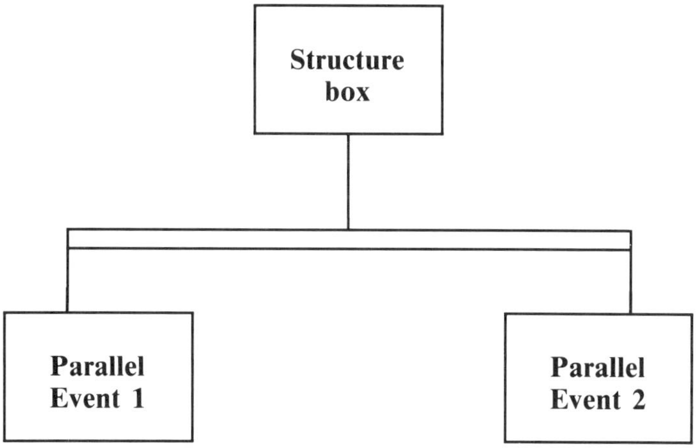

Figure 11.9 A parallel structure

In a Staff Records System, a person will have his normal career progression (promotions, transfers, etc) and, running parallel with this, his personal details may change (marital status, address, next of kin, etc). It is impossible to know which may come first. The events may happen concurrently, for example a transfer on promotion and a change of address. This is shown in Figure 11.10.

Quits and Resumes

There will be occasions when an event may occur which can legitimately upset the normal sequence of events. An obvious example is one that affects the representation of a person in a system. Regardless of what is expected to happen next, the person may die, giving a very literal example of a life history.

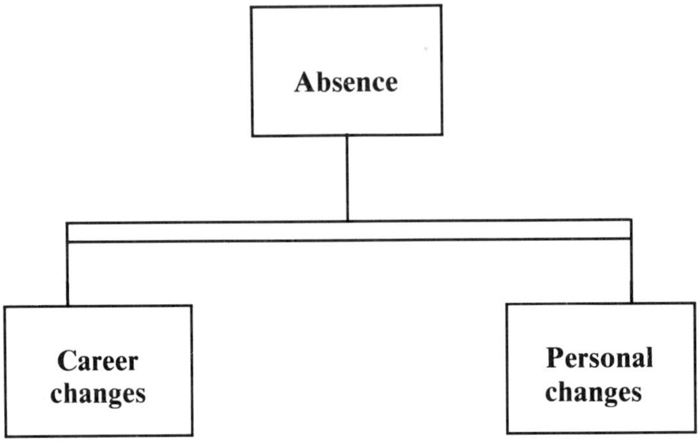

Figure 11.10 The parallel structure in a Staff Records System

Perhaps the next thing he should have done was to pay the next instalment on a hire-purchase agreement, but his demise would almost certainly delay payment while his executors sorted out his affairs The issue of an escalating range of threats to the deceased after his death has been notified is likely to hold a company up to ridicule, as well as to cause much distress.

To cater for this sort of event, it must be possible to discontinue the normal processing sequence and take some exceptional action. This is done by the introduction of quits and resumes.

Quits are shown by the entry of the letter 'Q' outside and to the right of a box. The resume can be elsewhere in the structure, or on a separate structure.

Figure 11.11 is an extract from such an ELH where the box *Payment of instalment* is at the bottom of a hierarchy and indicates that at that point it is possible to quit. Q2 shows that there is another quit somewhere else on the diagram (Q1). A Quit Q2 will be followed elsewhere on the diagram by a Resume R2, as shown in the example. (Similarly the Quit Q1 would be followed by a Resume R1.) As death can occur at any time, you would expect to find Q2 appearing in many places on the diagram.

Three quits, all to the same resume, are illustrated in the Library Orders and Acquisitions System diagram at Figure 11.16

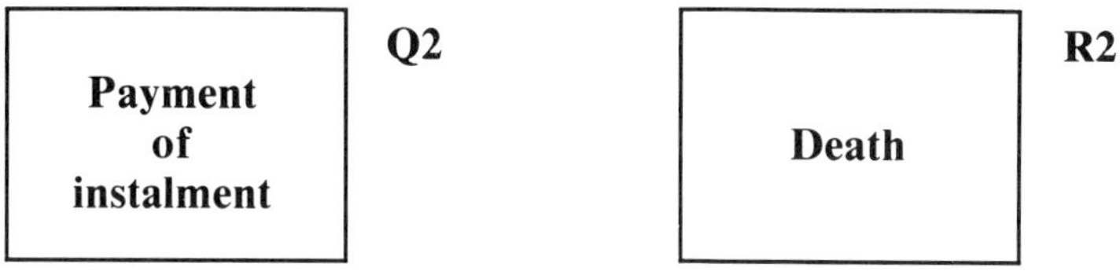

Figure 11.11 Quits and resumes

Null events

There will be circumstances where one of the options is for nothing to happen. This is illustrated in Figure 11.16, where an order is pending. During this waiting period it may be necessary to issue a reminder if there is an abnormal delay. Also during this period the bookseller may respond with some information about the order (out of stock, out of print, etc). However, the usual course of events will be for neither of these to happen, with the order being supplied within the usual time. This is shown by the null box, ie the box with no text, only a line. (Note that this is an artificial example to illustrate a null box. In practice it would not be necessary to show a null box on this diagram because an iteration (*Order life*) can be any number, including nil.)

ELHs IN PRACTICE

Whilst simple in concept, ELHs are time-consuming to produce. The work is detailed and painstaking, and can be expected to reveal a significant number of omissions from the DFDs. These omissions, in a 'traditional' approach to systems analysis, often only become visible during programming, user acceptance testing, or even after implementation. Changes during these later stages of system development can be very expensive indeed – far in excess of the time spent on constructing the ELHs. Among the complications are:

- some events can affect different occurrences of the same entity type in different ways;
- some events can affect the same occurrence of an entity type in different ways, depending on the state of the data in that entity at the time;
- whilst events will always occur in the correct order in real life, there is no guarantee that they will always be notified to the system in that order.

These possibilities are now considered under entity roles, effect qualifiers and state indicators.

Entity roles

In a banking system, payment of a standing order will result in a debit from one account and a credit to another account, ie two different occurrences of the same entity type are affected in different ways. The two are differentiated on the diagram by repeating the event and appending a description of the different roles within brackets in each. This is shown in Figure 11.12.

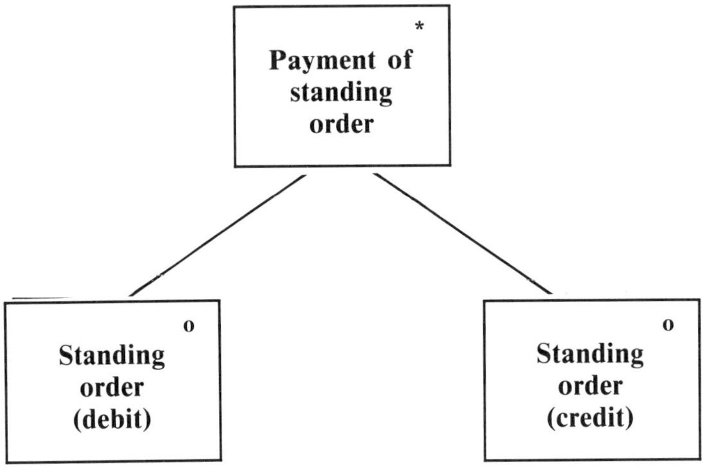

Figure 11.12 Entity roles

Effect qualifiers

Successful payment of the standing order will depend on whether there are sufficient funds in the paying account. There can thus be two different effects for the event *Payment of standing order.* These are illustrated in Figure 11.13, where the effect qualifier is shown in brackets. (Note the different shape of brackets to differentiate from those used for roles.)

State indicators

Although the valid sequence of events is known, errors can mean that events are notified to the system in an incorrect sequence. Perhaps something that should have been done was missed, due to a document being mislaid. Some way is needed of establishing that events are being notified to the system in the correct order, and this is done by the use of state indicators.

Each bottom level box on the ELH, which represents a state of the data, is given a unique number (the value is irrelevant, but conventionally the numbers

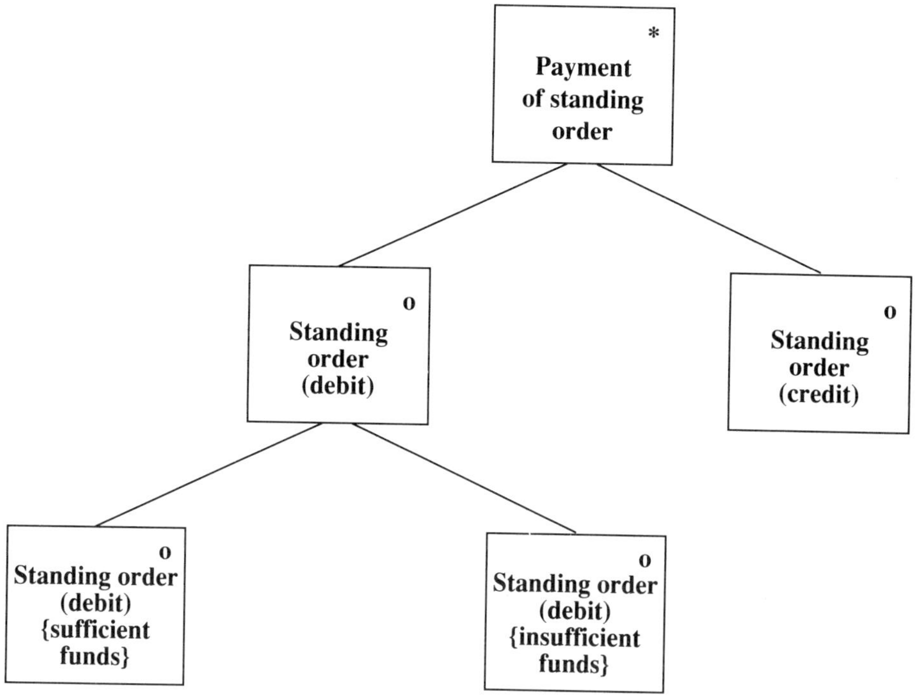

Figure 11.13 Effect qualifiers

are allocated serially). This number is held within the entity record as an attribute, indicating the current state of the data for that particular occurrence (ie where it is in its life cycle). It can therefore be tested when an event occurs, to ensure that the data is in its expected state.

State indicators are always shown in pairs, eg 2/3. This would indicate that a value of 2 is the only acceptable value for a particular event, and that after processing, the indicator will be changed to 3. Figure 11.8 is repeated at Figure 11.14, with state indicators added.

In this example, an indicator of 1, 2 or 3 in a book record would show that, according to the system, the book was available for loan. On presentation of the book at the issue desk, notification of the issue to the system would be accepted and the indicator would be changed to 4. On return, the system would expect to find an indicator value of 4 and would change it to 3 again, ready for the next loan.

If a book on loan was returned directly to the shelves without being notified to the system, when next it was presented at the issue desk the system would find an indicator of 4 which would show that somewhere, something had gone wrong. What the library would choose to do about it is one of the questions to be resolved during analysis, and then built into the design.

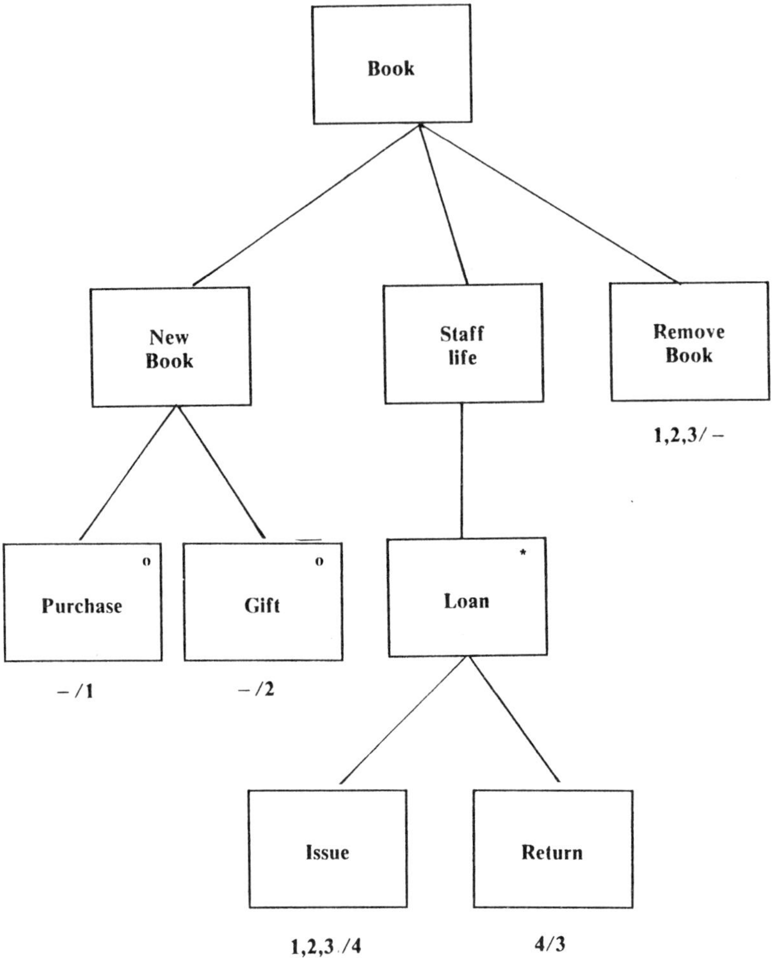

Figure 11.14 The use of state indicators

Considering all of the possible 'what ifs' is one of the reasons why the development of ELHs is so time consuming. You must accept that impatience at this point, a tendency to throw up your hands and leave it all to the system, will not work. The system can only do what it is told to do. If anything is overlooked, the system may do all sorts of unexpected things, and you may not even be aware that things are going wrong. The system could crash. Then you would know for sure that something was amiss. If the system is one on which your business depends, then losing it often, or for long periods, could be the first sign that you will be out of business before too long.

OPERATIONS

The diagrams are further augmented by the allocation of operations to the lowest level boxes. These cater for the birth effect, the amendment of records, and for the establishment and changing of relationships. A set of logical operations, using formal terminology, is set out in the *SSADM Manual.* Figure 11.15 shows the addition of operations to a birth event. Operations have not been shown on the remaining diagrams in this chapter because of the technicality of the expressions, and because their use is for the developers.

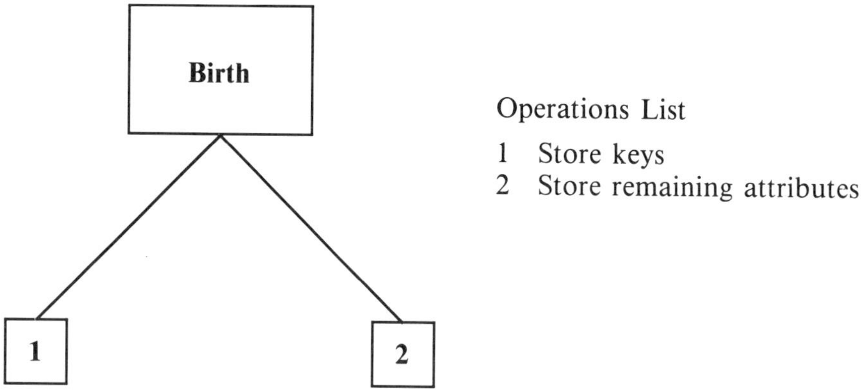

Figure 11.15 The addition of operations to the ELH

AN ELH WITHIN A LIBRARY ORDERS AND ACQUISITIONS SYSTEM

Figure 11.16 shows an ELH for the library system entity *Request Slip* from the Orders and Acquisitions System considered in the earlier chapters.

Note that the two events *Order required* and *No order required* are each shown twice on the diagram. In order to differentiate between them, effect qualifiers are shown in brackets for all four. This is necessary because the effect for each *No order required* will be different. In the first instance, the requester must be notified that the book is not going to be ordered. In the second, he can be told that a copy is already held or on order, and he will be notified when it is available for loan. Each of these quits to the last event, as does notification from the bookseller that the book is no longer available. This non-availability can also be notified to the requester.

Comparison with the DFDs

Once again a comparison reveals some missing data flows. The processing required as a result of the three quits is missing from the DFDs.

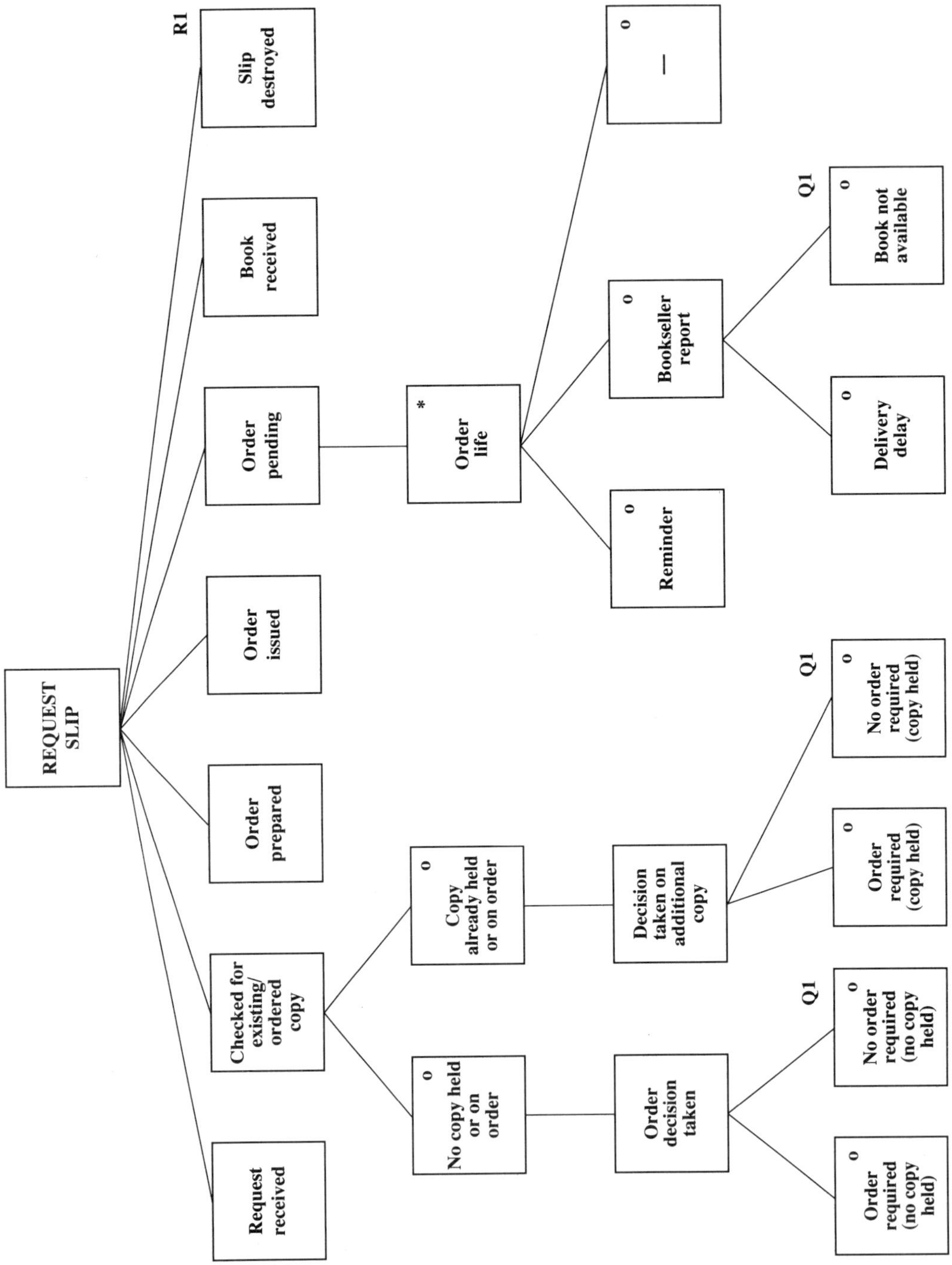

Figure 11.16 ELH for Library Orders and Acquisitions System Request Slip

EFFECT CORRESPONDENCE DIAGRAMS

Effect Correspondence Diagrams (ECDs) are the converse of ELHs.

An ELH shows how one entity is affected by many events. It establishes the correct sequence for the processing, and aims to ensure that no processing is missed.

An ECD shows how one event can affect many entities. Suppose that receipt of a Bookseller's Report notifying a delivery delay required three actions to be taken:

- add the information to the Order Record;
- add the information to the Request Slip;
- notify the Requester.

The same event would be shown on the ELHs for the three entities Request Slip, Book Record and Requester. (The ELH for the Request Slip is at Figure 11.16.)

The ECD is effectively a combination of a subset of the LDS and subsets of the relevant ELHs. It provides the information needed for the development of Update Process Models that go forward into physical design.

ECDs are prepared by and used by the developers. They are technical documents which should not come your way.

PRINCIPAL USES OF THE EEM IN SSADM

The principle may be simple, but there is no getting away from the fact that ELHs are hard work. The construction of ELHs requires a lot of thought and can be quite time-consuming. For this reason they are not prepared until the required Business System Option (BSO) has been selected and there is some prospect that the ELHs will be of value. An earlier construction may have included ELHs for entities that are ultimately excluded from the BSO.

The hard work is justified when it is realised that the ELHs, in providing a third view of the system, will usually be found to pick up quite a lot of detail that has hitherto been missed. The DFDs and other documents will need to be updated to reflect the additional information. This consequential updating may seem like a chore, but is invaluable later in development and in subsequent maintenance. ELHs also provide features in their own right, ie sequence of processing and checks against erroneous input.

The two steps which are most significant for EEM are:

– Step 360 ELHs and Effect Correspondence Diagrams are created.

– Step 520 State indicators are added to the ELHs. The Effect Correspondence Diagrams are converted into processing structures.

USER INVOLVEMENT

This third diagramming technique used in SSADM requires checking in its own right, and also cross-checking against both the DFDs and LDS.

Checklist

ELHs (form SSADMv4 19)

Check that:

- the diagram conforms to SSADM or installation standards;
- one diagram exists for each entity on the Required System LDS;
- each diagram includes all events affecting the entity *during its life in the system,* ie:
  - all creation events are shown;
  - all modication events are shown;
  - all deletion events are shown;
- the events are shown in the correct sequence;
- events which affect more than one entity occurrence for an entity type have been qualified by entity roles;
- events which affect an entity in mutually exclusive ways have been qualified by an effect qualifier;
- operations and state indicators have been shown;
- all events are identifiable on the DFDs as data flows.

12
Three three viewpoints

INTRODUCTION

The last three chapters considered the three main diagrammatic techniques used in SSADM. These techniques are complementary. Each has given its own view of the system. Each, alone, has helped to increase knowledge of the system, but each, individually, is an incomplete representation of the system.

The examples of diagrams created for a Library Orders and Acquisitions System showed that each of the later diagrams revealed omissions from DFDs. It can be argued that this would not be the case if the DFDs had been done 'properly' in the first place. Unfortunately, humans are fallible, and things do get missed.

CROSS CHECKS

Comparing the diagrams with each other helps to find discrepancies, and fill in blanks. There is absolutely no need to agonise indefinitely on fruitless attempts at getting each diagram to a state of absolute perfection that would usually be beyond attainment. You can confidently expect that what is missed by one approach will be picked up by one of the others. This is a good reason for not spending excessive amounts of time on any one of the individual techniques.

You could, for example, after taking your first studied consideration of DFDs, spend many more man weeks on them for a minimal gain in information, but reaching the stage where it seemed that perfection had been achieved. Then construction of ELHs could reveal perhaps another 25 percent of information that had been missed hitherto.

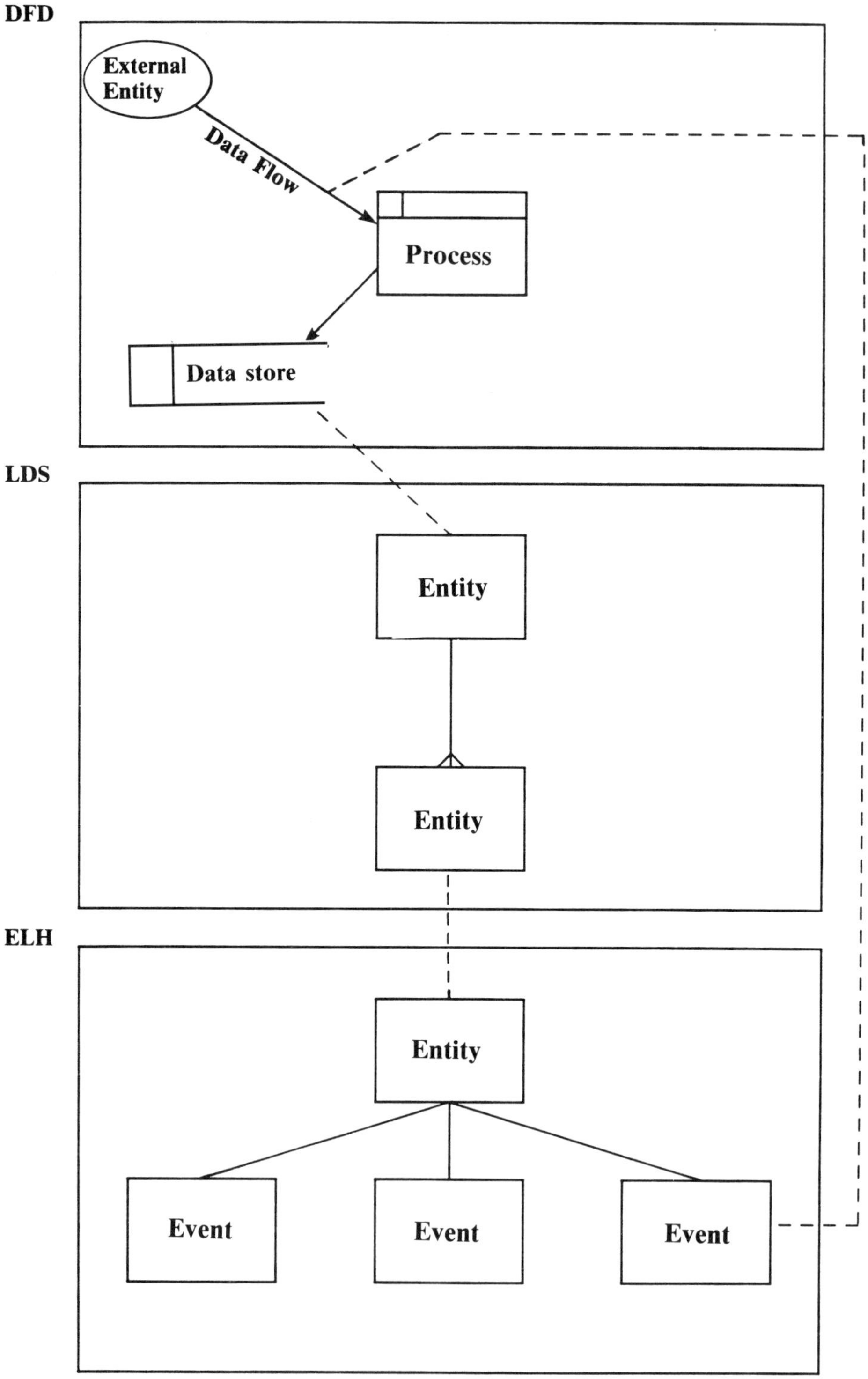

Figure 12.1 The three viewpoints

Whilst it might seem that the more detailed approach to analysis as required by SSADM will be unnecessarily time-consuming for you, there are two factors that prevent it from being so:

- the time spent on the individual tasks will not be excessive if full advantage is taken of their complementary nature mentioned above, given sensible management to keep things moving along;

- the time spent is, in fact, a displacement of effort from the later stages where it is wasteful, to the earliest stage where it is more cost-effective.

Information which can be cross-checked between diagrams is:

- entities on the LDS must be represented somewhere in the data stores on the DFDs;

- entities on the ELHs will correspond to entities on the LDS;

- events on the ELHs will match data flows which trigger processes on the DFDs.

The approach is very thorough. Not much should be missed. The relationships between these techniques are illustrated in Figure 12.1.

13
The Requirements Catalogue

INTRODUCTION

The Requirements Catalogue is the fourth major piece of the jigsaw that completes the picture needed by the system designers. The other three pieces are all diagrammatic ones – DFDs, the LDS and ELHs. The Requirements Catalogue is needed to allow for the entry of things considered wrong with the current system, and all the things it would be desirable to have in the new system. The system objectives, discussed in Chapter 6, will be among the items detailed in the Requirements Catalogue.

Entries are made in the Catalogue right from the start of the study, and concurrently with the application of the diagramming techniques. Each Catalogue entry is made on a separate sheet, thus permitting groupings such as priorities and related requirements.

INHIBITIONS

It probably goes without saying that you are not likely to get everything you want from your new system. There will be some limit to the resources. The real world considerations of what it would cost to develop, how long it would take, what the equipment would cost, and whether the development team has the necessary experience, are all factors that will come between you and the ultimate system.

Unfortunately, what no one can tell you at the start of the project is exactly what you can and can't have. The amount of time you can devote to the project, the clarity of your thought, the amount of senior management involvement and commitment, how long you can afford to wait, and what your competitors are doing, are all factors that will influence the decisions that must be taken when choosing Business and Technical Options in Stages 2 and 4 (Chapters 17 and 19).

The knowledge that you won't get all you want tends to serve as an inhibitor on what you should include in the Requirements Catalogue. It is easy to assume that some things are not possible, some would cost too much, some are too trifling to bother the developers with, and so on. The result of this could be that much that would be of value to you will not appear in the final system. But your assumptions could be wrong. It might be easy to implement. Or perhaps a very low priority item would get in on the back of one of higher priority and be included at negligible extra cost. Perhaps the bases for the assumptions may change while development is in progress.

Two things you can be sure of – if you don't ask for something, you won't get it, and nothing will happen if you don't mention it in the first place. So set down everything you can think of, no matter how trifling or how woolly it might be. As the work proceeds, you should add everything further that comes to mind. Consider the Requirements Catalogue as being a wish list - all that the system should do in a perfect world in which there were no restrictions, both now and in the future. Once you have something down on paper it is available for others to think about and comment on. Any entry, no matter how seemingly trivial, may spark off a thought by someone else that could prove to be vital. Everything is negotiable initially, and at least until the Business System Option is chosen. And if a requirement fails to make it into the first implementation, then it could feature in a later release.

A further reason for setting out all that you can think of, is that if you ask for something at the start, it is likely to cost very much less to implement than if you were to ask for it after the system has been installed. An entry in the Requirements Catalogue, even if not implemented initially, will alert the developers to a possible future enhancement. Hooks for it can be built into the initial design, so that later implementation of the feature can be done at minimum cost.

ALLOCATING PRIORITIES

Although you should have entered everything you could think of, the various entries will not be of equal importance. Implementation of some of your entries will be vital to the acceptability of the system. Others would be useful but not vital. Yet others are more in the nature of icing on the cake, and there are probably a few that embarrass you now that you have given them further thought. Don't be. Remember that the most brilliant developer might be unable to see beyond the end of his nose when it comes to thinking about what would be useful to you. The flights of fancy that could save your company much money in the future will almost certainly have to originate with you.

Accepting that not every item in the Requirements Catalogue will be implemented initially, it will be necessary to decide the importance of each.

When allocating priorities, it is easy to be too ambitious. Using a scale of 1 to 10 can lead to some intense soul-searching to decide whether something should be rated 3 or 4. There is nothing within SSADM to prevent you from using a highly sophisticated priority rating system, but for most practical purposes you should consider something simpler. To begin with, a very modest categorisation of priorities will usually be adequate, for example you could have priority levels of:

- mandatory;
- desirable;
- optional; or
- high;
- medium;
- low.

These priorities can then be set against the resource levels needed to implement the items, either initially or in later enhancements to the system. Items for initial implementation are likely to be those with either high priority or low cost, with a sprinkling of medium priority/medium cost items.

PRECISION IN REQUIREMENTS

The techniques of Data Flow Modelling and Entity-Event Modelling are excellent at identifying *what* the system is to do. It is often rather more difficult to deal with the non-functional requirements, ie *how well* the system is to perform, and what resource usage is permissible. Yet it is often the *how well* rather than the *what* that decides whether the system is acceptable to its users.

It was suggested above that the initial entries in the Requirements Catalogue could be quite woolly, eg 'More information is needed on the Despatch Note', 'The trial balance must be available sooner', etc. Sometimes systems are built on such requirements. They are seldom satisfactory. Imprecise requirements are fine as a starting point – a note to ensure that nothing is forgotten. They must be made precise when the contents of the Requirements Catalogue are examined in detail at Step 120 (Chapter 16) and when defining various Business System Options at Step 210 (Chapter 17). An entry such as 'The response should be faster', must be amplified to something like:

Within the peak times of	09.15 to 09.45
	12.00 to 14.00
	17.00 to 18.00

the response time must be less than 4 seconds. Outside those times the response must be less than 9 seconds.

This gives the designer a target to aim at. He will need to ensure that his design can meet these requirements. It will give you the yardstick against which you can measure the acceptability of the system that is delivered to you. Without such precision there can be endless arguments as to what 'faster' really meant. This is fine material for debate and for scoring points off the opposition. It is not very good for a team approach to doing something more effectively for your organisation.

The consequences of this are:

- You will have to specify the quality and resource requirements in a measurable form.

- A problem for the designer is that every effort to improve the level of performance for one feature is likely to affect other qualities. Often this will have a detrimental effect. It may prove to be impossible to meet all of your requirements. You may need to work with the developers towards an acceptable compromise.

- Ways of measuring the achievement of performance, quality and resource requirements will have to be built into the design, to prove that your requirements have been met before the system is accepted. This will add to the cost of the project, but provides a safeguard against the acceptance of an inadequate system.

SPECIFYING REQUIREMENTS IN A MEASURABLE WAY

The first step is to decide the quality and resource objectives that are critical to the development and performance of the system and to enter them in the Requirements Catalogue. These will vary according to the system. Some examples for which objectives may be considered were mentioned in Chapter 6.

For each of the critical objectives, it is now necessary to consider:

- a definition of the objectives;

- how they will be specified;

- the current situation, for purposes of comparison and to try to ensure that limits of tolerance are based on tangibles rather than on delusion or ignorance;

- a *precise* specification of the requirements. They should be stated in a way that is unambiguous, and measurable or provable where possible, avoiding generalities such as better, faster, more detail, etc. The limits of tolerance should be stated wherever possible, ie:

- least acceptable: anything below this would provide grounds for rejection of the system;
- the target level of performance;
- best usable: for example, a label printed in 5 seconds would exceed the best usable response if it would physically take 45 seconds to put ordered items into a container before affixing the label. Planning for such a short response would be a waste of resources, although the response would be perfectly acceptable if it happened coincidentally. Best usable may often be the same as target;
- references to other documentation that supports the facts and objectives.

It will be necessary to adjust the agreed levels of the various objectives until the stage is reached where a successful compromise has been reached between technical practicality and commercial necessity. The system should then be:

- meeting management objectives;
- meeting user requirements;
- implementable within known constraints.

The trade-offs should be possible within the range covered by the best usable and worst acceptable limits, but in the event of conflict it will be necessary to prioritise the objectives so that the most important ones are met and others are adjusted accordingly. This can only be done with close co-operation between management, users and developers, taking particular care where there is any possibility that an objective may fall below the worst acceptable level. If an acceptable compromise cannot be reached it may be necessary to abandon the project. Recognition of this unpalatable fact will then have been made at the earliest possible point, before further development work and expense has been wastefully incurred.

SECURITY, CONTROL AND AUDIT REQUIREMENTS

Security, control and audit considerations are all too often tagged on at the end, rather than built into a system from the start. This almost inevitably causes problems, so these essential system elements must be considered *before* the required system is specified. Version 3 of SSADM contained a step devoted solely to security, control and audit requirements. They are not mentioned separately in Version 4, being a subset of all the requirements. However, as they are of such importance to a system, you would be well advised to give them special consideration when completing the Catalogue.

Security requirements

Confidentiality requirements

Confidentiality is entirely your province, although the developers will give guidance. Requirements cover such items as:

- registration of personal data under the Data Protection Act;
- limitation of physical access to the system and to terminals;
- given physical access, who is permitted to:
  - access data (ie to look at it, but not to change it);
  - update data.

Integrity requirements

Integrity checks are aimed at ensuring that all data being entered into the system is correct. Typically they entail:

- validation procedures, ie what tests can be carried out to ensure that data or transactions are not obviously incorrect, eg:
  - a date of 32nd August can be recognised as invalid on input;
  - a diagnosis of pregnancy can be identified as invalid when matched against the record of a person who is shown to be male;
  - a diagnosis of pregnancy is worth querying for a female if the age is outside a specified range, eg under 15 or over 40; this does not mean that it is incorrect, but that perhaps the operator should be asked to confirm that it *is* correct;
  - a system calculation of a value can be checked to see that it falls within reasonable bounds. For example, net salary for the month should not exceed £1320 (or whatever value is relevant to that position), with any greater amounts being highlighted in some way on screen or printout;
- definition of the action needed to handle transactions which are to be rejected (errors, eg the first two examples above), and those which are valid exceptions (identified for further consideration, eg the last two examples above);
- definition of the action to re-input transactions which have been rejected.

Fallback and recovery requirements

Acknowledging that sometimes the system will fail, fallback and recovery requirements define what is acceptable to you in those circumstances. The requirements must be precisely specified, for example:

- A definition of an acceptable failure rate, ie what is the least acceptable average time between failures (mean time between failures, or MTBF)?

- What is the maximum time it can be permitted to take for the system to be recovered after a failure?

- What level of performance is required from a backup system in the event of failure of the main system?

- What level of user involvement is acceptable after the system comes back on line. For example, must all transactions input up to the time of failure be recovered automatically, or is some re-input by users at terminals an acceptable option, and if so, how much re-input, eg all day, the last hour etc?

- Is a totally manual backup system acceptable?

- Will it be necessary to make provision for a backup system to be operable from another site?

It is very tempting to ignore the finite nature of resources and request facilities that would be reasonable only in a moon shot, or the safe functioning of a nuclear power station. The greater the ability to avoid failure or to recover virtually instantaneously, the greater the cost, the longer the system will take to develop, and the more complex the system will become. A grasp of the realities is needed, ie what it will cost to give you what you would like to have.

Retention requirements

You will have to consider for how long you should hold the various computer records. If you wish to hold everything for ever, you could find that you have major storage problems. It is usually possible to move some data from the most readily accessible files after a time. Such items could be deleted and forgotten completely, or retained in a less accessible form, perhaps on archive disks or tapes that could be loaded specially onto the computer if required. You will need to think about:

- how to comply with legal requirements;

- what information is to be readily accessible;

- when records can be archived;

- how long it is permissible to take to process a record held in archives;
- whether archives need be on the computer, or whether they should be printed or output on microfilm.

Control requirements

Control requirements are of two types – those of relevance mainly to the developers, eg about performance of the system, and those of relevance to you, which could include:

- counts of records;
- reconciliation of processing, eg number of records at the start of the month, plus new records added, less old records deleted, is equal to the total of records on file at the end of the month;
- totals, eg of tax paid, to allow a cheque to be sent to the Inland Revenue.

Audit requirements

Audit requirements, rather obviously, require the involvement of the auditors at this early stage. Their requirements can be expected to cover such items as:

- information to control the handling of cash;
- special reports from the system;
- the availability of utilities to permit auditors to make their own enquiries of the system;
- audit trails, ie the documentation of the flow of data from its input, through all its processing, to its ultimate effect on the system, either internally or in the form of output information.

PRINCIPAL USES OF THE REQUIREMENTS CATALOGUE IN SSADM

The Requirements Catalogue features throughout the application of SSADM. Thoughts can occur any time, and the Catalogue is constantly available for enhancement. However, the principal times when it is at the centre of activities are described in Part 3, Chapters 15-21. They are:

- Step 010 when it is first set up.
- Step 020 when attempts are made to define problems and requirements.

- Step 030 for decisions on the minimum requirements of any new system.
- Step 110 when it is first set up if there has been no Feasibility Study.
- Step 120 where it is expanded as a result of more detailed analysis work, and priorities are assigned.
- Step 210 in which the Catalogue is again considered in the light of additions that have been made to it. Items and their priorities are checked, and possible solutions are considered and recorded. In particular, the base constraints are identified. These are the constraints that must apply to all the Business System Options.
- Step 310 to identify items that have been excluded from the Selected Business System Option and to note the reasons.
- Step 350 when some changes may be necessary following experience of the prototyping exercise.
- Step 370 during which each entry is checked to ensure that it has been fully defined.
- Step 410 when it is considered during preparation of the Technical System Options.
- Steps 640 and 660 where steps are taken to ensure that the design will meet the objectives specified in the Catalogue.

USER INVOLVEMENT

The Requirements Catalogue will be set up initially by the developers from the information they have been able to glean from the Project Initiation Document. It will therefore contain their interpretation of what they think that you want. It is up to you to check the entries with great care and remove any misunderstandings. You must then extend the list to include all the other items you think of as the study progresses. Eventually you have to:

- decide precisely on the nature of your requirements;
- allocate priorities to each item;
- decide whether each item should be in the system;
- help in finding solutions;
- keep the entries under regular review.

More precisely, reviews of the Requirements Catalogue should ensure that (so far as is appropriate for the stage being checked):

- all requirements and objectives are individually identified and clearly defined
- all entries affecting DFDs are cross-referenced;
- all entries affecting the LDS are cross-referenced;
- the individual entries are grouped in categories;
- priorities, ie the degree of seriousness/urgency have been entered from the start and refined subsequently;
- relative priorities of the objectives have been understood and made explicit;
- there is no duplication, by restatement of the same requirement in different ways;
- all requirements have been stated in a precisely measurable way;
- each requirement has a system function associated with it;
- solutions exist for each entry, including the specified levels of design objectives, and contain features that will allow the achievement of objectives to be visible to the users (ie where an objective is specified in measurable terms, a means of measuring must be available);
- tests have been planned to prove that the required levels of design objectives will be achieved by the operational system.

Part 3

SSADM Activities

14

Introduction to activities

ORGANISATION AND APPROACH

SSADM is organised into five modules:

- Feasibility Study (Stage 0);
- Requirements Analysis (Stages 1 – 2);
- Requirements Specification (Stage 3);
- Logical System Specification (Stages 4 – 5);
- Physical Design (Stage 6).

Two approaches to systems development are possible:

- to start with the Feasibility Study and continue into the full study;
- to go straight into a full systems study.

Of the seven stages of systems analysis and design, you will be most closely involved in the Feasibility Study, Requirements Analysis and Requirements Specification Modules, ie in Stages 0 to 3. Thereafter, much of the work is computer rather than business oriented, but the developers will still be asking questions, seeking clarification, discussing options, and seeking opinions on how the system should look to you (the Human/Computer Interface or HCI).

STAGE DIAGRAMS

The stage diagrams, featured in Chapters 15 – 21, are abridged only slightly from those in the *SSADM Manual*. They show *all* the documents produced in the

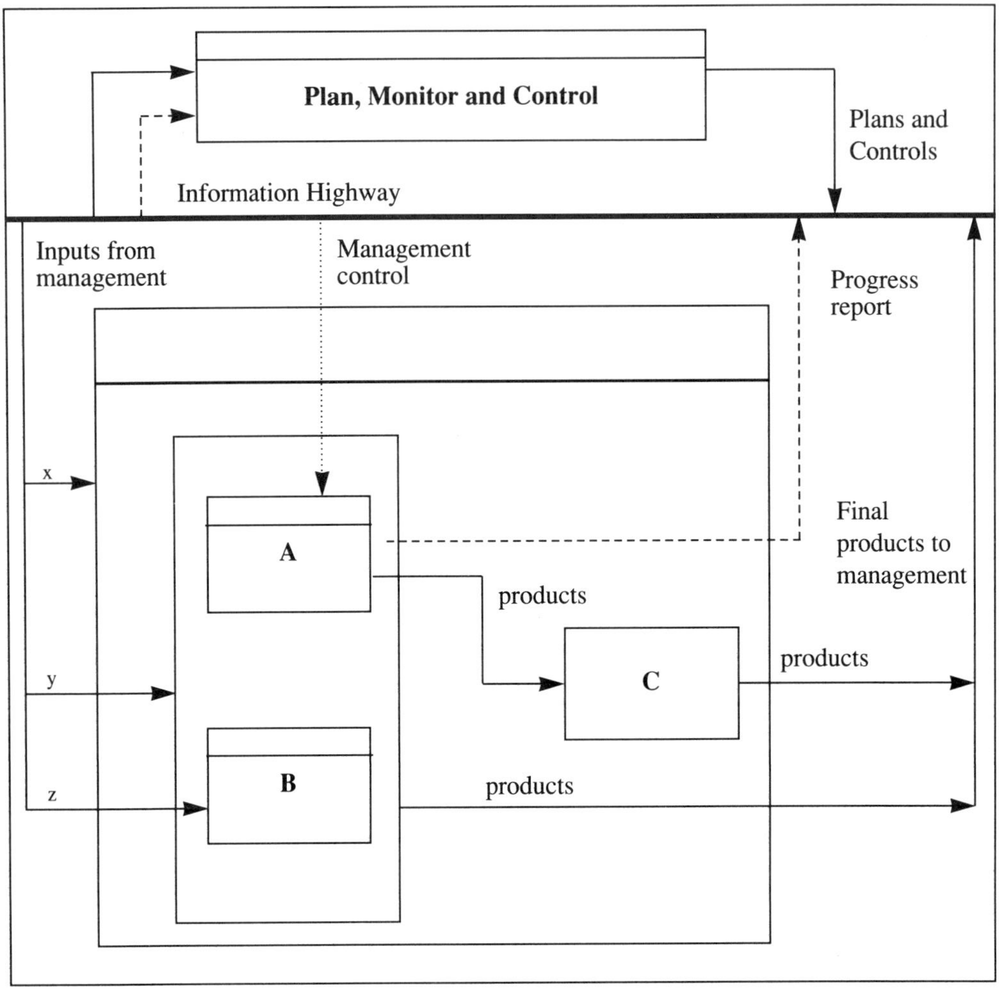

Figure 14.1 The SSADM stage diagrams

course of a complete SSADM development. Although only a selection of the documents has been discussed in this book (those most relevant to you), they are all shown on the diagrams. You do not need to work your way through the diagrams, but you may find them useful for reference during an actual development project. It will help you to see all that is going on, and how it all fits together.

The diagrams will appear confusing at first sight, but are not too difficult to follow once the principles are known. The general layout is shown in Figure 14.1.

Plan, Monitor and Control

Project procedures such as planning, estimating, and quality reviews are not a part of SSADM activities, but interface with them. The interface is the *Information Highway*. SSADM products and reports are shown as going from the activities to the Highway. To simplify the diagrams, the *Plan, Monitor and Control* box has been omitted from the diagrams in Chapters 15 – 21, but is implicit on all of them.

Information Highway

The Information Highway marks the division between the technical and the management processes. Flows of products between activities on the same diagram are drawn directly, but products and reports that pass between technical processes via a management activity are shown as being connected to the Highway. Thus all products going from one stage to the next go via the Highway as they progress via a quality review.

Inputs from management

Inputs from management are shown as coming from the Information Highway to the edge of a box. They are available to all the processes bounded by the box. Thus items shown as *x* are available to all three Steps A, B and C. Items noted y are available to Steps A and B. Items at *z* are available only to Step B.

Management controls and authorisation

Aspects of the development which are controlled by management are shown by dotted lines coming down from the Information Highway.

Progress reports

Progress reports are indicated by dashed lines from the processes to the Information Highway.

Parallel steps

Steps which are done in parallel are shown under each other. Steps to be carried out by the same team are enclosed in the same box. Thus in Figure 14.1, Steps A and B are done in parallel by the same team.

KEY POINTS FOR USERS

At the end of each step a list is provided of checks that can be made against the various documents in which you will be involved. Checks mentioned in early steps also apply to the same document in every subsequent step.

The developers will normally carry out the checks for conformance to standards, cross-references, and cross-checks between documents.

Feasibility Study Module

Stage 0

15
Stage 0 – Feasibility

INTRODUCTION

A Feasibility Study is, as its name implies, a preliminary study of a project to decide whether to go ahead with a full-scale development exercise. It attempts to ensure that projects that proceed into a full study are likely to be cost-effective ones for the company (however cost and effectiveness are measured in particular applications).

Although a Feasibility Study is regarded as optional within SSADM, you should *always* go through this phase unless there are very compelling reasons against it, for example:

- the system must be implemented regardless of costs and benefits (think what you are laying yourself open to here);
- because there is no alternative (can this really be true?);
- because it seems so small as to be scarcely worthwhile (and that has proved to be a false assumption on more than one occasion);
- because it is replacing an existing computer system for which the benefits are well known (but beware of the costs and availability of anything new).

Although the Feasibility Study is not mandatory in SSADM, its omission should carry a system health warning. In other words, you omit the Study at your peril, only after careful consideration, and with a willingness to accept the consequences.

Sometimes a Study may be regarded as delaying the start of the project proper (which is true), and adding expense (which is arguable). Although the start of the full study is delayed, time is saved subsequently, and though a cost is involved, most of that too will be recouped. (Much of the work done in the Feasibility

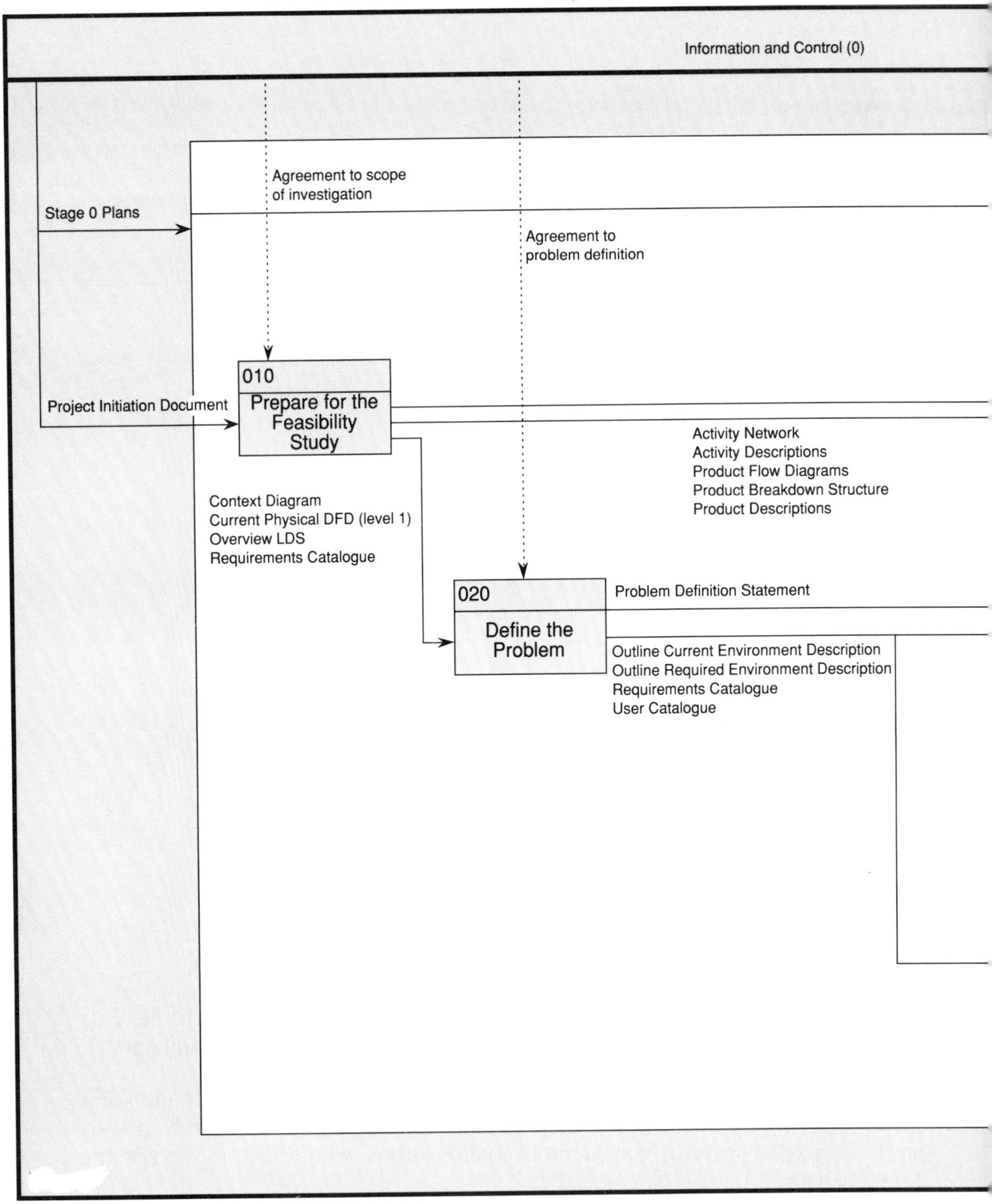

Figure 15.1 Stage 0

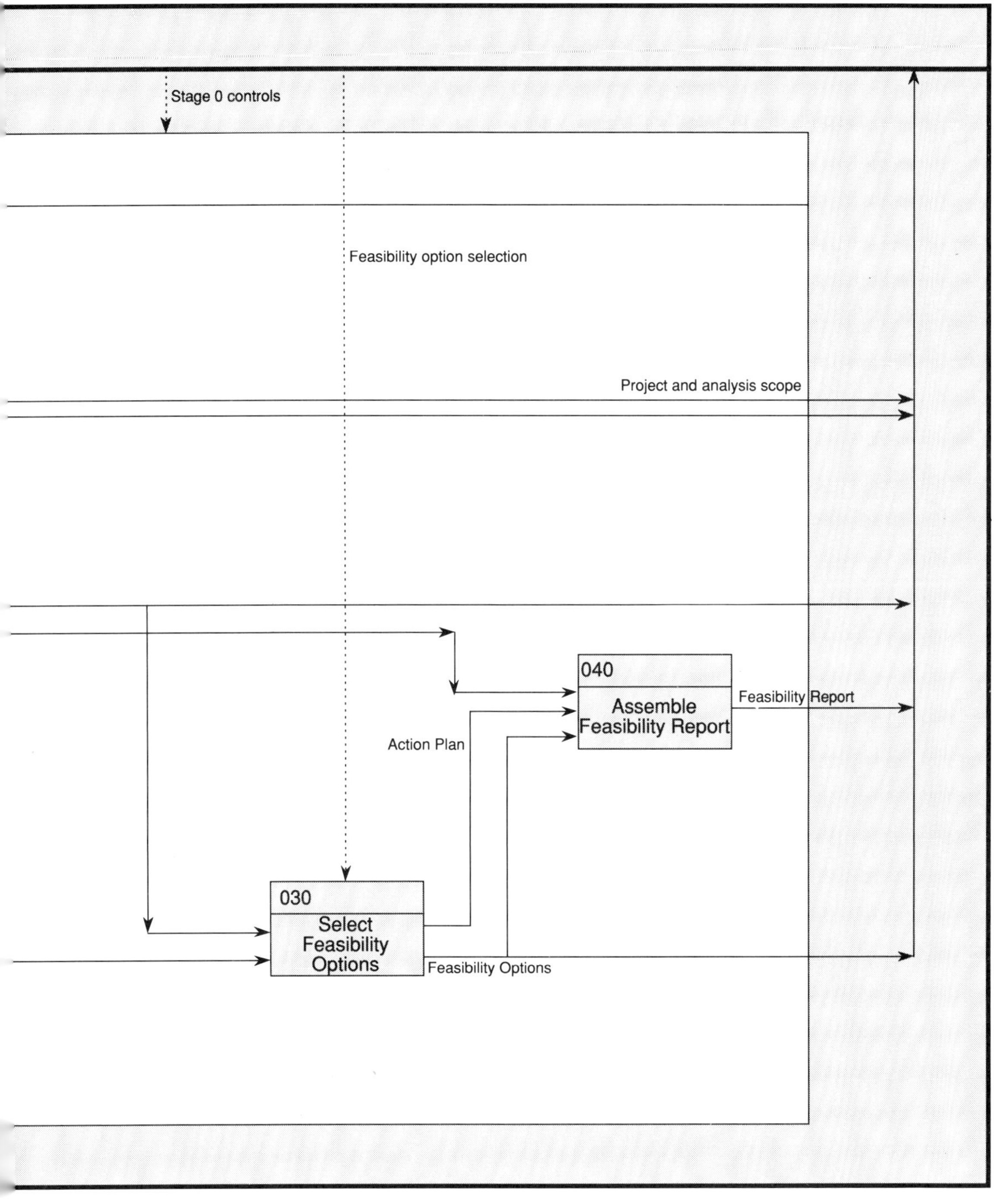
Stage 0 controls
Feasibility option selection
Project and analysis scope
040
Assemble Feasibility Report
Feasibility Report
Action Plan
030
Select Feasibility Options
Feasibility Options

Study will save a corresponding amount of work in a subsequent full study.) More importantly, it disposes, relatively cheaply, of some projects that are not cost beneficial and should go no further. Projects tend to gather momentum once they have got under way. It takes a brave decision to stop a full study that should never have started in the first place.

There is an authorisation point at the end of each stage of SSADM where the products are reviewed, rework can be required, an option selected, the development changed in some way, or the project even abandoned in exceptional circumstances. There should be less likelihood of things going so badly adrift if the project starts with a Feasibility Study. You must be very aware that without a Feasibility Study, abandonment at a review point must always be a decision that you (or someone) is more likely to have to take.

In SSADM, the Feasibility Study is essentially a high-level run through the work that is done in much more detail in Stages 1 to 4 of the full method.

The study consists of four steps. Its aim is to establish whether the proposed system development should go ahead (at least as far as the next stage). To do this it must decide:

- who will be involved;
- what options there are;
- what costs and timescales are involved;
- whether the system will be an effective one for the organisation.

A diagram of Stage 0 is given in Figure 15.1.

STEP 010 PREPARE FOR THE FEASIBILITY STUDY

This is the introductory overview step in which you will have considerable involvement. It takes a preliminary view of the proposed system, lays down the plans and schedules the work for the rest of the study.

The Project Initiation Document is reviewed to assess the scope of the project. The documents you will see include:

- Context Diagram;
- Current Physical DFD (level 1);
- Overview LDS;
- Requirements Catalogue;
- Study Plan.

The proposals are submitted for approval by the project board.

Key points for users

Context Diagram (form SSADMv4 3)

Check that:

- all of the external entities are shown;
- the data flows correctly indicate the scope of the system.

DFD (form SSADMv4 4)

Check that:

- all of the external entities are shown, as on the Context Diagram;
- the system boundary is correctly shown;
- the main system inputs and outputs are shown, as on the Context Diagram;
- all of the job functions are represented;
- all of the terminology, ie of external entities, data flows, processes and data stores, is meaningful to you;
- the diagram is only of the current physical system, ie future requirements should not be shown at this stage.

LDS (form SSADMv4 30)

Check for the correct identification of:

- initial entities;
- a unique identifier (key) for each entity;
- *direct* relationships between entities;
- the type of relationship, ie mandatory, optional, exclusive.

Requirements Catalogue (form SSADMv4 42)

Check that:

- it includes all items specified in the Project Initiation Document;
- all the requirements are correctly expressed.

Study Plan

Check that the proposals that involve you meet with your approval, and that you can accomplish the tasks within the times and costs as scheduled

STEP 020 DEFINE THE PROBLEM

Given project board approval for the study to proceed, more information is now gathered to add to the understanding of the business, its current problems and future requirements. This entails your involvement in:

- production of a Level 1 DFD for the required environment, proceeding to lower levels for processes where the situation warrants it;
- updating of the other documents;
- identification and entering of details for all the intended on-line users in a User Catalogue. (An on-line user is one who enters or obtains information directly at a computer screen rather than by referring to a printed list.) A Catalogue entry is required for each different job title, showing the tasks carried out by each of them.

The requirements are then set out in a Problem Definition Statement, which again requires the agreement of the project board before proceeding with the study.

Key points for users

User Catalogue (form SSADMv4 45)

- Check that all relevant job titles are shown.
- For each job title, check that all the tasks to be carried out have been noted.

STEP 030 SELECT FEASIBILITY OPTIONS

There are likely to be many ways in which a system could be implemented:

- the boundary between what the computer will do and what people (or other systems) will do can be drawn in different places;
- the current problems to be solved and the new requirements to be included can be varied;
- the system, if computerised, can be implemented in different ways – centralised or distributed, conventional files or database, PCs or mainframes, customised or packages etc.

In Step 030 several options are generated, first from the business viewpoint, then their technical implementation. Options will be discussed with yourself and other users to produce a short list, ideally of three options. Plans for the development of each of these are prepared and submitted to the project board for consideration. This may well produce a further composite option.

Key points for users

Feasibility Options

Each option should:

- be compatible with the scope and constraints as specified in the Project Initiation Document;
- meet the minimum requirements of *what, how well,* and *how much;*
- be capable of implementation by the available or planned resources.

Special consideration should be given to any equipment or software required for critical parts of the system, that is not currently and readily available.

STEP 040 ASSEMBLE FEASIBILITY REPORT

The Feasibility Study ends with the preparation of the Feasibility Report by the developers. Some revision is likely to be necessary because of the decisions made in Step 030. A final check is then made of all the current documentation. The documents are checked for conformance with SSADM and with organisational standards, and are cross-checked for consistency. When the work has passed these quality checks it is assembled into the Feasibility Report. A management decision to go ahead must then be taken before work can continue on the detailed full study that starts in Stage 1.

Key points for users

The Feasibility Report must propose a single system (the selected option) that:

- meets the terms of reference as detailed in the Project Initiation Document;
- adequately addresses your requirements as clarified during the study;
- can be developed within the time and cost budgets.

Requirements Analysis Module

Stages 1 and 2

16

Stage 1 – Investigation of Current Environment

INTRODUCTION

Stage 1 is the first stage of the full investigation. In initiating the detailed study it is concerned only in analysing the current system and its deficiencies. It observes what exists. It does not attempt to find solutions or to put together a new system. Your involvement throughout this stage is essential for the eventual development of a successful system.

Reference is made in the following sections to the creation of documents. However, when a Feasibility Study has been undertaken, some of this documentation will already be available.

Usually the system under consideration will be one that you are already using, but which is in need of improvement (or rescue!). This provides the starting point for the study.

Much of the first step is concerned with non-SSADM activities, ie the planning, estimating and scheduling of the work. The stage proceeds in Steps 120 to 140 with the SSADM techniques being applied by the developers in a top-down way, starting with high level views of the system, and proceeding down to detail. The physical elements will then be removed from the Data Flow Diagrams to give a logical view of the current system.

Stage 1 is illustrated in Figure 16.1.

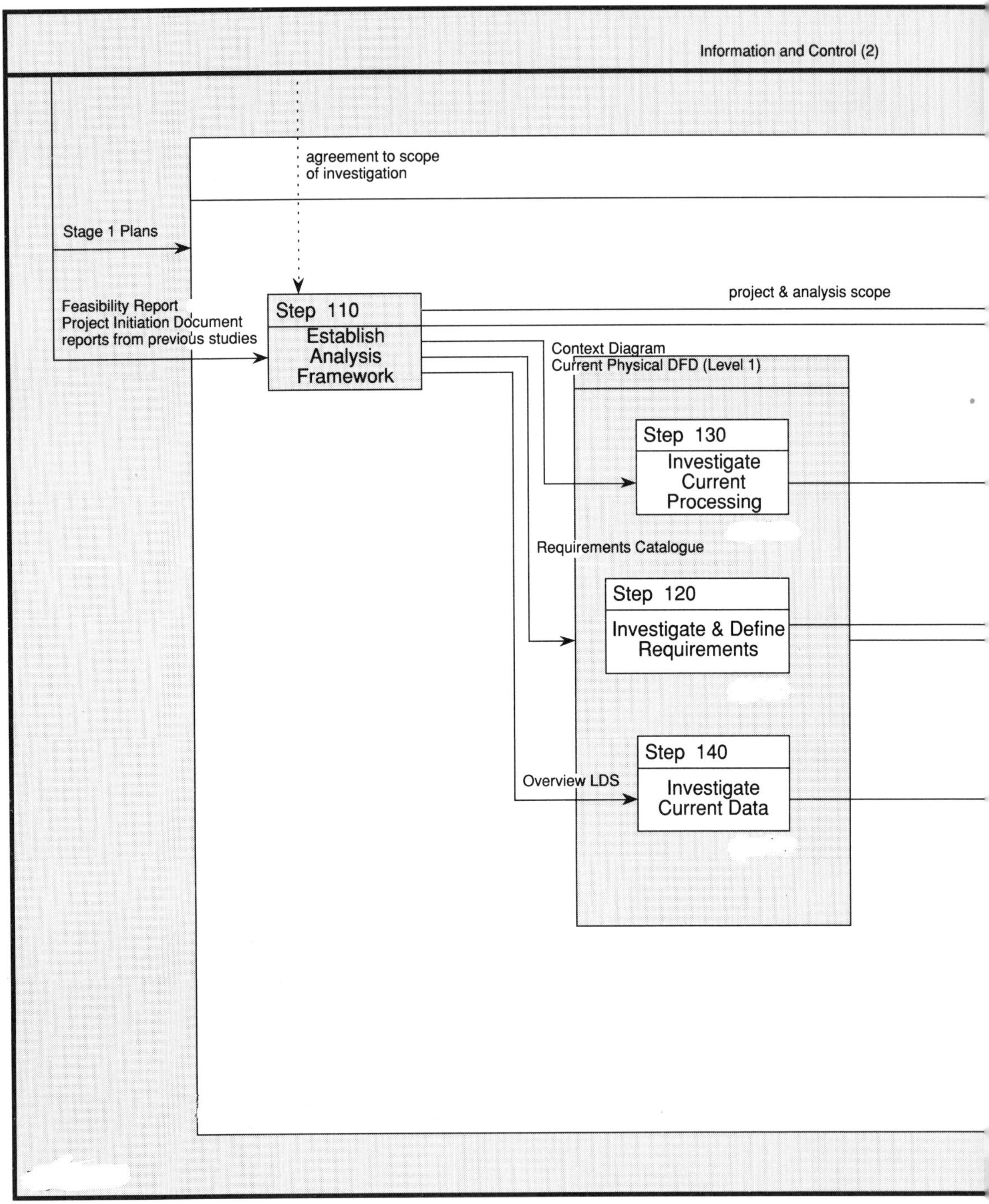

Figure 16.1 Stage 1

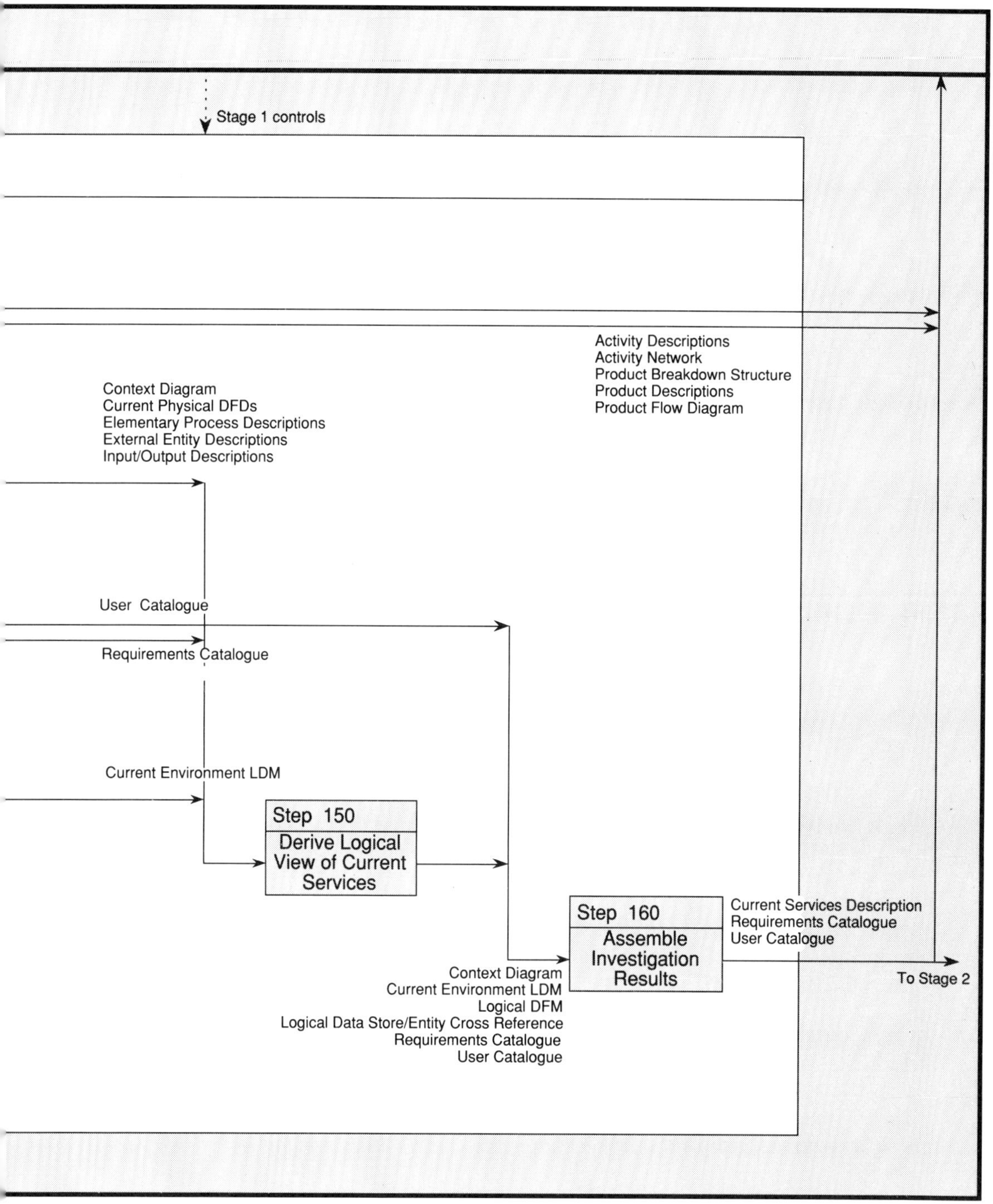
Stage 1 controls
Activity Descriptions
Activity Network
Product Breakdown Structure
Product Descriptions
Product Flow Diagram
Context Diagram
Current Physical DFDs
Elementary Process Descriptions
External Entity Descriptions
Input/Output Descriptions
User Catalogue
Requirements Catalogue
Current Environment LDM
Step 150
Derive Logical View of Current Services
Step 160
Assemble Investigation Results
Current Services Description
Requirements Catalogue
User Catalogue
To Stage 2
Context Diagram
Current Environment LDM
Logical DFM
Logical Data Store/Entity Cross Reference
Requirements Catalogue
User Catalogue

STEP 110 ESTABLISH ANALYSIS FRAMEWORK

This step takes an overview of the area of study, and prepares and plans the later activities. The work is very similar to that carried out at Step 010, and the analysis products are the same, although at a more detailed level, ie:

- Context diagram;
- Current physical DFD (Level 1);
- Overview LDS;
- Requirements Catalogue.

The developers will also prepare the planning documents, which you may not see, but that consist of:

- Project and analysis scope;
- Product Descriptions;
- Product Breakdown Structure;
- Product Flow Diagram;
- Activity Descriptions;
- Activity Network.

The starting point is the Project Initiation Document and plans, together with the documentation created during any study that may already have been carried out. If an SSADM Feasibility Study has been done, then the Feasibility Report will be reviewed at this point. Where there is a queue of work waiting to be done and it is a significant time since the initiation of the project, some of the stated requirements could be quite old. Where requirements have changed, some updating of the existing documents may be necessary, and estimates of the costs and benefits must be reconsidered.

A Context Diagram is created to give an overview of the system. It shows the elements in the real world (external entities) that must communicate (interface) with the system. It will also show communication with other computer systems. The primary inputs and outputs are indicated, thus putting the system into context and defining its scope.

A Data Flow Diagram (DFD) is created. This first diagram is a high level representation or overview of the system, and is known as a Level-1 DFD. It shows:

- a first idea about what is outside and what is inside the system, ie the boundary between the real world and the computer system;

- the most significant information that flows across this boundary, ie the principal system inputs and outputs;
- the main system functions.

Subsequently the information contained in the diagram will be analysed in greater detail. What is important at this point is to establish the scope of the project. Particular attention should be paid to ensuring that the boundary, which indicates the area for analysis (the domain of change, or the domain of computerisation as it is sometimes called), is in the right place. Much time can be wasted on studying areas that should properly fall outside the system, and whilst this may all be useful knowledge, it is none the less misplaced effort at this time.

The information contained within the diagram will be in your own terminology, referring to:

- what is done;
- who does it;
- where it is done;
- people and departments that currently exist;
- documents and other information that move from place to place, and where they are stored.

There is sometimes a tendency, particularly by experienced analysts, to solve problems and to design systems 'on the fly'. This can give a DFD that is a mixture of what is currently done and the analyst's perception of system solutions. There are very good reasons why this should not be done, not least of which are:

- it will be more difficult for you and other users to understand a composite diagram;
- the analyst's assumptions may be wrong, but may not be exposed because of the lack of understanding;
- it may lead to the omission of entries from the Requirements Catalogue which, in turn, will mean that they may not come to your attention subsequently.

An overview Logical Data Structure (LDS) is created. This shows a first stab at:

- an initial set of entities;
- how they are related to each other.

The project board (*see* Chapter 25) must be given the opportunity to consider the scope of the project. The board's approval is needed before any further work can take place. (Without approval, work may be done needlessly, adding to the cost of the project.)

The Requirements Catalogue is started. The entries are recorded as they are found, with no attempt at grouping them, finding solutions, allocating priorities, or specifying objectives in a quantitative way. Whilst all of this additional information may be included if known, no effort should be expended on getting it. These considerations come later, when the bulk of the entries have been gathered and they can be considered as a coherent whole.

The planning documents are essential for the control of the project and are a project management issue. A project management method must be in use. This is needed as being the alternative to anarchy and the wastage of resources. There are endless ways of frittering time away, and this will happen if the development process is not controlled. Both your involvement and that of the developers should be scheduled. Your time will be needed for fact finding, informal checks of the work as it progresses, and formal involvement in reviews.

Key points for users

Context Diagram (form SSADMv4 03)

Ensure that:

- all of the external entities are shown;
- the data flows correctly indicate the scope of the system.

DFD (form SSADMv4 04)

Check that:

- all of the external entities are shown, as on the Context Diagram;
- the system boundary is correctly shown;
- the main system inputs and outputs are shown, as on the Context Diagram;
- all of the job functions are represented;
- all of the terminology, ie of external entities, data flows, processes and data stores, is meaningful to you;
- the diagram is only of the current physical system, ie future requirements should not be shown at this stage.

LDS (form SSADMv4 30)

Check for the correct identification of:

- initial entities;
- a unique identifier (key) for each entity;
- *direct* relationships between entities;
- the type of relationship, ie mandatory, optional, exclusive.

Requirements Catalogue (form SSADMv4 42)

- Does it include all items specified in the Project Initiation Document?
- Are all the requirements correctly expressed?

Plans

Do the proposals that involve you meet with your approval, and can you accomplish the tasks within the times and costs as scheduled?

Project management

Ensure that an effective project management method is being used.

STEP 120 INVESTIGATE AND DEFINE REQUIREMENTS

Step 120 is carried out concurrently with Steps 130 and 140. During these three steps the overview of the system, taken in Step 110, is amplified as the investigation proceeds, more detail is obtained, and more requirements are identified.

User involvement is essential in this step, so one of the tasks for the developers is to identify all the users of the system. Details are entered in the User Catalogue, identification being by job title and the activities carried out by each. You will need to check that those relevant to your responsibilities are complete and correct.

The User Catalogue is used again when considering Business System Options at Steps 210 and 220. It also provides the starting point for dialogue design, which advances further at Step 310.

Step 120 is concerned with requirements and the consequent entries in the Requirements Catalogue. Initial information will come directly from you: details of problems you currently have, and the additional facilities that you need from the new system. This will be augmented by further problems and requirements that come to light as the processing is considered in more detail in Step 130 and the data structure is established in Step 140.

There are three main points to be made about entries in the Requirements Catalogue:

- The entries must be prioritised (this can be on any scale, although the more sophisticated the priorities, the more effort it will take for perhaps little payoff. Mandatory, desirable and optional may suffice, at least initially). These priorities will be taken into account when Business System Options are being proposed and selected at Steps 210 and 220.

- Entries relating to qualities and resources should be both quantifiable and measurable (how well and how much). Any vague entries such as 'faster', 'better', 'more', etc. must be made more precise. Note that more work may be entailed in providing a means of making the measurement.

- Possible solutions should be noted, and these may be either business or technical ones, supplied by users or developers as appropriate. You must pay particular attention to any critical requirements for which no practical solution has been noted. It would be rash to proceed in the hope that something will turn up. Your reputation could be on the line.

As the work proceeds, information is collected about all of the data used in the system. Each separate element of data is documented on its own Attribute/Data Item Description form. The collection of all the forms is known as the Data Catalogue.

The Data Catalogue is essentially a repository of data about data. Its aim is to define precisely each element of data in the system. The intention is to avoid misunderstandings between yourself and the developers, and not least, to avoid misunderstandings between the developers themselves.

The developers will need to obtain from you information about each data item (also called a data field or attribute) such as:

- name by which it is known to you;
- entity within which the data item is held (shown as the Cross-reference name/ID);
- synonyms by which it is also known;
- description, so that all those involved will know precisely what the data item is;
- validation information, for example:
  - logical format and length, ie what the data looks like, eg the date may be held as dd/mm/yy (English format), mm.dd.yy (American format), ddmmmyy, etc;
  - range, eg age of employees may be defined as being between 16 and 70;
  - permissible entries, eg sex may be shown as M or F;
  - cross-reference validation, eg if sex is shown as male, condition may not be due to pregnancy;
- derivation, ie how the information comes into the system, eg as basic data input (customer name), from a transaction (order item), derived by program (total value of order);
- access rights, eg who can see the data; who can update it;
- notes, for example:
  - use, ie for what purposes the data item is used within the system;
  - anything that requires further information, qualification or cross-referencing.

Key points for users

User Catalogue (form SSADMv4 45)

- Check that all relevant job titles are shown.

- For each job title, check that all the tasks to be carried out have been noted.

Attribute/Data Item Description (form SSADMv4 1) Data Catalogue

- Check that forms are held for all known data items.
- For each item, check that the document is complete and correct as far as the information for which you are responsible (or have knowledge) is concerned.

Requirements Catalogue (form SSADMv4 42)

Check that:

- forms are held for all items specified in the Project Initiation Document or identified in an earlier study;
- all the entries are relevant and valid;
- there is no duplication;
- related entries have been brought together, or suitably cross-referenced;
- descriptions are clear, expanding them where necessary;
- forms are held for all known functional requirements that are not in the current system;
- non-functional requirements (qualities and resources) are specified in a precise and measurable way as far as possible;
- the environment in which it must operate has been defined, eg considerations of space, climate or pollution;
- all requirements are correctly expressed;
- appropriate priorities have been allocated to each requirement, and those that are mandatory have been identified as such, eg:
    - mandatory processes, ie those which are essential to the acceptability of the system at the first implementation;
    - mandatory facilities, eg processes which require on-line access;
- limits have been expressed for:
    - development time, in terms of elapsed time;

- cost, in terms of man days, the purchase of equipment and software, and all other system-related costs;
- the number of people available to do the development work (this may be because of lack of staff or due to their having other commitments;
- effects on user staffing, in terms of likely redundancies, changes in organisation, and changes in geographical location;

– reasonable, practical solutions are suggested for each entry.

STEP 130 INVESTIGATE CURRENT PROCESSING

Step 130 is carried out concurrently with Steps 120 and 140. This is because investigation of the processing will reveal new requirements, and the data model developed at Step 140 must support the processing that is being investigated at Step 130.

At this time the investigation is of the system as it currently exists. The starting point for the documentation is the Current Physical Data Flow Diagram (Level 1), created in Step 110.

The processes, data flows, external entities and data stores are all closely examined, with the more detailed findings being recorded on lower level DFDs. This breakdown of information into increasing levels of detail is an aid to understanding: each individual diagram is relatively simple within a whole that may be extremely complex. Each user needs to see only the diagrams that are relevant to his responsibilities.

The DFDs prepared in the early stages of a system study are inevitably incomplete, and this is not self-evident from an inspection of the diagrams. As an aid to extracting the maximum amount of information as early as possible in the study, Document Flow Diagrams are developed from, and are used to enhance, the DFDs.

Elementary Process Descriptions (EPDs) are created for the processes on the lowest level DFDs to explain the detailed processing. An EPD will be needed for most of these lowest level boxes unless the processing is self evident (but what is self evident to users may not be so to the developers, and vice versa, so care is needed). EPDs are typically represented by about a half page or so of description. They would include business algorithms, eg how to calculate discounts for different categories of customers. It is useful to have EPDs available for your scrutiny early in the development process.

Input/Output Descriptions are produced for flows across the system boundary.

External Entity Descriptions are produced for the entities outside the boundary.

Key points for users

Document Flow Diagram (form SSADMv4 12)

The Document Flow Diagram is used only within this step, ie it is not an output product. Its purpose is to elicit information that should be on the DFDs, but that may have been missed. Once it has served this purpose it has no further use within the method. However, you will be involved in its production and checking.

- Are all the documents that are currently in use in the system, represented on the diagram?

- Do the data flows that represent the documents show *all* of the document movements, for every copy of each document, from initiation to final filing, to disposal outside the system, or to destruction?

DFDs (form SSADMv4 5)

Check all levels as for Step 110.

Ensure compatibility between the different levels of the diagrams.

Elementary Process Descriptions (form SSADMv4 14)

These forms amplify the information shown on the lowest level process boxes on the DFDs. One form is used for each lowest level process.

Check that the description of each process is both correct and complete.

Ensure that the LDS will support the DFD processes.

External Entity Descriptions (form SSADMv4 21)

One form is required for each external entity shown on the DFDs. Remember that these comprise real world people/organisations, other systems, and other departments/people within your own organisation who interface with the system.

- Check that a form is held for each.

- Check that the descriptions correctly specify the responsibilities or functions of the external entity, and any constraints on how it will interact with the system.

I/O Descriptions (form SSADMv4 26)

One form is required for each bottom level data flow that crosses the system boundary from an external entity.

On each form, check that all of the data items are listed.

STEP 140 INVESTIGATE CURRENT DATA

Step 140 is carried out concurrently with Steps 120 and 130. Completion of all three of these steps marks the end of the investigation into the current physical system.

The current Logical Data Structure to be documented is that needed to support the processing as it is shown in the Current Physical Data Flow Diagrams. It is independent of the way in which the data is currently organised. Data needed for new requirements is not included.

The technique of Relational Data Analysis, formally carried out at Step 340, may be used here if there is difficulty in establishing data groupings.

The overview LDS is examined and extended as necessary. The relationships are examined in greater detail, particularly any where a first view of the relationships seemed to suggest them as one-to-one or many-to-many. One-to-one relationships are suspect, but may be valid. Many-to-many relationships require particular attention because they are an indication that an entity may have been missed. The many-to-many relationships are *always* modified. Thus, after this step, it will be normal for *all* relationships to be one-to-many.

Entity Descriptions are created for each entity on the LDS. The Entity Description will ultimately contain comprehensive information about each of the entities. When first set up here, the entries are normally limited to:

- key, ie the data item by which an entity is uniquely identified;
- significant data items, ie those which come to mind on initial thinking about the entity;
- volumetric information, ie the average and maximum number of occurrences of the entity within the system. This should consider not just the current position, but also expected growth over the planned life of the system. (You should know what the planned life of the system is – stopgap, 5 years, 10 years, until present hardware is replaced, etc.) Peaks and troughs should also be recorded.

This work is likely to give rise to further entries in the Requirements Catalogue.

Key points for users

LDS (form SSADMv4 30)

- ensure that all many-to-many relationships have been satisfactorily modified to one-to-many relationships;

- ensure that any remaining one-to-one relationships are valid ones (at some point they must be changed to one-to-many relationships, to indicate which is the master and which the detail);

- ensure that the LDS will support the DFD processes.

Entity Descriptions (forms SSADMv4 17 and 18)

- ensure that Entity Descriptions show significant data items and volumetrics.

STEP 150 DERIVE LOGICAL VIEW OF CURRENT SERVICES

The diagrams produced up to this point have been derived from the investigation of the current physical system, with all its inadequacies. Little is achieved by computering a mess, other than to obtain a computerised mess. The first step towards improving the situation is achieved by removing the physical constraints from the work done thus far. This process is known as *logicalisation.*

Logicalisation is done on the lowest level DFDs, with changes being carried back up into the higher level diagrams.

The Data Flow Diagrams of the current *physical* system show *what* is done and also *how* it is done, *where* it is done, and *who* does it. The new system will be doing much the same of the *what* element. However, the *how, where,* and *who* are historical and must not be allowed to inhibit the design of the new system. They are therefore disposed of in this step. Further, the current system is likely to have many deficiencies. Typically it will have been found to contain:

- data duplicated in more than one data store;
- entities split over more than one data store;
- data being held in the system but never used;
- physical transformations of data, ie the same data but in a different sequence;
- enquiries which do not change the state of the data;
- existing physical constraints, eg different geographical locations, or split storage due to limitations of space;
- data being used within the system without its apparently having been entered or derived in the first place, in which case further investigation is required.

This step aims to remove the physical aspects, to correct the deficiencies, and to give a clean, logical starting point for the building of the new system.

The actual process of logicalising the Data Flow Diagrams (DFDs) is undertaken by the developers, but you are likely to be closely involved in resolving misunderstandings and uncertainties, all of which add to the knowledge of the system being gained by the analysts. The DFDs, after logicalisation, are still of the *current* system. No attempt should yet have been made to move it towards the *new* system. The diagrams will probably have a rather tidier appearance than on the physical DFDs. It is possible that many process boxes will fall into a line beneath each other. Remember that this does not indicate sequence or priority. If they appear like this, it is for clarity and for no other purpose.

During logicalisation, any entries on the DFDs that relate to enquiries and do not change the data in any way, will usually have been removed and transferred to the Requirements Catalogue.

A Logical Data Store/Entity cross-reference is created, showing the correspondence between data stores on the DFDs and entities on the LDS.

The supporting documents (Elementary Process Descriptions, Input/Output Descriptions, External Entity Descriptions and the Requirements Catalogue) are also amended as necessary to reflect the logical view of the system.

Solutions to existing problems, and new requirements, are built into the logical system in Stage 2.

Key points for users

DFDs (forms SSADMv4 4 and 5)

- ensure that all physical aspects have been removed from the DFDs;
- ensure that all retrievals removed from the DFDs have been entered in the Requirements Catalogue.

Logical Data Store/Entity cross-reference (form SSADMv4 29)

- ensure that all data stores from the logicalised DFDs, and all entities from the LDS are represented;
- ensure that the matching of data stores and entities has been done correctly;
- check that no entities are split between two or more data stores.

STEP 160 ASSEMBLE INVESTIGATION RESULTS

The final step in Stage 1 is a comprehensive review of all the documentation that has been produced. Up to this point, checking has been principally of individual documents. One of the strengths of SSADM is the way in which the different documents complement each other, and so Step 160 carries out comprehsnvie cross-checks between them. These checks will be made by the developers.

A review procedure may already exist in your organisation. If not, you should adopt one of the formal approaches to this task. (Inspections are outlined in Chapter 23.) Errors and misunderstandings will be vastly cheaper to correct at this point than if discovered at a later stage of development.

Both users and developers must satisfy themselves that:

- all of the information is accurate;
- the work has been done to the required standard;
- the project is a viable one;
- the plans for the rest of the analysis phase are acceptable.

Corrections required as a result of the review are completed. The project can then advance to Stage 2.

The Data Flow Diagrams (DFDs) require particularly careful study. They must correctly show *your* perception of the logicalised current system. The system boundary, originally identified in the Project Initiation Document and perhaps modified during the Feasibility Study and again at Steps 110 and 130, must again be scrutinised, possibly changed again, and formally agreed.

The plans will require review now that:

- more is known about the system;
- the boundary is more firmly established (but still subject to further consideration when Business System Options are proposed and selected in Stage 2).

Key points for users

- agree system boundary;
- review all documents;
- agree updated plans.

17

Stage 2 Business System Options

INTRODUCTION

The aim of systems analysis and design is to produce a system that will satisfy the user's requirements. However, real world pressures of time and cost will almost certainly inhibit the grand design. It is unlikely that all of the existing problems will be solved and all of the new requirements will be built into the initial implementation of the new system.

When a system solution appears on the horizon, there can be a tendency not to look any further, but it would be rare indeed to find that there was only one possible solution that would be of use to the users. Stage 2 (Figure 17.1) recognises this and sets out specifically to generate several different solutions, all satisfying any mandatory constraints and requirements but with different variations on system boundaries, facilities included, other requirements satisfied, and problems solved. There are choices to be made, and these are considered at Step 210 when Business System Options are generated, and at Step 220 when an Option is chosen. The logic of this chosen implementation is then considered in detail in Stage 3.

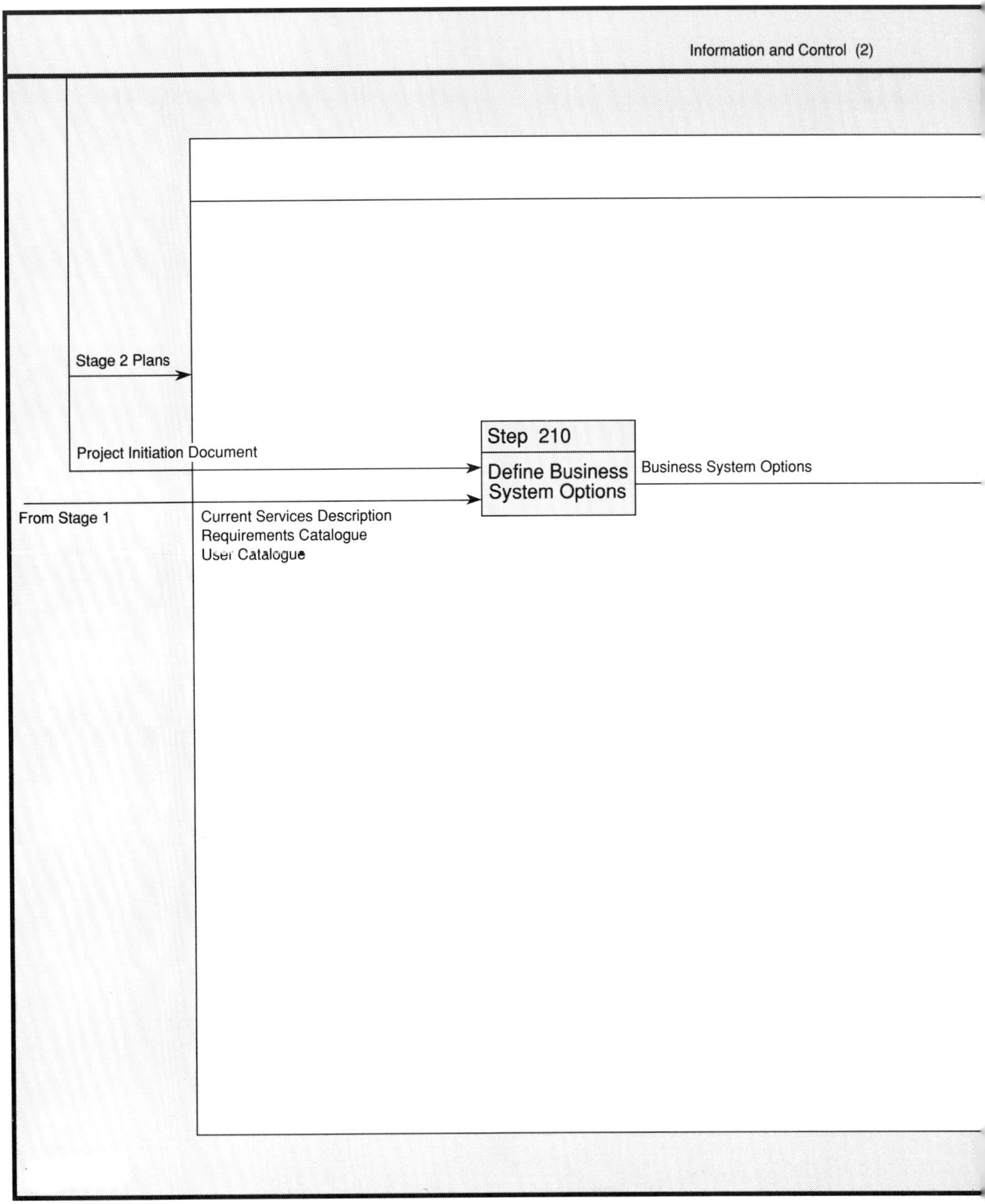

Figure 17.1 Stage 2

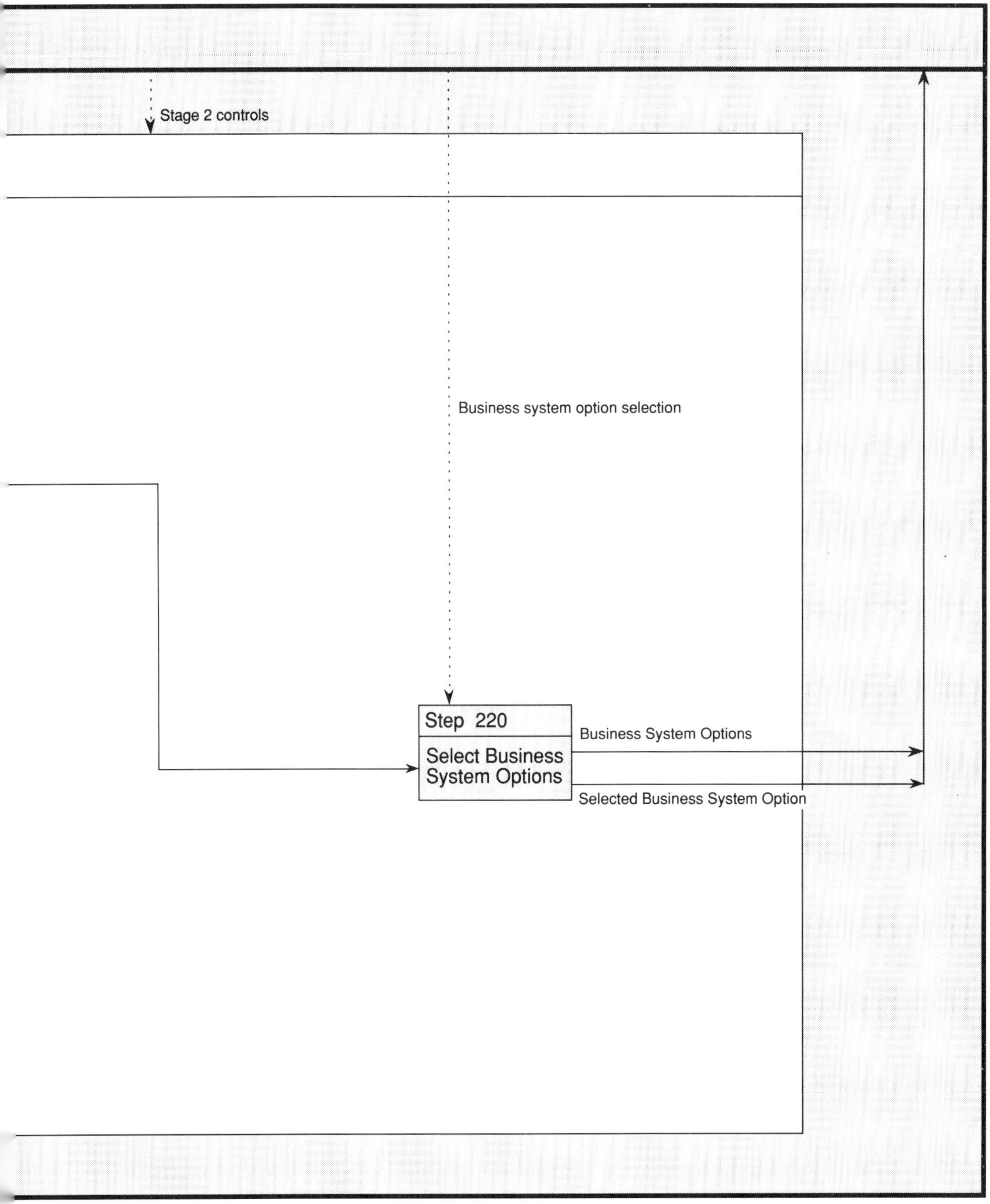
Stage 2 controls
Business system option selection
Step 220
Select Business System Options
Business System Options
Selected Business System Option

STEP 210 DEFINE BUSINESS SYSTEM OPTIONS

At Step 120 you will have set the different priorities for the various requirements of the new system. These priorities will most likely range from those that are essential to those that it would be nice to have some day. You must now identify the requirements that are *essential* to you. All solutions put forward by the developers must satisfy these mandatory features. However, even within these constraints there are likely to be many possibilities, each with its own unique costs and benefits.

The work involved in this step can be very time consuming for the developers. From the information they have gathered during the investigation they will now develop several possible scenarios or Business System Options (BSOs). All the possible variables must be considered:

- The boundary will be reviewed again and could be drawn in various places.

- Each entry in the Requirements Catalogue may be omitted, partially implemented, or fully included.

- The system could be left unchanged, modified within its existing framework, or replaced by a new system.

Computerisation is not the only solution. There is no such thing as a single correct solution. The possible solutions cannot be considered as right or wrong – only as acceptable or unacceptable for your particular organisation at this particular time.

Each of perhaps six possibilities will be put forward in outline and discussed with yourself and other users.

Essentially, what has to be decided here is *how the system will appear to you,* ie what it will do, how well it will do it, and what it will cost for it to be developed and operated. Only very broad estimates can be given now. The estimates are refined in later stages as more is established about your required system in Stage 3, and how it will actually be implemented is considered in Stage 4. (Inevitably, the technical implications during Stage 4 may require some rethinking of the chosen Business System Option.)

After these discussions any non-starters are rejected. This should still leave about three options for further consideration and development. Typically, these could be:

- a basic system, dealing with perhaps about 80% of the work, ie the routine, non-complex transactions;

- a comprehensive system, doing most of what has been suggested, including many low priority items, probably exceeding the desired cost, but showing the sort of system and facilities that could be made available;
- a reasonable compromise, containing the high priority items, some of the desirable ones, staying within the base constraints, and achieving the minimum specified levels for qualities and resources.

Each of these outline BSOs is a textual document which will include:

- identification of the system boundary;
- an indication of the requirements that will be addressed;
- a brief description of organisational implications;
- an outline cost/benefit analysis;
- an estimate of training needs and costs.

It may be supported by:

- DFDs indicating the system boundary;
- a Logical Data Structure (LDS), which may differ for each option (different options may require different combinations of entities, with consequent changes in relationships, data volumes and access paths).

Key points for users

Select a short list of possible BSOs with agreed boundaries, and with the requirements for inclusion defined, after considering:

- alternatives;
- effects on your organisation;
- cost/benefit analyses;
- policies for future expansion or contraction of the business;
- market opportunities;
- whether it provides a viable and acceptable way of working.

STEP 220 SELECT BUSINESS SYSTEM OPTIONS

The Requirements Analysis Module culminates in the presentation of the short-listed Business System Options to the project board, and to a wider audience where appropriate.

The analysts can only present the options and their implications. The actual selection is a business decision to be taken by the sponsors of the project. Their aim must be to select the best possible compromise in the existing circumstances.

The selected option could be one of those presented, but is more likely to be some variation entailing consequent rework. It could contain elements from more than one of the options presented, and maybe some new ideas that arise during the presentation process.

After the choice has been made, a description is developed for the selected option, and this goes forward to the Requirements Specification Module.

Key points for users

The points for consideration are the same as those listed for Step 210, but as the audience is different, so too will their perception be different. The position of the boundary and the requirements for inclusion will be selected after considering:

- alternatives;
- effects on your organisation;
- cost/benefit analyses;
- policies for future expansion or contraction of the business;
- market opportunities;
- whether it provides a viable and acceptable way of working.

Requirements Specification Module

Stage 3

18

Stage 3 – Definition of Requirements

INTRODUCTION

Stage 3 is the only stage in the Requirements Specification Module. During this stage, the selected BSO is transformed into the logical system Requirements Specification. Further work on the Data Flow Diagrams provides the source of information about functions. The data structure is improved by Relational Data Analysis, a technique that assists the grouping of data elements into simple, logical, structures. Further detail about events, their effects on the data, and therefore on the consequent processing, are obtained by the development of Entity Life Histories.

Stage 3 is illustrated in Figure 18.1.

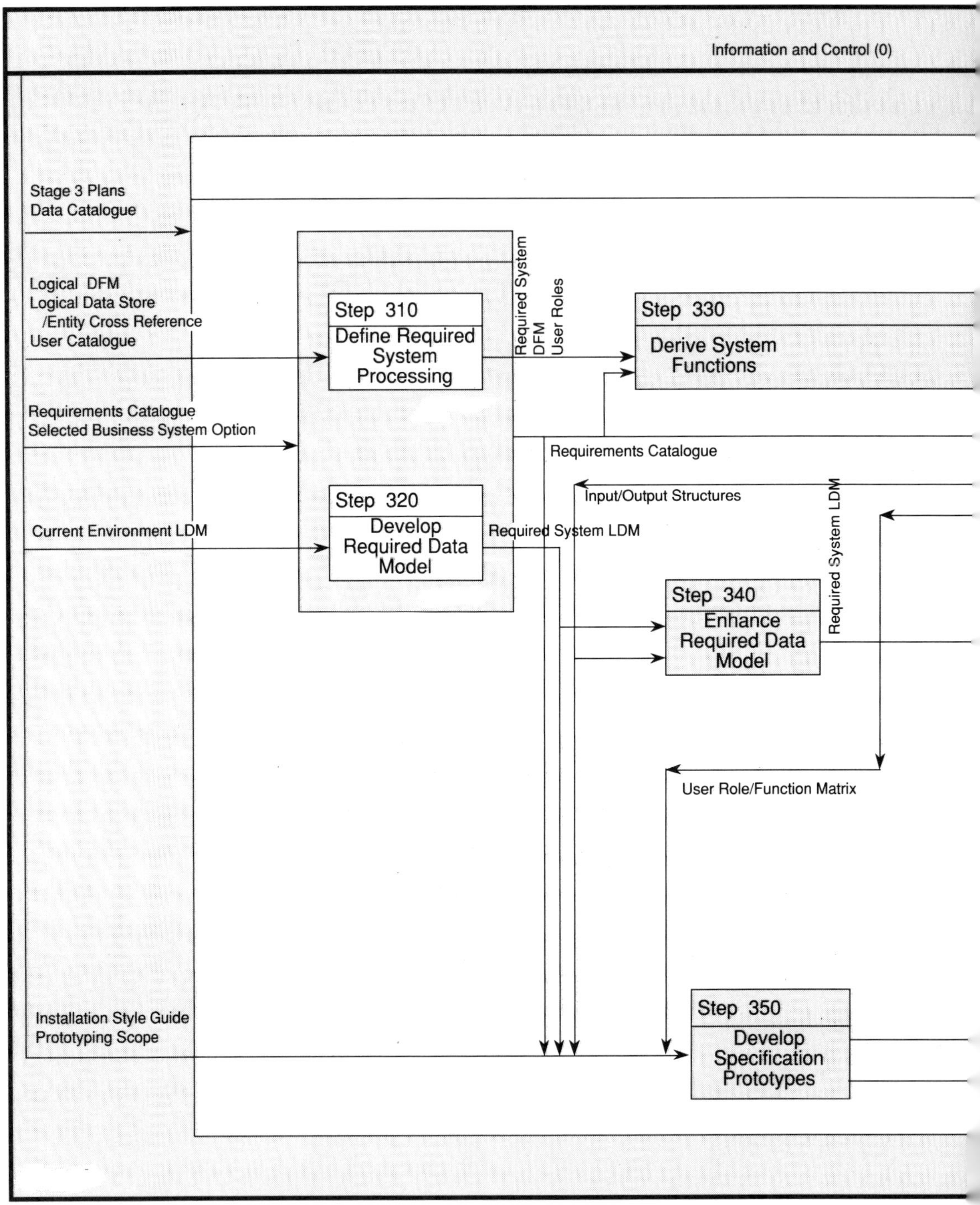

Figure 18.1 Stage 3

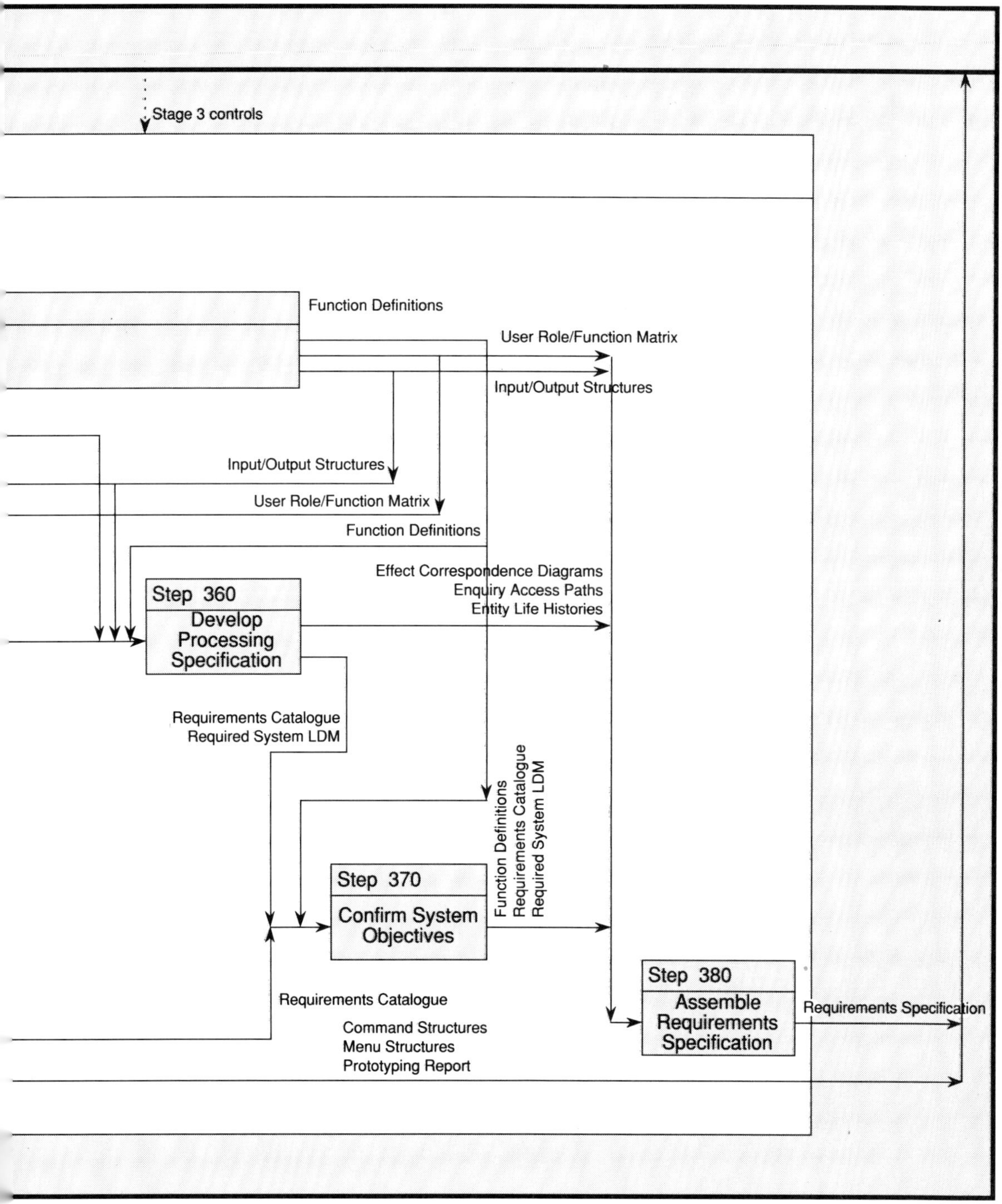

Stage 3 controls
Function Definitions
User Role/Function Matrix
Input/Output Structures
Input/Output Structures
User Role/Function Matrix
Function Definitions
Effect Correspondence Diagrams
Enquiry Access Paths
Entity Life Histories
Step 360
Develop Processing Specification
Requirements Catalogue
Required System LDM
Function Definitions
Requirements Catalogue
Required System LDM
Step 370
Confirm System Objectives
Step 380
Assemble Requirements Specification
Requirements Specification
Requirements Catalogue
Command Structures
Menu Structures
Prototyping Report

STEP 310 DEFINE REQUIRED SYSTEM PROCESSING

Steps 310 and 320 are very similar to Steps 130 and 140, ie they are carried out in parallel and consider processes, data flows and data structures. Whereas in Stage 1 a high level view was taken, with little idea of how the new system was going to look, they are now done in detail for the required system.

Items in the Requirements Catalogue that have been excluded from the ongoing development are noted with reasons for their omission. (The design should, so far as is practical, allow for these to be included at some time in the future. This particularly applies to any that may have been specifically earmarked for inclusion in subsequent enhancements to the system.) There may be new requirements to be entered.

The DFDs are updated in the light of the selected Business System Option. The Level-1 DFD, which was the basis of the BSO, is decomposed to give lower level DFDs, this decomposition being carried out as far as necessary to investigate fully the data flows and processing. All of the facilities provided by the current system should have been incorporated, unless their omission was deliberate, justified and agreed. The DFDs should incorporate those items from the Requirements Catalogue that were chosen for incorporation in the BSO, and any new requirements identified during the selection process.

The changes noted in the Requirements Catalogue and DFDs will also affect the Elementary Process Descriptions, Input/Output (I/O) Descriptions, and External Entity Descriptions.

The Elementary Process Descriptions (EPDs) will need to be reconsidered in the light of the chosen BSO. Further EPDs may need to be created, existing ones amended, and some, for processes excluded from the BSO, will be dropped.

Up to this point, screens, prints, data flows and documents have only needed to be mentioned in a high level way, usually by name, for example, order screen, payroll print, outstanding credits, invoice, etc. More details are now required, and these are entered on I/O Descriptions. In these, the individual data items that go to make up the inputs and outputs to the system are entered by name and detail.

Changes to the system boundary may require the creation of new External Entity Descriptions, the abandonment of others, and reclassification of any which have moved within the system boundary and ceased to be external entities.

Data store contents are compared with the parallel development of the Logical Data Model. All the items of data in each data store must be represented in the data flows to the store, ie all the data must have a source outside the store, and must be used somewhere in an output data flow.

User Roles are defined in the required system. There is likely to be considerable duplication of information with the User Catalogue, but the purposes are different. A person with one job title may have several different responsibilities (roles). (For example, the night porter in a hotel may also cover the roles of receptionist and room service at certain times.)

Knowing these different roles is important to the developers for dialogue and menu design, to ensure that the necessary information is available to those who need it. (What a user enters, and how the computer responds, is known as a dialogue or conversation. A dialogue is likely to consist of a series of screens of information being passed between the user and the computer. A menu is a list of possible choices of actions from which the user can select what to do next.)

The recording of roles is also of direct use to you, identifying where a single responsibility is shared by several people, or where one person has too many responsibilities.

Note that in systems requiring high levels of security, such as financial systems, having one person responsible for too many roles is a potential security risk. To have the same person responsible for authorising the purchase of new supplies, issuing orders, approving payments, feeding invoices into the system and issuing cheques, could make a considerable hole in the company finances, discovered only on receipt of a picture postcard from South America. The division of responsibilities will require collusion for the same risk. A lower level risk still exists, of course, in which case you may get two cards from South America, but the chances of fraud are less.

Key points for users

Requirements Catalogue (form SSADMv4 42)

Ensure that:

- all items have been correctly identified for inclusion or exclusion;
- adequate solutions have been noted for requirements that have been included;
- reasons have been noted for items that have been excluded.

DFDs (forms SSADMv4 4 and 5)

Ensure that:

- all required facilities in the current system have been included;
- all new requirements are represented.

Elementary Process Descriptions (form SSADMv4 14)

Check that:

- an EPD exists for each lowest level box on the DFDs;
- the processing is correct as described.

I/O Descriptions (form SSADMv4 26)

Check that:

- a form exists for each data flow crossing the system boundary;
- details of the data content are both complete and correct.

External Entity Descriptions (form SSADMv4 21)

Check that:

- one exists for each external entity;
- the data contained is correct.

STEP 320 DEVELOP REQUIRED DATA MODEL

Step 320 is carried out concurrently with step 310. The Logical Data Model and Requirements Catalogue are updated and the structure of the LDS is checked to ensure that it supports the processing shown on the DFDs and described in the Elementary Process Descriptions for the selected BSO.

The data structure that existed before selection of the Business System Option (BSO) is unlikely to have emerged unscathed from that selection process. In this step it is examined in detail and modified as necessary to ensure that it supports the processing that has been chosen for the BSO. The developers will have redrawn the Logical Data Structure so that it matches the processing requirements that you have chosen. They may have used Relational Data Analysis, formally used at Step 340, to help in establishing data groups. They will wish to check with you that any assumptions they have made are correct.

The Entity Descriptions may also have been subject to change. However, the most significant action in this step is to complete the forms so that they include every known item of data (individual items of data, such as name, address, date of birth, nationality, etc, are often known as attributes).

The system cannot be designed unless it is known how much storage is required. This information is needed both to assess hardware requirements and also to calculate how long it will take to retrieve data (the access time) when it is needed for a process. This information will be entered by the developers on the Entity Descriptions, but they will be dependent on you for the information. Great care is needed. Wrong information may well lead to the design of a system that is not the optimum one. It could lead to a system that will exceed the available capacity in a short time. Then, if there is no suitable upgrade path, a complete rewrite of the system may be needed to allow continued operation on different equipment.

It is possible that you may not have all of the necessary information, and the figures you supply may thus be estimates or, worse, guesstimates. Consequently you should inform the developers of the amount of confidence you have in the figures you supply to them, eg:

> 11500, plus or minus 10 percent
>
> 124000 as at August 1992
>
> 200000 (guess).

Key points for users

LDS (form SSADMv4 30)

Ensure that:

- the LDS structure will support the processing shown on the DFDs and Elementary Process Descriptions.

Entity Descriptions (forms SSADMv4 17 and 18)

Check that:

- the forms identify all the known attributes;
- the volumetric information (ie the number of occurrences) is correct;
- the user role information is correct;
- the access rights meet with your security requirements.

STEP 330 DERIVE SYSTEM FUNCTIONS

A significant transformation takes place in this step with the Data Flow Diagrams and much of the information in the Requirements Catalogue being superseded by Function Definitions.

The Required System Data Flow Diagrams provide the source of information for the creation of update Function Definitions (more are likely to be found later when Entity Life Histories are created at Step 360).

Enquiry Function Definitions are also completed. They are derived mainly from the Requirements Catalogue (although some of the more critical or complex enquiries may have been shown on the DFDs.)

At this point all the processing that has been identified so far in the investigation has now been transferred from the Data Flow Diagrams to the Function Definitions. This work will have been done by the developers.

With the functions established, you will now be involved in defining how you will communicate with the system. This user interface, as it is known, is recorded in Input/Output Structures. For updates, these come from the Input/Output Descriptions. The enquiry interfaces are established from discussions with yourself and other users. These dialogues, cross-referenced to user functions, are documented on the User Role/Function Matrix. Critical dialogues are identified.

Service levels (ie the quality of service required) are defined for each function.

Key points for users

Function Definitions (form SSADMv4 22)

Check that:

- the volumetric information is correct;
- the service levels meet your requirements.

I/O Structure Descriptions (form SSADMv4 27)

Check that:

- a Description is held for each box shown on the I/O Structure Diagrams;
- the data items shown for each structure element will meet your information requirement for the function.

I/O Structure Diagrams (form SSADMv4 28)

Check that the diagrams illustrate an acceptable way for you to interact with the system.

User Role/Function Matrix (form SSADMv4 46)

Check that:

- all on-line functions are shown in the column headings;
- all user roles are shown in the row headings;
- all the functions required by each user role have been correctly identified.

STEP 340 ENHANCE REQUIRED DATA MODEL

The Logical Data Model has been derived from the top down, and structured to ensure support for the processing shown in the Required System Data Flow Model. This may not be the most efficient structure, so Relational Data Analysis (RDA) is now applied to groups of data items.

The LDS was essentially a top down approach to data analysis in that it started with entities and was gradually filled out (on the LDS and on Entity Descriptions) to show an increasing level of detail of the data elements (attributes) held within the entities. RDA is exactly the opposite. It starts with the data attributes and is a technique for organising these individual items of data into simple, logical, related groups that are less prone to change and better able to cope with change when it does occur. Processing of simple data groups is itself simplified.

The technique of RDA is also known as *Normalisation* and *Third Normal Form* (TNF or 3NF). (After RDA, the data groups are said to be in Third Normal Form, ie they are TNF relations. This rather strange name is because RDA is a three step process, putting the data first into First Normal Form, then into Second Normal Form, and finally into Third Normal Form. The technique can be carried on to Sixth Normal Form, but this is a rarety.)

The steps to convert the data into TNF are:

- Remove any repeating groups to put the data into First Normal Form.
- Ensure that all data items are dependent on the key. The data is then in Second Normal Form.
- Ensure that all items other than the key are independent of each other. The data is then in Third Normal Form.

Data in Third Normal Form is therefore a grouping of items in which:

- there are no repeating groups;
- all the data items are functionally dependent on the key and independent of each other.

The technique of RDA is applied by the developers. Your involvement in this step is likely to be in answering queries that arise when documents are analysed in the sort of detail that this technique demands. The technique itself is entirely automatic and does not require any great experience. It can, however, require a lot of effort when there are many items to analyse. It will often speed up the work considerably if it is done by teams of two – a user and a developer. The developer can go very quickly through the RDA techniques given a user at his elbow to resolve the queries as they arise.

RDA is carried out on the Input/Output Structures, but because it is a time-consuming task, it is not carried out on all of them. The ones selected are based on their complexity, volume, frequency and importance.

The selected structures will be entered on RDA Working Papers (forms SSADMv4 40). These are documents for the developers, but they may well ask you to check them for completeness, and to add any further items that may occur to you.

When the chosen data structures have been normalised, they are set out as LDS type structure diagrams. These are compared with the Required System Logical Data Structure, and differences are considered and resolved. (RDA, by giving an alternative view of the data, can usually be expected to identify some aspects of the system that have been missed, even given the thoroughness of the analysis techniques that have been used up to this point.)

The aim of the comparison is to combine the access paths to data indicated by the LDS, with the simple, flexible structure of TNF. Inevitably there will be some compromises, some of the decisions will be subjective, and experience is invaluable. There is no single 'correct' structure. Different practitioners would be likely to produce different structures, each of which would be capable of supporting the system in their different ways.

Although TNF structures are the most flexible, they may be further modified during physical design in Stage 6 for reasons of performance. However, everything has its price, and improvements in performance are likely to be at the expense of greater programming effort, less flexibility in the system, and more costly and time-consuming work during maintenance and enhancement.

STEP 350 DEVELOP SPECIFICATION PROTOTYPES

This step is optional, depending on the complexity and novelty of the system, and your own previous experience of computer systems. The boundaries and objectives of the prototyping exercise are defined by the project board.

There are various types and different approaches to prototyping. (The subject is discussed in Chapter 26.) It is not the intention at this point to build the system from the prototypes in an incremental way, although this is a perfectly valid approach to system development. Prototyping as considered in this step is for the purpose of identifying errors and misunderstandings that have remained hidden until now, and as an aid to the development of screen menus and dialogues for on-line systems. Prototyping is also used to test the interfaces with other systems, for example to check that a magnetic tape containing salary payment details is acceptable to BACS (the Bankers' Automated Clearing System).

The Business System Option will have identified work that is to be done on-line, ie by a person sitting at a computer or terminal. What the operator enters, and how the computer responds, is known as a dialogue or conversation.

A dialogue is likely to consist of a series of screens being passed between operator and computer. Related screens in a dialogue were linked together by the I/O Structure Diagrams.

I/O Descriptions were created initially at Step 130, and consist of lists of data items. Those which are for on-line transactions must now be laid out in screen formats that will be easy for the operator to use, for example:

- by making the impression of the screen acceptable, ie easy on the eye and not cramped;
- by laying out the areas in which data is to be entered in the same sequence as in forms that the operator is using as input documents;
- by making provision for default values, so that if the data to be entered has the normal value, then merely pressing a single key will present the normal value to the system.

There is much more to screen design. The important thing is that the screen must be acceptable to you, even if this is at the cost of some complication to the technical development work. It also should be noted that screen designs may be affected when the technical option is chosen in Stage 4. To do it as you really would like it may be impossible given the software in use, may take too long to transmit, or may initiate processing that could effectively close the system down to other users for an unacceptably long time. Screen design should also conform to any standards already in use, for example:

- the position of help and error messages, how you get to them, and how you get back to the system from them;

– meanings of codes, eg 'A' is always for an additional record, 'D' is always a deletion, 'N' is always the next record, etc.

The prototyping is done on a selection of dialogues and report formats. The exercise will have served its purpose when you are happy with the menus and command structures as demonstrated to you by the developers, and any changes have been incorporated into the Requirements Catalogue and Requirements Specification. Any dialogues and report formats not considered for prototyping will be dealt with later at Step 510.

Key points for users

The parts of the system that you should see demonstrated in prototype form are those most critical to the success of the system. It is worth remembering that:

– The way the system seemed to you on paper is going to be different from the way it seems on a computer screen. You may wish to modify your earlier thoughts.

– Performance of the prototype will not be that of the delivered system (unless the developers choose to build delays into the prototype). There will be very little processing going on in the background, and probably only a handful of records stored for demonstration purposes. Don't let this lull you into a false sense of security.

– Because you have seen a demonstration, this doesn't mean that the project is almost complete, and that delivery of the finished system will come after a minimal amount of further work. There may well be nothing in the prototype that will be of use to the developers in the production of the final system. It will have achieved its purpose if it has finalised your interface design.

STEP 360 DEVELOP PROCESSING SPECIFICATION

Step 360 requires very detailed consideration of the processing to be carried out in the required system. The Data Flow Diagrams showed the processing without any regard to the sequence in which it is done. Sequence is now established during the construction of the Entity Life Histories (ELHs). It can be expected that this exercise will reveal a significant number of omissions from the DFDs. This is not a reflection on the effort that has been put into the development of the DFDs, but is the consequence of looking at requirements from a different viewpoint.

ELHS may be drawn directly, but an optional and useful initial step taken by many developers is first to complete an Event/Entity Matrix. This is a simple table in which the:

- column headings are entities, identified from the required system Logical Data Structure;
- row headings are events that have been identified from Function Definitions.

Each cell in the table is then considered in turn to decide whether the entity is affected by the event. If it is, the effect is noted in the cell, ie:

C = creation

M = modification

D = deletion

From the completed table it can immediately be checked that:

- each entity is affected by at least one event;
- each event affects at least one entity.

Also, the entity columns show the events that must be included in a logical sequence on the ELHs.

The process is carried out by working up from the bottom of the Logical Data Structure to create the ELHs for the normal lives of all the entities.

ELHs show the sequence in which events must occur if they are to be acceptable to the system. In real life, mistakes are made, and so information is not necessarily received in the correct sequence. Thought must be given to the action to be taken when events occur out of sequence. It is up to you to decide what you wish to do when the system identifies an error condition, for example when:

- a library reader wishes to borrow a book whilst he has an unpaid fee outstanding;

- a patient is discharged from hospital who was not shown by the system as being in hospital;

- a reinstatement is received for a member of staff who is not known to have previously left.

These abnormalities are included by working down the entities from the top of the LDS structure.

A single event can have several different effects, and can affect more than one entity. All of these effects are shown on Effect Correspondence Diagrams, with one for each event. Construction of these may lead to changes in the Requirements Catalogue and the Logical Data Model. Specifically, volumetric information is added to the LDS.

Work on the ELHs relates to updates, ie things happening to the data to change its state. Processing relating to enquiries is now covered by the creation of Enquiry Access Paths, with one for each enquiry.

Events which have been missed are added to the ELH and should also be entered on the DFDs. (Although the DFDs have now served their main purpose within SSADM, they are nevertheless useful for reference in later stages. They also provide the best way for anyone new to the project, or to its subsequent maintenance, to gain an understanding of what the computer system is designed to do.)

Key points for users

Event/Entity Matrix (form SSADMv4 20)

Check that:

- all the entities shown on the LDS have been entered as column headings;

- all known events have been entered as row headings;

- the effects of events on entities are correctly recorded;

- a creation and deletion are shown for every entity;

- every event affects at least one entity.

Entity Life Histories (form SSADMv4 19)

Check that:

- an *ELH* has been created for each entity;

- all creation events are shown;

- all modification events are shown;
- all deletion events are shown;
- events which affect more than one entity occurrence for an entity type have been qualified by an entity role;
- events which affect an entity in mutually exclusive ways have been qualified by an effect qualifier;
- the events have been shown in the correct sequence.

Effect Correspondence Diagrams (form SSADMv4 13)

Check that:

- one diagram is held for each event;
- all entities affected by an event are shown on the same event diagram.

Enquiry Access Paths (form SSADMv4 15)

Check that:

- one diagram is held for each enquiry;
- all entities to be accessed by each enquiry are shown;
- the structure exists on the LDS.

STEP 370 CONFIRM SYSTEM OBJECTIVES

This step provides a final review of requirements before considering their implementation in Stage 4. Up to this point, entries have been made in the Requirements Catalogue as the need for them has been identified. The objective of this review is to ensure that all requirements have been identified and fully defined and that the performance levels specified for them are still valid and realistic. The Requirements Catalogue is considered in conjunction with the Function Definitions and the required system Logical Data Model.

Much of the work needed by the end of this step will already have been done – some of it much earlier, even as far back as Step 110 or the Feasibility Study (Stage 0).

It is important to ensure that the non-functional requirements of resources and qualities (*how much* and *how well*), which are critical to the success of the system, are specified in a measurable form. Without this, performance will be down to the discretion of the designers or, regrettably, to pot luck. Design objectives therefore appear here yet again to ensure that all the items that should have been defined quantitatively, have been so defined. You cannot hope to get the performance you need unless you have said what it is. It is likely to cause extra costs if the right levels of performance are not built into the initial design.

Items to be considered include:

- storage criteria, for which the maximum file sizes will need to be known;
- function timing criteria, paying particular attention to:
  - times when interactive use is heaviest;
  - transactions where the on-line response is most critical;
  - those which have the largest batch volumes;
- information objectives, to ensure that all the information required can actually be obtained from the system;
- fallback and recovery requirements, ie:
  - reliability criteria, being the shortest acceptable time between failures;
  - the maximum amount of time that it can be allowed to take to recover the system after a failure;
  - the performance level of the backup system;
  - procedures for the operation of a backup system at another installation;

- how users are involved in any rerunning after system failure, errors, or loss of output;

- what is entailed given the necessity to revert to a manual backup system.

You must also check all other performance elements that you have been able to specify in a measurable way.

Provided that performance objectives have been agreed, you are reasonably entitled to reject a system that fails to meet them. This is a most important point in any circumstances, but particularly so when development is being done by an outside contractor.

Key points for users

There is nothing new here. The importance of this work has been stressed before. It is your last opportunity to ensure that your requirements are correctly recorded and understood by the developers. You must reconsider everything carefully before agreeing to allow the work to proceed to the next step.

- ensure that all objectives are precise;

- for measurable objectives, ensure that an acceptable means of measuring will be available;

- check for confirmation that all objectives, as specified, will be attained.

STEP 380 ASSEMBLE REQUIREMENTS SPECIFICATION

Step 380 completes the work of Stage 3. All the documentation is reviewed to ensure that:

- all of the information is accurate;
- the work has been done to the required standard.

The products are cross-checked and assembled into the Requirements Specification, which comprises:

- Data Catalogue, containing:
  - Attribute/Data Item Descriptions
  - Grouped Domain Descriptions
- Requirements Catalogue
- Processing Specification, consisting of:
  - User Role/Function Matrix
  - Function Definitions, containing:

    Function Definitions
    I/O Structures
    Enquiry Access Paths
    (Common) Elementary Process Descriptions
  - Required System LDM, consisting of:

    LDS
    Entity Descriptions
    Relationship Descriptions
  - Entity Life Histories
  - Effect Correspondence Diagrams.

Key points for users

Most of the work in this step will be done by the developers, but you will be involved in the resolution of any problems that may arise while they are assembling and checking the products.

The project board members must satisfy themselves that the project continues to be a viable one and that the plans for the future work are acceptable.

Logical System Specification Module

Stages 4 and 5

19

Stage 4 Technical System Options

INTRODUCTION

A Business System Option was chosen in Stage 2, and the requirements were then comprehensively analysed in Stage 3. This gave a Requirements Specification that set out the requirements as agreed by management, the business areas concerned, and the computer department. At the start of Stage 4 the requirements are precisely known, but the actual implementation will present a further range of choices. Just as there were many possible ways of designing the system from your point of view, so there are many technical ways of providing the system you require. Some examples are shown in Table 19.1.

Stage 4 is devoted to finding the best technical implementation of your system within the constraints of your particular organisation and circumstances. Considerations now may change the perception of the required BSO and cause some reworking of Stages 2 and 3. There is a possibility of the Business and Technical Options each modifying the other until a satisfactory compromise is reached.

Several possibilities are considered in Step 410, with perhaps three being developed in more detail. One is then chosen in Step 420.

In-house	v	**Bought-in development**
Package	v	**Customised development**
4GL	v	**Procedural language**
Centralised	v	**Distributed**
Mainframe	v	**Micros**
Conventional files	v	**Database**
Evolution	v	**'Big bang'**
Some combination of these or other possibilities		

Table 19.1 Some possible technical options

Stage 4 is shown in Figure 19.1

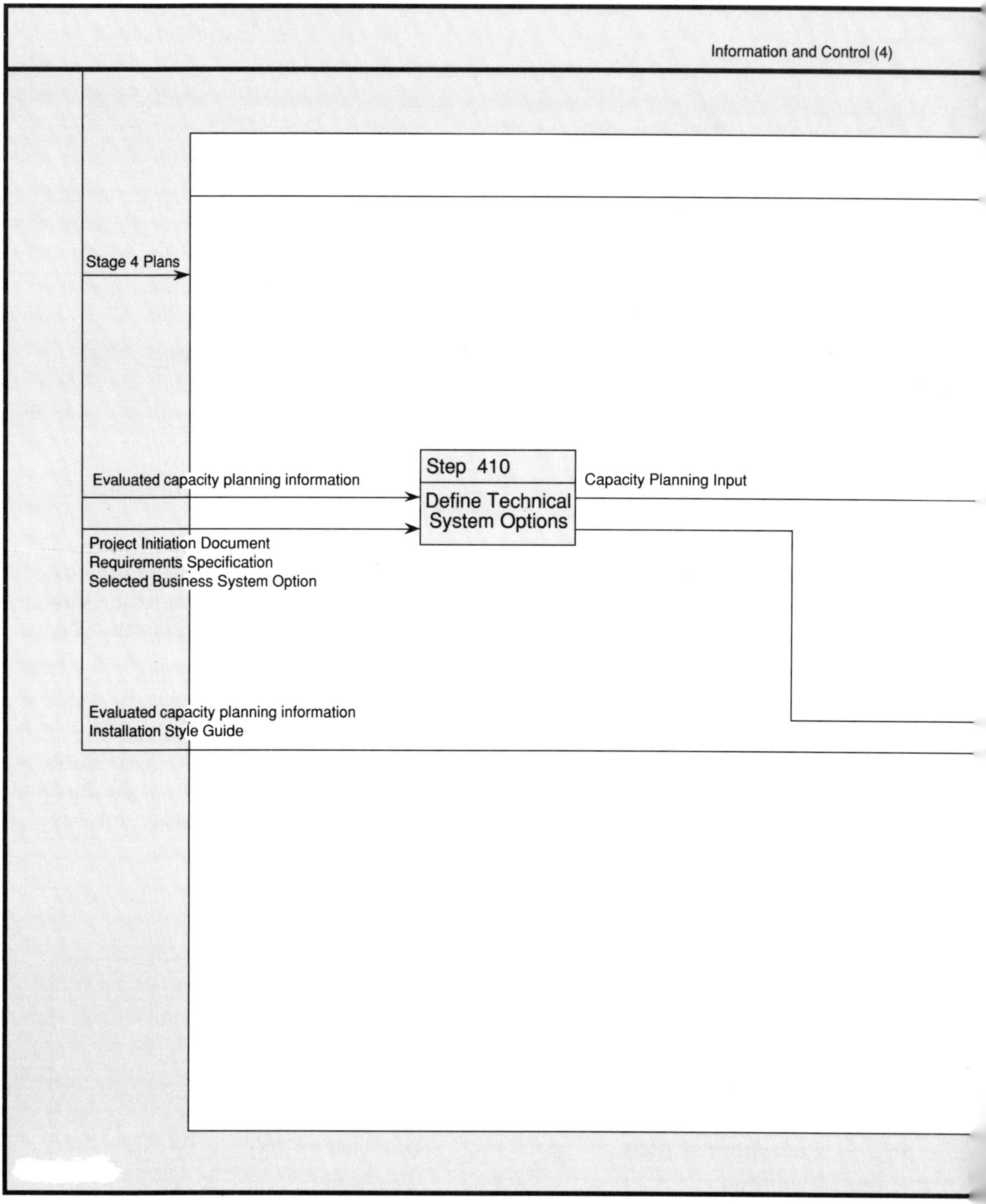

Figure 19.1 Stage 4

- Impact Analysis, defining the effect on the user environment, including:
  - how the work will be taken on;
  - an outline of testing;
  - changes to organisation, working practices, and staffing;
  - training requirements;
  - savings;
  - comparison with other options;
- Outline Development Plan, to provide information about the required resources, skills, times and costs, and their planned availability, covering the rest of the development, ie for the remainder of design, for implementation and for live running;
- Cost/Benefit Analysis, showing the estimated costs (development and running costs), the savings as compared with the present system (ie tangible benefits). Intangibles are always tricky and require subjective judgement. They include better service, greater customer satisfaction, improved staff morale, earlier access to strategic information, etc.

STEP 420 SELECT TECHNICAL SYSTEM OPTION

The Technical System Options developed at Step 410 are formally presented to the project board, and to a wider audience where appropriate. It may be worth inviting people to attend who are only on the fringes of the proposed system, or who are not directly involved but have some knowledge of the work. This will broaden the discussion, and may raise some ideas that have not been considered previously.

Documentation to support the various options is issued before the presentation. It may be advisable to hold a separate presentation for each option, depending on the complexity of the system. Presentation is considered vital, choice from the documentation alone being open to misunderstandings.

One of the options (or a hybrid) is selected. As for the Business System Option, the selection is a business decision to be taken by the sponsors of the project. The chosen option must be capable of achieving the quantitative targets that have been agreed.

As the implications of the choice are technical, the project board will be dependent on the advice received from the developers. The choice must, however, be made by the board. It will need to consider such factors as:

- estimated development and running costs;
- estimated development time;
- facilities to be implemented;
- performance and other quality levels to be achieved;
- benefits expected;
- impact on the organisation.

So far as hardware choice is concerned, there are two contrasting dangers to watch out for:

- Over-specification. Some computer departments have been known to suggest more powerful equipment and software than is necessary. This can be quite attractive to them technically, and also looks good on a CV.
- Under-specification. If you outgrow the initial system, for example, by requiring faster processing or more data storage, it can be very costly to circumnavigate a system dead end. The board will need to consider the system for several years ahead and ensure that there is scope for expansion, ie that an upgrade path is available.

If the provisional choice is a variation on one of the options presented, it may be necessary for the developers to rework some of the material, to reassess the costs and benefits, before a final decision can be taken.

After the decision has been made, the documentation must be updated to describe the choice.

Key points for users

The Technical Option is selected after considering:

- alternatives;
- effects on organisation;
- cost/benefit analyses.

20

Stage 5 – Logical Design

INTRODUCTION

In Step 330 a start was made towards the definition of dialogues and of update and enquiry functions. At Step 340 the logical data design was built. The optional prototyping Step 350 continued the work on the dialogues and menus. The technical implementation selected at Step 420 took all this information into account. Stage 5 now completes the logical design of the system by concluding the work on:

- Dialogue Design (Step 510);
- Update Process Design (Step 520);
- Enquiry Process Design (Step 530).

You have no formal involvement in Steps 520 and 530, but you will doubtless find more questions coming your way, and be asked to check work that has been done. The review at Step 540 also may involve you.

The stage diagram is shown in Figure 20.1.

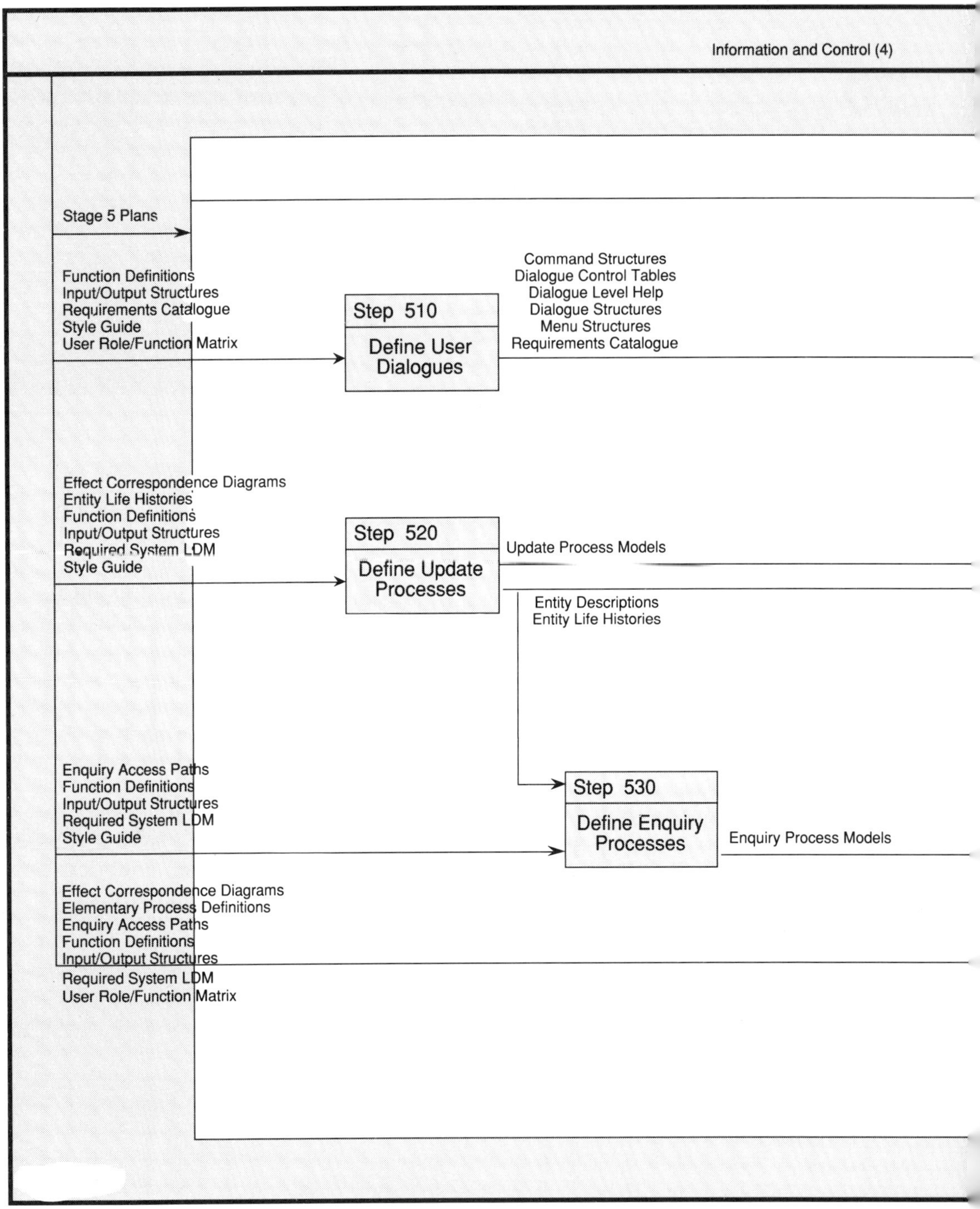

Figure 20.1 Stage 5

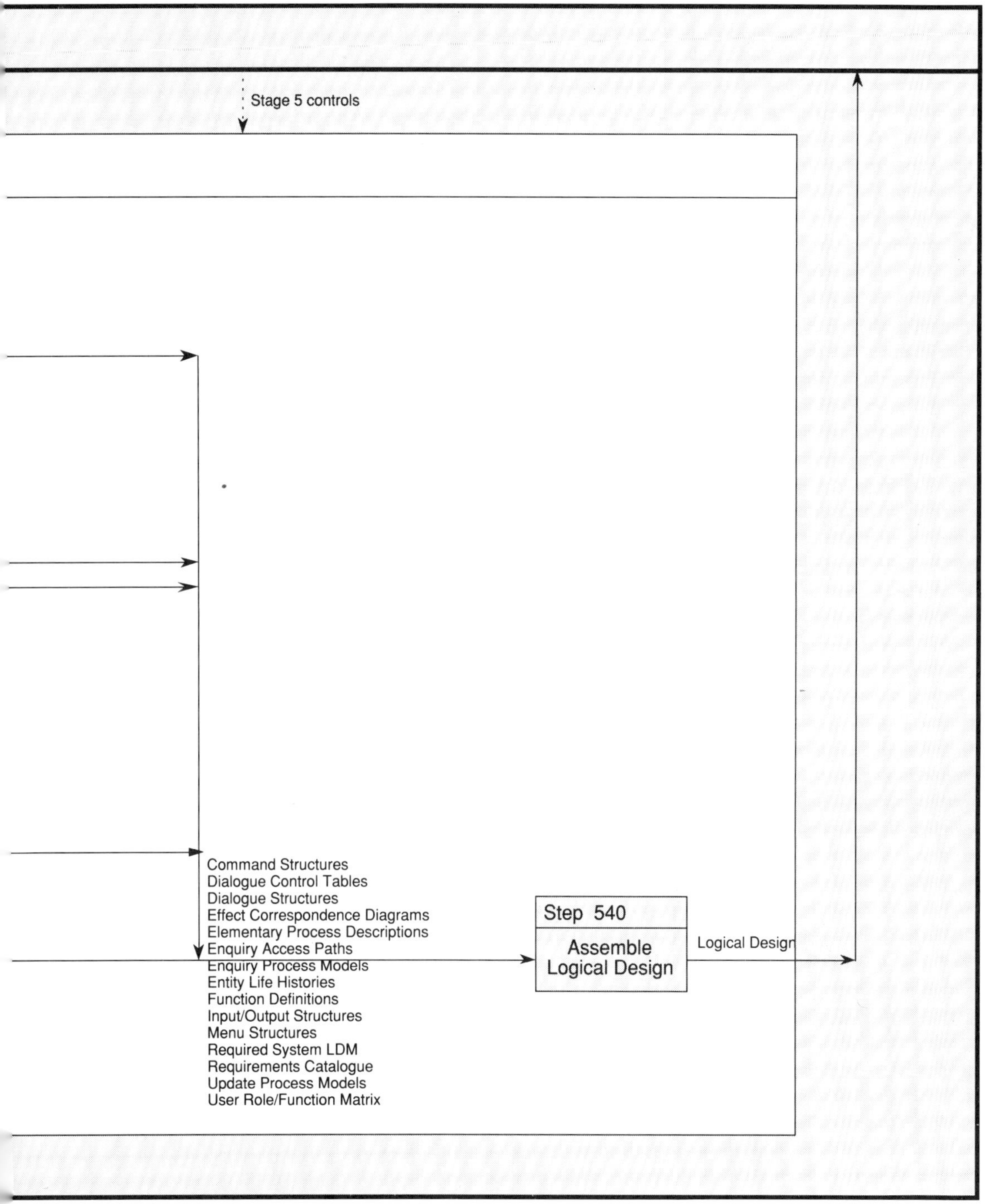
Stage 5 controls
Command Structures
Dialogue Control Tables
Dialogue Structures
Effect Correspondence Diagrams
Elementary Process Descriptions
Enquiry Access Paths
Enquiry Process Models
Entity Life Histories
Function Definitions
Input/Output Structures
Menu Structures
Required System LDM
Requirements Catalogue
Update Process Models
User Role/Function Matrix
Step 540
Assemble Logical Design
Logical Design

STEP 510 DEFINE USER DIALOGUES

The User Role/Function Matrix created at Step 330 identifies what dialogues are required. This step deals with the further logical aspects of dialogue design, ie the structure of each dialogue, and the relationships between different dialogues. It is therefore interested in the logical groupings of dialogue elements, and these are documented in Dialogue Control Tables. Other details to be considered are the menu structure and help facilities.

All aspects of dialogue design are heavily dependent on the type of person using the system. Regular users will soon want something faster than nested menu structures, and will need little help. Casual users will need much more assistance when using the system. A mixture of the two types of user will require more ingenuity and flexibility in the design.

How easily you can work with the system, and what lengths you have to go to in order to extract the information you require, is critical to acceptance of the system. Pay attention to this step. You are likely to have to live with the results for a long time.

In approving the interface to the system, you should consider:

- Ease of use of the system.
- The sequence in which data will logically be entered.
- The experience of the different user roles, and of different users fulfilling the same role. An example was mentioned earlier of a night porter covering reception duties. He may not be anywhere nearly as proficient as the daytime receptionists.
- The environment in which the equipment is to be sited. A keyboard in a workshop, being attacked by oily fingers and in danger of having cups of coffee on it, may be the wrong device for the environment.

Key points for users

This is *your* system. Be tenacious in challenging and pursuing any reasons put forward as to why you cannot have the interface that you really need. It may be necessary to reconsider the technical option, even if this causes a significant amount of rework.

STEP 520 DEFINE UPDATE PROCESSES

Steps 520 and 530 constitute the logical database process design. The emphasis is on *logical*, and does not assume that a database management system (DBMS) will be used for the physical implementation.

All updates result from events that are shown on the Entity Life Histories. The ELHs show the events in the sequence in which they occur. The developers must build in the processing checks to ensure that this sequence is obeyed. The first step is to add state indicators to the ELHs. The sequential information contained in the diagrams is then transferred to processing specifications.

The Effect Correspondence Diagrams are converted into Update Process Models (one for each event). Operations, derived from the ELHs and including the state indicator checks, are listed and added to the Models. Conditions governing selection and iteration are then added, and error outputs specified. The completed diagrams thus show completely detailed processing structures.

STEP 530 DEFINE ENQUIRY PROCESSES

Enquiries include those operations that are purely enquiries, and also the enquiry elements of updating operations.

For each enquiry, the Enquiry Access Paths are converted into processing structures that represent the structure of the input data.

Output data structures are created from the Input/Output Structures.

For each enquiry, the input and output structures are merged to give one Enquiry Process Model. Operations and conditions governing selection and iteration are added to the structure, and error outputs are specified. The completed diagrams thus show all the processing detail required for each enquiry.

STEP 540 ASSEMBLE LOGICAL DESIGN

The final step in Stage 5 marks the end of the logical design of the system. The work done thus far must now be reviewed and the quality, progress, and further plans accepted by the project board before proceeding to the physical design of the system in Stage 6. Any changes to the logical design once physical design is under way can prove to be expensive beyond all proportion to the apparent insignificance of the change. Consequently this is a critically important step.

The review by the design team is for completeness and consistency. The documentation is then assembled as the Logical Design, which comprises:

- Logical Process Model, which contains:
  - Dialogues
  - Effect Correspondence Diagrams
  - Enquiry Process Models
  - Function Definitions
  - Update Process Models
- Menu Structures
- Command Structures
- Requirements Catalogue
- Data Catalogue, containing:
  - Attribute/Data Item Descriptions
  - Domain Descriptions
- Required System LDM, consisting of:
  - LDS
  - Entity Descriptions
  - Relationship Descriptions

The project board must be satisfied that:

- All of the information is accurate.

- The work has been done to the required standard.
- The project continues to be a viable one. (It would be a courageous decision to abandon the project at this point, but there may be times when this is the right decision to make. Senior management may well wonder why such a decision had not been reached earlier. However, always remember that the system should be for the good of the company, not for the continued entertainment of those involved in developing it.)
- The plans for physical design are acceptable.

Physical Design Module

Stage 6

21
Stage 6 – Physical Design

INTRODUCTION

Stage 6 is concerned with the physical design of the system. It consists of seven steps, and is illustrated in Figure 21.1. It takes what is needed logically (the logical design created in Stage 5) and relates it to the physical environment in which it will operate (the Technical System Option selected in Stage 4). The practicalities of real life implementation may well require some compromises that will move the design away from its logical perfection. If earlier work has not been done as thoroughly as it should have been, there will also be the possibility that design objectives will need to be redefined. This is considered at Step 630.

In this stage, some work is also started (it may have been started earlier) in readiness for the later stages of development.

There is minimal involvement for users in many of the steps in this stage.

The output is the Physical Design, which goes forward to the production stage of the development cycle.

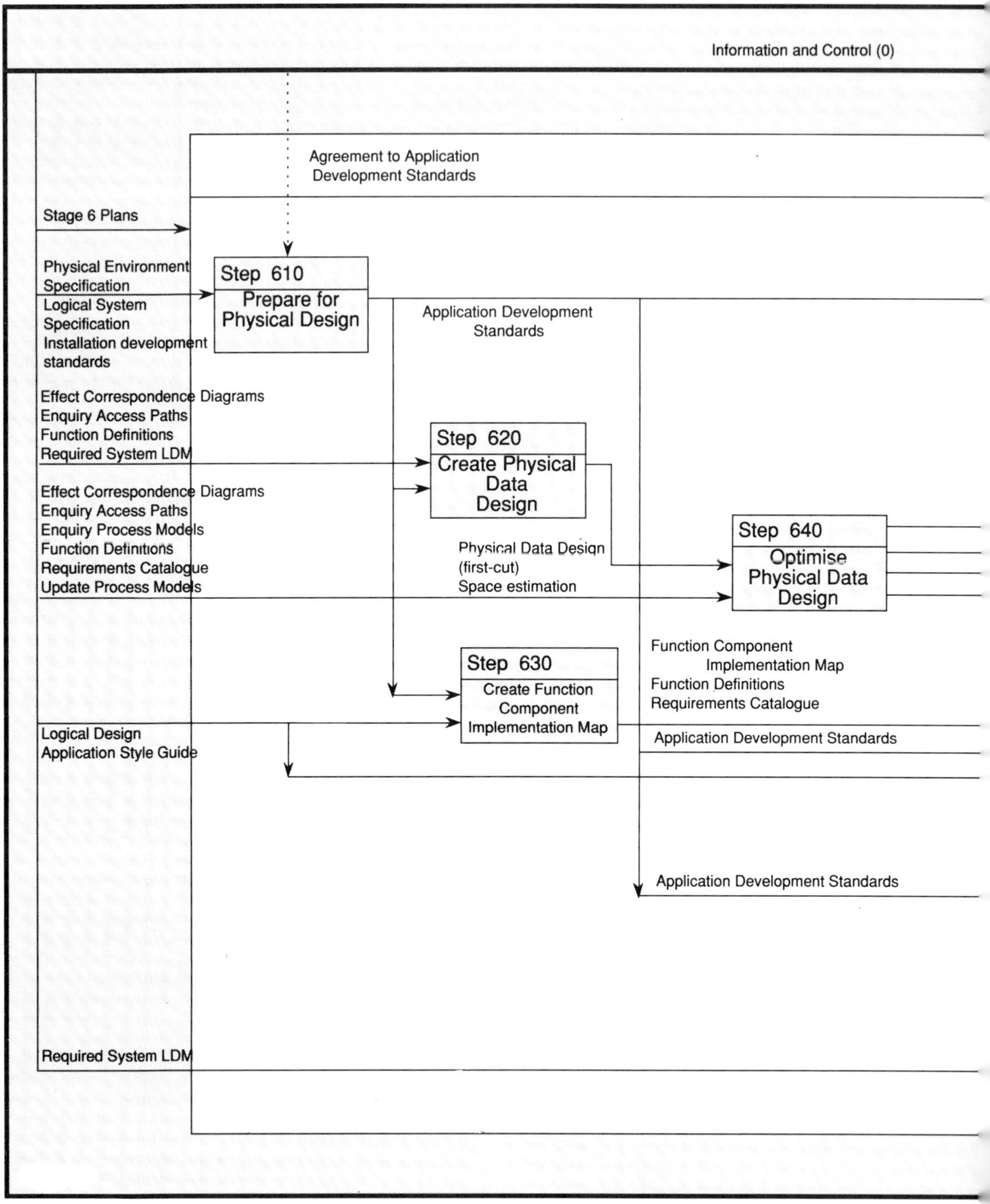

Stage 21.1 Stage 6

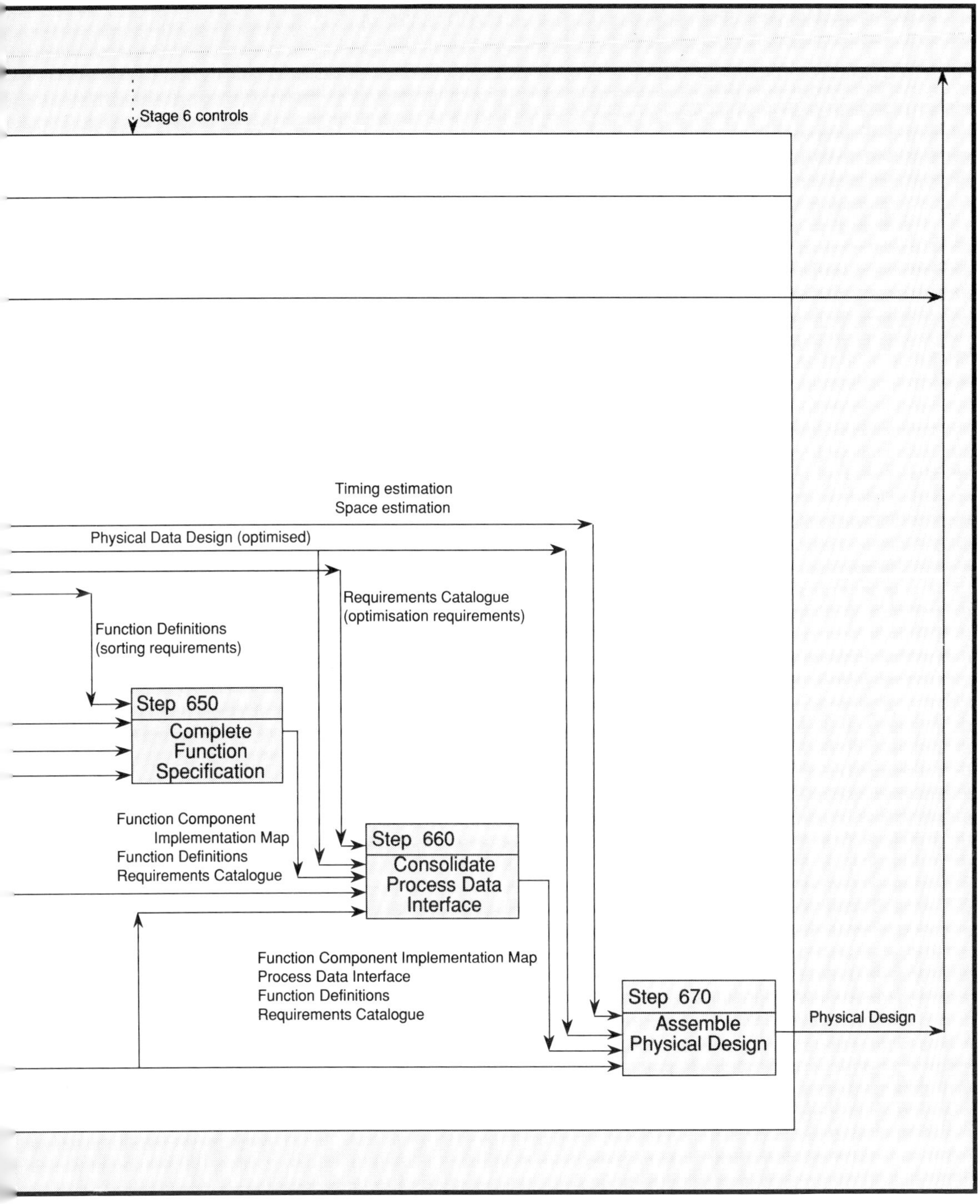
Stage 6 controls
Timing estimation
Space estimation
Physical Data Design (optimised)
Requirements Catalogue
(optimisation requirements)
Function Definitions
(sorting requirements)
Step 650
Complete
Function
Specification
Function Component
Implementation Map
Function Definitions
Requirements Catalogue
Step 660
Consolidate
Process Data
Interface
Function Component Implementation Map
Process Data Interface
Function Definitions
Requirements Catalogue
Step 670
Assemble
Physical Design
Physical Design

STEP 610 PREPARE FOR PHYSICAL DESIGN

This step draws up the plans and makes the rules for the rest of the work in Stage 6. Physical data and process design starts by taking stock of the facilities provided by the tools that are to be used for development. The facilities they provide are classified against parameters regarding processing, storage and performance. The plans are agreed with the project board.

Standards are established for:

- use of the physical processing system;
- data base management system (DBMS) facilities;
- data design rules;
- names;
- program specification.

An Activity Network and Activity Descriptions are prepared to cover the work of the remaining steps in physical design.

A start is made on the preparation of user, operation and training manuals.

The *User Manual* should be in the standard format as agreed within the organisation. Typical contents will include:

- a schedule specifying:
    - times when on-line systems will be available;
    - deadlines for data entry, and for correction and reinput of errors;
    - restrictions on use, for example at times of peak loads on other systems using the same computer processor;
- user instructions detailing, for every user role:
    - how to operate on-line systems;
    - emergency procedures in the event of system failure, specifying the work to be done while the system is down, and the involvement of users during recovery of the system;
    - contacts within the computer department in the event of problems or queries;

– supporting information, such as:

- screen formats and dialogues;
- example formats of reports and other printed documents;
- details of error codes, where used (as a principle, identification of errors is preferably by text rather than code; errors should always be identified precisely rather than grouped in any way);
- definitions of other codes used within the system;
- manual procedures that form a part of the business system, as distinct from the computer part of the system.

Some of the User Manual will be in narrative, but supplemented by diagrams wherever possible. They may include DFDs for external entities to show details of their interaction with the system.

Facilities may be provided to enable you to create your own enquiries (end user facilities). This will normally be by use of suitably generalised and easy to use software such as report generators or interactive query languages. If such facilities are available, then suitable instructions must also be available for their use. This may utilise the proprietary manuals and other documentation, but only if the information they contain is expressed in terms that are understandable to non-computer people. A regrettable amount of documentation remains obscure even to computer specialists, containing information that is incorrect, incomplete, incomprehensible or difficult to find. Some translation or notes may be required.

The *Operations Manual,* for use within the computer department, defines such items as:

- times when the system is to be available;
- the data that is to be on-line;
- the operation of batch systems;
- security and recovery requirements;
- distribution of reports and other documents that have been printed.

These operational aspects should all be discussed with and agreed by you.

Key points for users

Ensure that the plans for the continuing development are acceptable to you.

The manuals, started but not completed at this point, should be planned to contain:

– all that you need for your involvement with the system in the User Manual;

– your operational requirements in the Operations Manual.

STEP 620 CREATE PHYSICAL DATA DESIGN

In Step 620 the Required System Logical Data Model is converted into a physical data design conforming to the rules established in Step 610.

The physical environment may rely on conventional files or may be under the control of a database management system (DBMS). There are many different DBMSs. The structure that works efficiently with one may not (probably will not) work so well with another. It may even not work at all. It is an area where experience on the part of the developer is essential.

This first-cut design will be a legitimate structure that will work in the environment at which it is aimed, but will not be expected to give the optimum performance. At this point it may well not even perform adequately. Performance targets are considered at Step 640.

STEP 630 CREATE FUNCTION COMPONENT IMPLEMENTATION MAP

Physical process specification continues with Step 630.

The Logical Design produced during Stage 5 covers all the processing required by the users. It is now given further consideration. Processing may now need to be defined for:

- controls and control error handling;
- physical input and output formats;
- syntax error handling (where the structure of the data input to the computer is not as expected).

There may be duplication and common processing.

System failure must be considered. In the event of failure, some transactions may be only part processed. The dangers are:

- a process that has only been part actioned at system failure may be fully repeated when processing is resumed, thus leading to duplicate updating of some files;
- a process that has been part completed may be left incomplete, with some updates missing.

In either case, the data will be wrong. These are problems for the developers. Units of processing that must be fully complete are known as *success units*. The developers must build in the procedures needed to ensure the correct and full processing of each success unit, and hence the integrity of the data, when processing is resumed.

Development tools may permit some processing to be specified non-procedurally (ie specified by defining *what* must be done rather than *how* to do it). This should be done now. Processes which are defined procedurally are dealt with at Step 650.

Database access components are specified at Step 660.

STEP 640 OPTIMISE PHYSICAL DATA DESIGN

The physical data design, when implemented, must achieve the quality targets (how much and how well) set out in the Function Definitions and the Requirements Catalogue. These relate to the space taken up by the data, and the time taken to carry out the processing.

The first-cut physical data design created at Step 620 is unlikely to meet these objectives. Problems can be expected in some areas that will require changes to the first-cut work. The difficulty for the developers is that changing any one system element will have repercussions on others. For example, improving recovery procedures to make them faster or more automatic could well require additional processing to be done on every transaction, with more information being recorded each time (logging). This would have a detrimental effect on response time and on the amount of available storage capacity.

Compromises have to be reached that will enable all of the agreed objectives to be reached, to at least the required lowest acceptable levels, and Step 640 is concerned with achieving them. To this end, the data design may need some modification to make it more compact, or able to respond to the processing more efficiently.

These design compromises are normal, and should permit the required performance to be achieved. Failure will mean reconsideration of the performance objectives themselves. This is a last resort rather than something that can be expected as part of a normal development process. It indicates that something was not done properly earlier on. It is principally (but may not be solely) a reflection on the developers.

There may be reasons, of course. If the project required technical expertise beyond that already known to the developers, and if the cost of employing an expert for that particular aspect was requested but turned down at the time, then the developers are not entirely to blame. Whatever the reasons, it is regrettably late in the development cycle to be finding that the system will not perform. Changes to performance objectives will upset the projected cost/benefit calculations, and could lead to a considerable waste of money. If the situation should arise, you will inevitably be involved in the reconsideration of objectives.

Failure to achieve the objectives at this late stage will prove costly. There may be time penalties resulting from the need for:

- fundamental rethinking of the design;
- reassessment of the objectives themselves.

Other possibilities are likely to be even less palatable:

- the need to purchase more hardware and/or software;
- abandonment of the project.

Businesses have been known to fail through ill-considered computerisation projects. SSADM has offered many opportunities to avoid nasty surprises at this late stage in development.

Although compromises in the first-cut data design are expected in this step, the other measures are not. None of them will enhance the reputation of the computer department, and there is likely to be some blame coming the way of those users associated with the project. The possibility of failure here is an excellent reason for not skimping on any of the comprehensive checking that is specified as needing to be carried out in all the earlier stages of SSADM.

Incidentally, it should be noted that the work done at this stage is theoretical. When the system is first installed it may not perform exactly to the levels expected, and some fine tuning will still be needed. This is perfectly normal. The performance levels should, however, be achievable if not actually achieved initially.

Key point for users

Obtain confirmation that the design will meet the objectives.

STEP 650 COMPLETE FUNCTION SPECIFICATION

Functions that could be described non-procedurally were actioned at Step 630. Step 650 now continues with physical process specification by dealing with the specification and design of the procedural components. These procedural specifications provide the detail required by the programmers. Logical processes are combined into physical programs or run-units with each carrying out a range of related functions.

Database access components are dealt with at Step 660.

STEP 660 CONSOLIDATE PROCESS DATA INTERFACE

Physical process specification concludes with an investigation of mismatches between the optimised Physical Data Design and the Required System Logical Data Model from which it has been developed. Processing is specified to provide an interface between the two. The whole design is considered for:

- effective use of development software;
- ease of implementation of future changes, both to requirements and to the physical environment;
- components which fail fully to meet the requirements and which have resulted in design compromises.

STEP 670 ASSEMBLE PHYSICAL DESIGN

The final step in SSADM is concerned with a review of the products of Stage 6 for completeness and consistency. The documents are then assembled as the Physical Design. This consists of the:

Physical Data Design, including:

- Space estimates
- Timing estimates

Physical Process Specification, consisting of:

- Data Catalogue, including:
  - Attribute/Data Item Descriptions
  - Grouped Domain Descriptions
- Function Component Implementation Map
- Function Definition, including:
  - I/O Structures
  - Enquiry Access Paths
  - Elementary Process Descriptions
- Requirements Catalogue
- Required System Logical Data Model, comprising:
  - Logical Data Structure
  - Entity Descriptions
  - Relationship Descriptions
- Process Data Interface

Part 4

Implementing SSADM — Considerations for Management

22
The Ingredients of Success

Taking on SSADM will change the way the work is done. More effort is put into analysis, which inevitably delays the start of subsequent work. Managers who fear that no real progress is being made until programming is under way will be worried. It requires an act of faith to believe that there will be savings later, on program design, coding, testing, implementation, maintenance, and user satisfaction.

SSADM has the potential to solve many problems of systems development, but there are provisos:

- It does not guarantee that the right systems will be developed. That is a matter of strategic judgement for company management.
- It is not a panacea. Its use will not automatically guarantee better systems. Nor is it aimed at the development of systems other than for data processing. However, for data processing systems it is very effective.
- Whilst it is freely available, assimilating the method will take time, even for experienced computer people. Training is going to be needed if the developers are to understand it and to get the best out of it, and training would also be of considerable help to you.
- Much of the early-day struggles with the method can be avoided by the judicious employment of experienced consultants. This has a cost, atlhough their employment does not necessarily have to be for long periods. Short visits at strategic points in the application of the method can be very effective.
- Your close involvement, and that of other knowledgeable users, is critical to the successful development of systems (as it is with any method).
- The potential gains of high quality design may be lost if the developers do not use similarly proven and effective methods throughout the remainder of the development cycle.

The remaining chapters in this part consider some of the subjects that will require your attention if you are going to be involved in the competent use of SSADM and the successful development of your systems.

Quality control is essential to the success of the method. SSADM does not specify how to go about it, on the assumption that it is a fundamental task that is already being carried out. Chapter 23 is for those organisations for which this is a false assumption. Most of the points raised in Chapter 23 will apply equally to any method.

System development failures when using SSADM can be due to many factors some of which are:

- inexperience;
- lack of training;
- bloody mindedness by those involved because of the imposition of a new method;
- merely paying 'lip service' to the use of the method;
- lack of effective user involvement, commitment and dedication;
- lack of control.

These are problems for management, the first four of which require general management skills and interest to resolve. Chapter 24 is about the last of these – project management. SSADM is not a substitute for management. It does not manage itself, but it does provide a firm basis for effective management. As with quality control, many points raised are general ones, but are critical for the success of a project. It is all too easy to blame SSADM for a failure when the real failure was lack of control.

Some practical suggestions are made in Chapter 25 for those who decide to go ahead with the introduction of SSADM. If followed, these suggestions should help towards the successful development of the first project. This will in turn lead to the general acceptance of the method, and its use for further projects. The payoff will be seen in systems that are more robust and do more of what you really need.

Finally, Chapter 26 moves beyond SSADM. There are all sorts of ways of tackling a system development. This is missionary work about how to approach your task. It is an attempt to get away from some of the problems that so often seem to plague computerisation projects. Its aim is to help you with the design of systems that will be effective ones for your company, by developing the right projects in the right way, and appreciating that implementing your system only reaches the horizon that you saw at the start of the project. But as you sail into the sunset, the horizon gets ever further away. You will always find more that you could do to your system to make it even better. Implementation is not the beginning of the end, but rather the end of the beginning. It marks the starting point for what the future might hold. There are great savings to be made by intelligent anticipation of what may happen in the future.

23
Quality Control

INTRODUCTION

This chapter is concerned with reasons for and attitudes towards quality control.

As a system investigation proceeds, all the information will be set down as it is gathered. Unfortunately, that does not mean that what is set down will be correct. There will be misunderstandings, mistakes and omissions. If these are not picked up, they will be reflected in the design of the system.

It has long been known that design errors and omissions that remain undiscovered until testing or after implementation may cost 100 times as much to correct compared with the cost of errors found before moving on from design (*Boehm,* 1976). Certainly the cost can be out of all proportion to the apparent triviality of the problem. Any effort spent trying to pick up these errors and omissions can therefore be regarded as an investment.

There is one basic and inescapable fact. The quality of the system, and all that that means, ie:

- doing what you want;
- performing to the standards that you require;
- with development staying under control;

cannot be achieved without your involvement. Involvement takes time, and the time must be available when required. The time needed should be planned ahead with the project manager and built into the development schedule.

You will need to be involved in quality control at two levels:

- informally, as work progresses and is discussed between the analysts and yourselves; and
- formally, at significant points in the development process.

Quality reviews are required within an SSADM development. Their prime purpose is to detect errors in the products. They are concerned with ensuring that:

- the method is being used correctly;
- the specified products are available;
- the products are complete in themselves and cross-checks against other products show no inconsistencies;
- the work conforms to installation standards;
- the system will do, functionally, what it is supposed to do;
- the required levels of the design objectives are achievable, ie how well the system is to perform, as distinct from what it must do.

LEVELS OF QUALITY CONTROL

Quality control procedures can be considered at two levels:

- Informal, for products that do not go forward from the end of a step. This may be either because they are development documents leading to a final document that will be subject to a formal review, or because they are internal to a step.
- Formal, ie checkpoints that involve the setting up of meetings that are subject to documentation, and rework if necessary.

INSPECTIONS

Although quality control is required during the application of SSADM, and a review procedure is described in the *Manual*, exactly how it is done is left to individual organisations.

Many organisations will already have their own procedures that may be applied to the SSADM products. Government computing uses procedures laid down in the PRINCE Project Management Method. Another commonly used approach is the Structured Walkthrough, although the practice is variable.

The method that has been shown to give the best results is the Inspection method, pioneered by Michael Fagan of IBM (for which he was awarded $50,000, the highest award ever made by IBM). It is applicable at any time, with any method. Reported results suggest that Inspections can find 70 percent to 80 percent of design and coding errors. A comparative test with a structured walkthrough showed that the Inspection sample contained 38 percent fewer errors (*Fagan,* 1976). The effectiveness of Inspections grows with repeated use, as checklists are developed and refined.

The Inspection method is described briefly below. PRINCE uses similar (but different) terms and procedures.

THE INSPECTION METHOD

Inspection is an attempt to introduce the disciplines of engineering into software development. Its objective (in common with other approaches) is to detect errors as soon as possible in the project life cycle. It can take place after any control point in the development process has been reached. This will normally be the availability of a product on completion of a task. As a separate Inspection of each product would often be impractical, some grouping is necessary in practice, and depends on the volume of work and the interval since the last Inspection.

Basically, Inspection is a comparison method. It tries to find differences between the product of work carried out at one level and the product of the previous level. Ultimately the aim is to confirm that the two are exactly equivalent. A product cannot be used as the basis for further development until an Inspection has been satisfactorily completed. Rigorous rules are laid down as to what should be examined, when this should be, and against what criteria.

Inspection principles

The features of the Inspection method are listed in Table 23.1.

- **Do at prescribed checkpoints**
- **Inspect for all defects**
- **Inspect by colleagues**
- **Do in a prescribed way**
- **Limit to two hours**
- **Led by a Moderator**
- **Inspectors have roles**
- **Checklists are used**
- **Inspect at the optimum rate**
- **Statistics maintained and analysed**

Table 23.1 Inspection principles

Checkpoints

Inspections are carried out at a number of points in the development. Major ones are set by the project board; others by the project manager.

Defects

Inspections are for all classes of defects – both in the business and technical aspects of the development, and in the clarity of the documentation. Defects include basic logic errors (misunderstandings of what is done or required to be done, for example how to calculate discounts), failure to conform to standards, omissions, possible ambiguities, inadequate thought given to ways of achieving quality objectives, in fact anything where there is any possible room for doubt or misinterpretation.

People involved

Inspections are carried out by colleagues at all levels of seniority, other than the top people whose involvement is at a higher level on the project board (*see* Chapter 25). The inspectors should be experienced people who know the system, and who have been given the authority by the project manager or user management to comment on the work. Inspectors should preferably be from different teams (the documentation should be self-explanatory). Ideally a meeting should involve from three to five people including a Moderator. Exceptionally there may be more, if each has something unique to offer. They should also be aware of policy decisions about the system that have been taken by senior management.

Procedure

Inspections are carried out as a series of prescribed steps (*see Inspection practice).*

Time

Meetings are limited to two hours. Experience shows that they lose some of their effectiveness after two hours, so it may be necessary to hold more than one meeting to get through all of the work at any point in the development.

Moderators

Inspections are led by a moderator. This can be a specialist role within a company, or a role carried out by the project manager or a user manager. Ideally he should have had formal training. This is given in some organisations. Courses are available but rare, and for many moderators, training consists of learning by experience.

The Moderator is responsible for the administrative arrangements, leading the meeting, noting and classifying the defects, arranging follow-up action, and checking that it has been done.

Responsibility for this role should be allocated early in the project.

Roles

Inspectors are assigned particular roles to increase their effectiveness, with different people each concentrating on a different aspect. The roles will depend on the type of work being inspected, for example:

- Does it follow the agreed standards?
- Is it logically correct?
- Are there any discrepancies as compared with the source documentation?
- Are detailed procedures correctly defined?
- Is the volumetric information correct?
- Will it meet objectives as specified?
- Is it complete?
- Is it presented in the agreed format, and on the agreed media?

Each role should have its own checklist.

Checklists

Checklists are used detailing items to be examined. These help to define the work, and to increase the number of defects found. The checklists are created initially by giving careful consideration to checks that can be made. Detailed lists are provided in the *Product Descriptions* section of the *SSADM Version 4 Reference Manual (NCC, 1990*). These should be augmented from experience, with particular attention being paid to those errors that are found to occur most frequently, and identification of where and how they originate. The lessons learned on each development should be carried forward into future projects.

Rate of Inspection

Material is inspected at the optimum rate for error finding. Going too slowly wastes time. If the meeting is driven along too quickly, the number of errors found will drop. (It may be possible to save 20 minutes on an Inspection. It might cost many hours later on to resolve the defects that have been left in the system.) The appropriate rate for any organisation can only be found from experience, as revealed by analysis of the statistics.

Statistics

Statistics of numbers of errors found and types of defects are maintained and analysed. This helps in the building up of the effectiveness of the Inspection procedure by additions to and improvement of the checklists, and by finding the optimum rate for the Inspection process.

Inspection practice

- **Planning**
- **Overview**
- **Preparation**
- **Meeting**
- **Rework**
- **Follow up**
- **Third hour meeting**

Table 23.2 Inspection procedures

Planning

The moderator obtains the documentation at each checkpoint. Then he will:

- decide who will inspect it;
- arrange the meeting;
- distribute the documentation to those involved.

Overview

The overview is to give a broad knowledge of the project to the inspectors before they look at the detail. It is a presentation of anything from half an hour to an hour, and is given by someone with an adequate knowledge of the requirements. This can be a senior manager, a user or a developer, or perhaps some combination of these. It is not necessary to hold an overview meeting if all those involved are already familiar with the project.

Preparation

Initially, inspectors work alone to familiarise themselves with the material and prepare to put forward all the defects they can find (defects are inconsistencies between two different sorts of documentation). Sufficient time must be allowed to permit inspectors to check up on anything on which they may have doubts or lack of knowledge. About one and a half hours are usually considered necessary and should be scheduled. You might be tempted to regard this preparation as an unnecessary chore, but it has been found to give a net increase in productivity at the meeting itself.

Meeting

The meeting is attended by the nominated inspectors and by the moderator. This will normally be a total of three to five people. The amount of work to be handled during the meeting is limited and specified. Ideally the originators of the work should not be present. The documentation should be self-explanatory to those using it.

The inspectors identify suspected defects for the moderator to set down in writing. There is no discussion as to whether the defect is *real*. If an inspector *feels* that something is wrong, then the lack of clarity must be resolved by rework. Otherwise someone else involved in later stages may also misunderstand what is really required.

Solutions are not discussed during the meeting as this has been found to be neither productive nor necessary.

Rework

After the meeting, the moderator arranges for rework to clear the suspected defects. Some may be nothing more than ambiguous documentation, but ambiguity is itself a fault that must be rectified.

Follow up

The moderator is responsible for ensuring that all the defects noted have been resolved. The documentation is not permitted to go forward to the next stage of development until the moderator has ensured that all the points raised have been satisfactorily cleared.

Third hour meeting

The discussion of solutions or improvements is not permitted during the main meeting as detailed above. In order not to lose any good ideas, the inspectors can hold a third hour meeting to express their personal views on errors and improvements.

References

More information on Inspections can be found in *Fagan* (1976), and *Gilb* (1988).

QUALITY CONTROL AND SSADM

The formality and frequency of the reviews are matters for managerial judgement. It must be accepted that reviews take time, but not so much as building on work that is eventually found to have been defective.

The basic principles are:

- All documents created since the last review must be reviewed for a first time.
- All documents changed since the last review must be reviewed again.
- All references on all forms and diagrams must be checked for accuracy and relevance.
- Some documents that have not been changed will also need reviewing, where they could have been affected by changes made elsewhere.
- The end of a step provides a logical review point.
- The size of the system will have a direct bearing on the frequency of the reviews. For a small system it may be sensible to group together more than one formal review. For a large system, it may be advisable to carry out some reviews at task or even at product level. The main criteria are the amount of work done since the last review, and the optimum time of two hours for a review meeting.

MAINTAINING QUALITY AFTER SSADM

The work done during the competent application of SSADM will have resulted in a well-structured system design, from which an equally well-structured system can be built. However, without the use of effective program design techniques, continued quality control procedures, and well-planned tests, it is still possible to destroy the quality that has been engineered into the design. This is the responsibility of the development staff.

It is reasonable to assume that developers who care sufficiently about quality to use SSADM will not want to jeopardise their efforts by being less efficient during the later stages of development. However, it is worth checking that this is not a false assumption. The Inspection principles must be applied throughout the remainder of development.

NATIONAL QUALITY STANDARDS

Many organisations are now registered as being accredited to BS5750 (British Standard) or ISO 9000 (International Standards Organisation) relating to quality. (The two standards are identical.)

These standards require an organisation to specify the procedures for its work, and to be able to demonstrate that these procedures are being followed.

SSADM provides a procedural approach to the task of systems analysis and design. Any organisation using the method in the prescribed way will be able to show that they are working to these national and international standards, so far as that aspect of their work is concerned. In order to be registered, they must first be accredited. To achieve this they would have to show similar well-documented standards for the other aspects of their work, to show that their staff are adequately trained and actually work to those standards, and to accept that the initial accreditation will be followed by regular reviews by an external assessor.

Preparing for registration can be time consuming and costly, but there really isn't any substitute for quality. If your organisation is not already registered, you should consider whether it would be in your best interests to do so. The local office of the Department of Trade and Industry will be able to advise. Registration will prove to the world at large that your working practices have been impartially examined and approved. Among the benefits of this are:

- it gives greater job satisfaction to the staff to know that they are part of a high quality organisation;
- there will be fewer problems with your customers;
- your reputation will be enhanced;
- it will give you an advantage over non-accredited organisations when tendering for work.

You are part way there already with SSADM. Why not go for the rest?

24
Project Management

INTRODUCTION

This chapter considers project management in relation to the area of development covered by SSADM, and also introduces some other important but more general points. Those who would like to implement the NCC approach should refer to the *Project Management and Control Manual* (NCC Publications 1988). Within central government the approved project management standard is PRINCE, and this is an approach that is increasingly being used in the private sector. Many installations will already have their own methods of project management.

THE NEED FOR PROJECT MANAGEMENT

If a computer system is to satisfy the anticipated cost/benefit estimates and to be of real use to you, it must be brought in:

- within time;
- within cost;
- doing what you need;
- at the right quality.

The chances of satisfying time, cost and need without control are remote. Project management aims to provide this control. Unfortunately the reality is that all too often these criteria of successful development are not achieved even with a control method. A standard development method is also needed, and SSADM gives this. It provides the following aids to the effective management of projects:

- the same approach to every project, which permits the building up of a statistical base to improve the estimating process;

- the Module/Stage/Step/Task structure, which gives the basis for estimating and monitoring progress;

- the products, which provide the basis for reporting progress.

Remember that project management activities must themselves feature in a project management system, ie they:

- take time;

- cost money.

These resources must be used effectively. It is possible to spend large amounts of time making returns, collating figures, drawing graphs, updating schedules, etc. Project management is a means to an end, not an end in itself.

TIME WASTERS

Before proceeding to project management activities, it is worth considering how time can be wasted during an SSADM development. These misuses of development time should be guarded against or resolved as soon as possible into the project. Immense amounts of time can be spent on:

- Failing to establish the initial scope of the study (allowing work to be done that will be irrelevant to the system as eventually agreed).

- Permitting detailed work to be done on elements of the system that are beyond the agreed scope (interesting diversions no doubt, and quite possibly of value in the future, but of no real use to the work in hand).

- Expecting, encouraging, or permitting the redrawing of diagrams to the point where they become works of art or draughtsmanship rather than working documents. Diagrams are adequate if you can understand them, except perhaps for the formal quality reviews and final documentation.

- Allowing iteration to continue unchecked, within or between tasks, in the search for the totally complete specification.

- Failing to organise people to be available at the appropriate times for interviews, meetings, and reviews (the alternatives being either waiting for people, or the potentially even greater time waster of making decisions without consultation).

Experience has shown that these time wasters can easily double the cost and timescale of a project with no increase in benefits. Good project management must be constantly on guard against such irrelevancies.

AVOIDING PROBLEMS

If the work is to be done within schedule it is essential that:

- Any potential growth in the content of the system is identified and notified to management *before* extra work is done.
- Any slippage is identified and corrected as it occurs. There is a frequent hope, seldom realised, that time lost during a project can be made up at the end. This is often attempted in a 'traditional' development environment by omitting the documentation and skimping on testing. Documentation cannot be omitted in SSADM as each task depends on earlier documentation. Being less than thorough with testing leaves errors and omissions for you to find after implementation, and this represents a financial loss to the organisation. In this event, the price will be paid later.
- The technical staff must not take it upon themselves to build in extra facilities that they think would be useful. No changes should be made without considering their effect on time and cost, without agreeing it with you, and without obtaining the necessary level of approval before starting. Failure to do so could prove to be very expensive. In extreme cases it could result in your rejection of the system. *See Change Control.*
- The developers must not become consumed by the technical challenges. The effort required to save a couple of hundred bytes or to save a few microseconds is not worth the effort as a technical exercise. It can only be justified if the saving is essential for storage or performance purposes. Similarly the convoluted logic of a development genius can take an extraordinary amount of time for lesser mortals to understand subsequently.

Any potential difficulties, problems or delays should be reported for consideration at the earliest possible moment, whilst it is still possible for the project manager to do something about it.

If as a project proceeds it begins to get behind schedule there comes a point, often fairly early, when no amount of extra resources will bring it back on schedule. The effort of training people and the increase in lines of communication becomes counter-productive.

ELEMENTS OF PROJECT MANAGEMENT

Project management is not an integral part of SSADM, but is essential for the success of an SSADM project (and any other project). It consists of a range of activities:

- planning;
  - estimation;

    - scheduling;
    - evaluation;
- monitoring, of:
    - progress against time and cost budgets;
    - quality;
    - user involvement;
- authorisation;
- change control;
- rescheduling;
- collection of statistics.

These activities are considered in more detail in the sections below.

ESTIMATION

The Problems

As work proceeds on any system, more is known and less remains to be done. It is possible, and usually essential, to refine estimates regularly as work proceeds, and this is done in SSADM. Even so it can still be difficult, in what is theoretically the last week of a project, to be sure that nothing will be carried forward into the following week.

If estimating when near the end of a project cannot be done with total confidence, then early estimates are obviously much more prone to error. Estimation in the early stages of system development is a classic example of the *Catch 22* situation – an estimate cannot be made with any great hope of ultimately being proved correct by events until the work involved is known in considerable detail. On the other hand, management is understandably reluctant to sanction work to go ahead to this level of detail in the absence of some estimate of what the costs are likely to be.

The figure that may stick in your mind is the one first given, but this is almost invariably lower than actual cost. Projects all too often exceed their early estimates by 100 percent or more. The detail needed for any sort of accuracy in estimating is missing until the requirements have been fully identified. Regrettably, this is often a little late to be producing estimates that would show that the project should not have been started in the first place. There is always the temptation to continue with a project once a significant amount of money has been spent on it, even though the cost/benefit calculations, when reconsidered, would show a totally different picture. Management must be prepared to stop a project if that is the best decision for the business. (Revision of estimates is considered further below under *Monitoring with SSADM*.

The first problem is that of producing time and cost estimates during the Feasibility Study that will bear some acceptably close resemblance to actual subsequent experience. At the same time you must be aware of the degree of error that is likely in these early estimates, and the basis on which they have been made.

Estimating is not easy. There are many approaches, all eminently capable of producing figures that are well wide of the mark. Unfortunately there is no infallible tool that will give an accurate estimate, or anything near to it, without considerable effort on the part of those making the estimate. Consider just some of the many factors involved:

- type of project;
- complexity of system;
- team organisation;
- experience of team;
- methods used;
- availability of equipment;
- availability of software.

and so on.

Other factors that are also needed are:

- sufficient statistics of past performance in similar circumstances on which to base the estimates;
- major features of the proposed system known in reasonable detail;
- no changes to requirements to be actioned during development without prior re-estimation.

If all of these and any other relevant items are taken into account, then there is hope of producing estimates that bear some resemblance to the subsequent reality. Being pinned to a hopelessly optimistic estimate is a situation that ultimately gives satisfaction to no-one, and has a detrimental effect on morale. The development staff may then choose to take all sorts of short cuts, making decisions without consultation, and being less than thorough with testing. This destroys much that has been gained by the use of a structured method. Targets must be realistic.

Making Estimates

Estimates can be made in several ways:

- by calculation (*Putnam* 1980, *Boehm* 1981);
- by Function Points (*Albrecht* and *Gaffney* 1983, *Behrens* 1983);
- by breaking the development process down into its constituent parts and estimating for each of them separately.

Estimating is not only a management task. Involving members of the team (both developers and yourselves) in estimating can prevent some of the initial over-optimism, and is more likely to lead to acceptance, commitment and motivation of the team.

The basis of each element of the estimate should be recorded, so that future estimates can be refined in the light of experience.

Software is available that can help with the task of estimating. Such packages are built on statistical bases derived (inevitably in the first instance) from experience in other organisations. They can thus be taken as a guide, but require customisation from statistics that are installation-specific. Inevitably this takes some time and effort.

Estimating and SSADM

A work breakdown is readily available from the SSADM tasks, customised as necessary, and giving clearly defined start and end points in terms of inputs and products. (These must be augmented by estimates of the non-SSADM work that must also be done.) Estimates on this basis are also needed for scheduling purposes. It is sensible to have an estimate by an alternative approach for purposes of comparison. Any significant discrepancy between the two estimates would serve as a warning, and would clearly indicate the need for some further thought.

Estimates are drawn up, reviewed, authorised, monitored against actual performance, and revised as necessary.

In SSADM, estimates are included in the Module Plans for approval by the project board.

SCHEDULING

Purpose

The purpose of scheduling is to take the estimated resource requirements for each activity, together with the known resource availability. Then, allowing for the logical interrelationships of activities, it is possible to establish start and end dates for each of them.

Bases for scheduling

Scheduling may be done in one of two ways:

- by allocating available resources to the tasks, to decide how long the project will take;

- by taking the time available and deciding what resources are necessary to meet the target dates (remembering that the target may be impossible; if it would take a five man team an estimated 40 weeks to complete (a total of 200 man weeks) then 200 people could not complete it in a week, and it is unlikely that 20 people could do it in 10 weeks).

Uncertainties

It is important to beware of dependence on external factors, eg:

- deliveries of hardware;

- performance of new equipment and software.

Late deliveries or failure to perform can have a dramatic effect on plans, and the possibility of this happening must be considered when formulating the plan. Items which are particularly vulnerable to delay are those that do not yet exist. Delivery of any item that is under development by a supplier must be open to doubt. The supplier may run into problems, or his priorities might change.

All other areas of uncertainty should be identified and documented so that particular attention can be paid to them. They will include such items as:

- searching for anything, eg suitable software;

- communicating between different items of equipment for the first time;

- gaining effective practical experience after receiving training.

The scheduling process

Scheduling is done by matching the resources known to be available to the customised SSADM tasks, to which the estimates have been assigned.

From the SSADM task estimates, a further breakdown may be required so that each activity:

- has a clear boundary with defined inputs and products;
- can be performed by a single individual or a small team;
- will last for only a short period – ideally no more than two weeks;
- must include your involvement in the detail.

In establishing the relationships between the various activities it will be necessary to identify:

- activities which must be performed in sequence;
- activities which can take place in parallel.

The relationships are best shown diagrammatically on a network analysis diagram, eg Critical Path Analysis or PERT (Programme Evaluation and Review Technique), which permit identification of the critical path. The act of drawing up such a network is itself a check on the completeness of the analysis, and usually reveals omissions.

In preparing schedules, factors to be considered are:

- known absences, such as training courses, meetings, presentations, seminars, vacations, bank holidays, etc (for practical purposes it may be wise to assume that no progress will be made for two weeks at Christmas, and very little in August; whatever the good intentions, there is major disruption during these periods);
- an allowance for the possibility of unscheduled absences due to sickness, the intrusion of non-project activities, etc;
- training of new staff due to turnover or promotion;
- contributions of team members to the planning process;
- involvement of team members in quality control;
- turnround time for development work on the computer;

– the management element;

– allowances for uncertainties (contingency time).

A fairly common practice is to assume a three and a half or four day week for estimating purposes.

When activities have been assigned to people (with or without a network diagram) they can be entered on a bar chart.

Contingency and management time

The term *Contingency,* as used here, is an allowance for the uncertainties that are inherent in any system development. It is additional to the basic resource estimates for the expected work content of a project, and may be defined as a reserve resource that must be carefully controlled. Some organisations may wish to delegate different percentages of the total allowance for contingency to different levels of control.

Both contingency and management time must be considered as separate elements when making estimates, ie they should not be built into the estimates for individual tasks.

Multiple projects

Where an individual is working on more than one project, the demands of each must be taken into account on the schedules. This may require a separate staff schedule for the individual. An allowance must also be made for 'lost time' due to continually switching between projects.

Software aids

All but the simplest schedules are difficult to modify or maintain on paper, and the use of software should be considered. Many software packages are available with considerable variations in facilities provided, costs, and the equipment needed for their operation.

EVALUATION

When the scheduling has been completed, the project delivery time and cost must be reviewed. If there is any indication that either of them is likely to exceed the resource objectives, then further high level consideration will be required. Options for management are one or more of the following:

– accepting a smaller system by redrawing the system boundary;

– accepting a simpler system by omitting some of the requirements;

- accepting a simpler system by requiring fewer of the problems to be solved;
- relaxing some of the design objectives to accept a lower level of performance;
- accepting an increase in time and cost.

Short cuts through SSADM should not be taken. This would risk a loss in the quality of the product. The apparent saving of analysis and design time would then prove to be a short term saving, with greater costs in the later stages of development, its acceptability to you, and subsequent maintenance costs. (Don't confuse this with the planned omission of tasks which, after consideration, have been found to be unnecessary for a particular project.)

MONITORING

Purpose

The purpose of monitoring is to:

- check that work is proceeding according to plan, ie by both developers and users, within time and cost;
- ensure that work is aimed at achieving the required levels of performance specified in the design objectives;
- ensure that the work is being done to SSADM and installation standards;
- take corrective action where appropriate;
- reschedule the work when necessary.

Monitoring with SSADM

SSADM aids monitoring by virtue of the prescribed tasks which break the project down into small units of work with end products for each step. Monitoring can thus be done against:

- work actually done (end products produced and tasks completed);
- time taken to date (allocated to each task);
- estimates of the time needed to complete the tasks currently in progress.

Estimates of time to complete tasks should be in man days. Experience has shown that less thought tends to be given to estimates by percentage.

Estimates of time to complete the system must be subject to careful review by senior management as represented in the project board. The board must always have the option to suspend, abandon or significantly change the development in the event of unacceptable growth in the estimates.

Regular checkpoint returns from team members should be as simple as possible whilst providing the information needed by the project manager. There should be no need to report data that is available from other sources, or to report the same thing more than once.

The project board also monitor the development in all its aspects and implications for the organisation. This is done at the end of each module, but may be needed at other times if it becomes apparent that the planned targets will not be achieved.

AUTHORISATION

In SSADM, the Project Plans and all Module Plans require authorisation from the project board. Any comments or recommendations made by the board must be taken into account before work can continue with the next module.

CHANGE CONTROL

Changes may be imposed by external factors, or at the request of users or senior management. Some may be initiated by the developers. Where a proposed change arises from within the computer department, the proposal must, of course, be agreed by the users. All changes should be recorded.

Changes will usually affect budgets. They may:

- affect work still to be done, which will have a future cost, but will not entail any rework;
- have a more fundamental effect, where later work has been based on elements that are to be changed.

Whilst both types of change have their cost, rework represents a waste. Consideration should be given to the causes of such changes with a view to trying to anticipate or avoid them in future developments.

As with every other element of the system, the cost/benefit should be considered and the decision taken whether to:

- Include it forthwith.

- Put it with other change requests, in order of priority.

- Shelve it for the present, but keep it under review for possible future implementation. It will be one of the considerations when trying to anticipate change, and the design should be left as open-ended as possible to accommodate the proposal with the minimum of additional cost in the future.

- Reject it, although even if it is decided that it will never be implemented, never is a long time. The proposal could be resurrected under different circumstances in the future. It is advisable to treat it in the same way as those that have been shelved.

Sometimes the imposition of a 'freeze date' is attempted. This is a date after which development will continue with any further changes being ignored until development as specified on the freeze date has been completed. This notion of an inexorable freeze date is seldom workable in practice. Nevertheless it is a good idea to hold all but essential changes and plan to incorporate them in later releases, after the initial implementation. Of course, anything that entails a major design change should be incorporated as soon as possible to minimise reworking.

The responsibility of deciding whether to implement a change rests ultimately with the project board, but for practical purposes some levels of decision on change may be delegated, depending on cost and time factors:

- Up to some agreed level of cost and delay, the project manager should be authorised to make the decision. Within this control limit, set by the project board, he should have complete responsibility for managing the project. He must report any possibility of exceeding this budget.

- Above these agreed limits, the decision will be a matter for the project board itself.

Decisions to be made by the organisation are:

- agreed levels for delegation to the various decision makers;

- how changes should be recorded;

- how to rate priorities.

Changes are inevitable during all but the shortest of developments. These are caused by:

- changes in the business environment;

- imposed changes, eg due to legislation;

- changes in the technical environment;
- changes or extensions to user requirements.

One of the problems is that in addition to the disruption caused by the change itself, every change is also likely to extend the development time, and the longer the development time, the more opportunity there is for further changes (a good argument for evolutionary development with short timescales for each increment of the system).

Each proposed change requires:

- a specification of the change;
- an estimate of the cost of implementing the change;
- a consideration of the costs of *not* implementing the change;
- an estimate of the effect on the project and on other projects;
- a reconsideration of the relationship between costs and benefits;
- entry in a Change Control Log or Register;
- authorisation, at the appropriate level, to go ahead.

It may be decided to implement a change in the next release of a system, but to include some preparatory work in the current version.

RESCHEDULING

As development continues, the eventual significance of any divergence between actual progress and estimates becomes more obvious. On a project of any significant size, it would be normal for some rescheduling to be needed in the light of actual experience.

DOCUMENT CONTROL

Throughout an SSADM development, new documents are being created and earlier ones amended. It is easy to lose control of the situation, particularly on projects with many team members. Before starting the work, a control system should be devised so that it will be known how many copies there are of every document, who has them, and what changes are incorporated in each new version.

Every different version should have a unique identifier, and arrangements should be made to cancel or recall earlier versions. Much time can be wasted by people working from out of date documents. They are like time bombs lurking in the project.

STATISTICS

Introduction

Data collected during development work forms the basis for estimating and scheduling. Without statistical data, both:

- the refinement of estimates for on-going work; and
- estimates for future work;

can only be based either on guesswork or on someone else's experience.

Statistics, then, are necessary either for the development of one's own estimating method or to permit the calibration of a commercially available model. But this is not the only use of statistics. For example, it is sometimes suggested that they may be used for comparing the performance of different teams, or assessing the impact of different development methods. However, some experience suggests that this is very difficult to do in practice, as each project is different and results are too difficult to interpret.

Among the aspects to be considered are:

- What data is necessary to permit better estimating?
- Who should provide it?
- When should it be obtained?
- How should it be collected?

In the absence of standards and statistics there is no basis for estimates. If the next project will not be developed in the same way that an earlier one was done, then any statistics collected will be of only limited value.

SSADM lends itself admirably to the accumulation of statistical data. Every system is developed in the same way, and past experience will therefore give an excellent indication of likely future performance.

Management considerations

It takes time to collect data and to store, maintain and analyse it. Adequate time must be allowed for this, or either the statistical work or the development work (or both) will be skimped. The outcome will be either a poorer system or unreliable statistics.

Management must:

- consider the potential problems of self-recording of performance;
- see what statistics can be obtained automatically, eg from systems software or specially written programs;
- constantly monitor the indicated results to watch for trends and potential problems;
- find why and where actual performance is differing from estimates.

Classification of statistics

The statistics should be classified or annotated to indicate the environment in which they were collected, for example:

- type of system;
- size and complexity of system;
- size of team;
- experience of people involved;
- strategy, eg evolutionary development, prototyping, etc (*see* Chapter 26).

Collection of statistics

There are many factors that can influence development time and cost. Statistics will normally be collected by the project manager and be collated and analysed by the computer department. For the benefit of other users involved in future developments, you will need to record and contribute details of your own involvement in the various tasks.

Use of statistics

Once statistics are available it is possible to come up with some rules of thumb to give very rapid initial sizing. For example, it may be found that in one particular installation:

- on everage there are 1.8 program modules per screen;
- on average a module takes eight days for a programmer to code and test;
- therefore an average screen takes 14 days to code and test;

- programming takes 30 percent of total development time;
- therefore a screen represents 47 days of development work;
- therefore a 20 screen system will take 940 days of development effort;
- allowing for absences, effective man days are 3.5 per week;
- the work would therefore take one (average) developer 940/3.5 = 269 weeks;
- user involvement represents 5 percent of total development time, ie 5 percent of 269 = 13 weeks approximately.

(WARNING: These figures are for illustration only. They have not been researched.)

This is not very sophisticated, but does give an early indication of likely time and cost. To provide a closer estimate of elapsed time it will be necessary to consider the non-average people who will be doing the work, how many of them will be available, what work can be done in parallel, and the relevance of the environment in which the statistics were collected (*see Classification of Statistics*). The comments of Fred Brooks in *The Mythical Man-Month*, that time is not divisible by the number of people available, should always be borne in mind. Projects have a basic time that cannot be reduced. The classic example is: If it will take one woman nine months to have a baby, how long will it take nine women?

25
Using the method

INTRODUCTION

There are many good reasons for using SSADM, and they were considered in detail in Chapter 3. However, taking SSADM on board is a major step for any organisation. The effects are far-reaching. The work pattern will change for all those involved, some of whom may never have taken an active part in system development activities before.

It follows that using SSADM is a course of action that is not to be undertaken lightly. It requires the commitment of all concerned if systems to be developed using SSADM are to be as successful in practice as they are in potential.

CORPORATE MANAGEMENT

The effect on corporate management of using SSADM depends on how it views its own responsibilities within the organisation. As computerisation is a voracious consumer of resources, then total lack of involvement in system development is an abdication of responsibility.

It is a duty of higher levels of management to ensure that work within the organisation is carried out in an efficient and effective manner. With this aim in mind, senior management involvement should initially be at the strategic level to ensure that:

- the right systems are computerised;
- they are taken on in the best sequence.

The development of a corporate IT (Information Technology) strategy lies outside the scope of this book. However, techniques provided by SSADM can be used to help in the development of a strategic plan.

Subsequently, during system development, involvement is needed to ensure that:

- the best methods are being used;
- project management control has been installed;
- quality control procedures have been defined and implemented;
- the emerging systems are meeting corporate objectives.

Organisations tend to get the computer systems they deserve. If development is left to the technical people, then technically oriented systems are likely to emerge. Systems are much more likely to meet corporate and user objectives if their development is overseen by corporate and user representatives. Projects should have senior managers as sponsors. The sponsors should be represented on, or delegate authority to, a project board.

USER MANAGEMENT AND USERS

User management must have a clear understanding of both corporate and system objectives, and should be deeply involved in the organisational aspects of an SSADM project. The two aspects in which they may expect to take part are the project board, in which representation should be mandatory, and in project management – a role that can usefully be taken on by a user if he has the appropriate skills.

The most important point to understand and accept, for all those involved in a development, is that systems belong to their users. All major decisions must be made by the users, rather than their merely taking part in the decision making process. When systems fail to succeed as well as they should, it may be because users:

- will not co-operate;
- do not know how to co-operate;
- are not given the chance to co-operate;
- are not asked the right questions;
- do not know precisely what they want;
- are insufficiently aware of the capabilities of computer technology.

SSADM is designed to involve users from the start of systems analysis, and will overcome all of the above reasons for failure, other than wilful refusal. Yours will be the key role in:

- supplying information about what you do (the current system);
- thinking about what could be done better (solving existing problems);
- specifying additional facilities to be incorporated in the system (new requirements);
- specifying in measurable terms how well the system is to perform (quality objectives);
- specifying in measurable terms the time and cost limits on development and operation of the system (resource objectives);
- ensuring that your requirements are met (informally by your involvement with the checking and preparation of diagrams, and formally by participation in quality control).

It is a responsibility of user management to ensure that both they and their staff:

- are agreed on the project objectives;
- co-operate in developing a project plan;
- agree user involvement as specified in the plan;
- ensure that the appropriate users are available when required;
- take part in informal checking as work progresses;
- know what is expected of them during development;
- understand what is given to them for discussion and quality review;
- take part in the formal quality control procedures.

This involvement in the analysis, decision making and quality checking processes will take up more of your time than the 'traditional' approach. User management must be made aware of the need for this commitment in sufficient time to permit the allocation of resources.

THE PROJECT BOARD

Representation

Membership of the board should comprise people with sufficient responsibility to take high-level decisions based on what has been done, and to decide whether further work should be carried out. Consequently they are people at senior management or board level who are financially and politically responsible for the project.

Representation on the board is a matter for the organisation and will depend on the project. The *SSADM Manual* suggests the composition of the board as:

- Executive representation to ensure that corporate interests are always considered and that financial resources are available.

- User department representation to ensure that user resources are available and that the emerging system meets the needs of the department. Where the work involves more than one department it may be advisable to extend the user representation accordingly. (Some organisations consider it advisable to have the user who is sponsoring the system as chairman.).

- Computer department representation. This is to cover the technical aspects and the availability of technical resources for the project.

Finance department representation should also be considered to monitor progress against the planned budget, and to see that the projected returns on the capital investment remain within acceptable limits.

For a sufficiently important project, further independent corporate representation may be deemed to be advisable.

In all circumstances, this senior project management group should be as small as possible commensurate with the decisions that must be made. Three to five people is probably ideal. A single person would have no formal forum in which to discuss ideas and recommendations. More than five would be in danger of being counter-productive.

It is possible that some smaller projects (or smaller organisations) may choose to have fewer people controlling a project. In this case the responsibilities will remain the same, but they will be represented by fewer people.

Corporate interests should always be the concern of all those who attend, no matter what the size of the board.

Responsibilities

In addition to their parochial concerns, the board members will also have total authority for ensuring that the project (sometimes more than one project) is under control, ie:

- the development work completed has not diverged from what was authorised;
- the project is staying within the agreed constraints of time and cost;
- there are no significant changes to the cost/benefit ratio;
- the project is redirected if external factors (eg changed needs) render the current project deliverables to be out of date (redirection should be carried out only if absolutely *essential* as it will add to time and cost);
- proper consideration is given to whether further development should take place;
- detailed plans for the next stage of the work are properly authorised, paying particular attention to any significant divergence from estimates made earlier; each organisation must decide for itself what *significant* means, for example 10 percent from budget.

Authorisation to continue the project

Continuance to the next development module is based on the detailed plans that have been submitted for approval. This is a critical responsibility. It is never easy to kill a project when much money has already been spent. Sometimes it must be done in the best interests of the company. The senior managers must not let work continue unless confident of the success of the project, by whatever criteria success will be measured. They must have the authority to do this.

Selection of options

Computer options are considered during the Feasibility Study, during Requirements Analysis when Business Options are presented, and during Logical System Specification when Technical Options are put forward. How the selection is done will vary from organisation to organisation. It will be mainly dependent on the constitution of the quality control review team and the project board (and any other committee that the organisation may deem necessary for adequate control to be maintained).

The principles of selection should be seen as funnelling down from the informal range of possibilities put forward initially, to the three (or whatever) for formal selection. The short-listed options are developed in more detail, and then go to the project board for final selection. If the earlier work has been done thoroughly and in full knowledge of corporate objectives, then the project board may have little need to do more than rubber stamp one of the options, with some hybrid option always being a strong possibility.

Any major change deemed necessary at project board level would be likely to result in the discarding of detailed work already done, with its attendant cost. Consequently proposals going to the project board should always be based on realism, not optimism.

THE PROJECT MANAGER

Project management will involve a project manager and one or more team leaders. For a small project the activities may be combined and be the responsibility of a single person.

The manager is responsible for the day-to-day control of a project.

The manager must appreciate that SSADM does not replace management, but is an aid to it. An SSADM project needs strong and effective management as much as does any other approach to systems development.

The project manager will report to the project board.

Basic skills

As the job title implies, the task requires management skills. Besides these, the manager must also:

- be experienced in project management techniques;
- have an adequate knowledge of SSADM;
- have experienced advice available to him.

The management resource

It is essential that the project manager should be allocated sufficient time to manage the project effectively.

In a small project, the team leader will normally be the manager. He may also be responsible for some key elements of the work that require experience beyond that of the other team members.

A larger project, with more than one project team, will need a management structure. In this case the manager may well be fully occupied with management activities. More detailed involvement with the technical work is likely to have a detrimental effect on the control activities and hence on cost and delivery date.

Background experience

Given the basic skills mentioned above, the project manager need not necessarily be a technical expert in systems development. A user who has adequate training can effectively manage the Feasibility Study and Requirements Analysis Modules. A user manager will also be able to resolve many queries that arise, that would otherwise require a more time-consuming expedition to the user department.

Areas Requiring Particular Attention

Areas where control is needed are:

- In the effective customisation of the tasks defined in SSADM to meet the requirements of the project, and in estimating time and resource requirements. If a user is the project manager, he may require technical assistance in this area.

- In deciding when to stop the application of a technique and regard the work on a task as having been taken as far as necessary for that stage in development.

- In ensuring that the diagrams serve the purpose for which they were intended, ie as working documents and not as art forms.

- In the close monitoring of performance, ensuring that any slippage is caught early enough for something to be done about it.

- In ensuring a sensible approach to quality control. The method specifies the appropriate checkpoints, but common sense is also needed. There may need to be several separate checks at the same checkpoint in a big system, or maybe some checkpoints will need to be brought forward to task levels within a step. Maybe more than one checkpoint should be combined for a small project. The essential feature is the assessment of the amount of rework that may be necessary if something has gone wrong since the last check. The manager must also ensure that appropriate people are identified and available for the quality control work.

THE TEAM LEADER

For a small project, the team leader may also be the project manager.

The team leader needs to have:

- training in and experience of team leadership;

- an expert knowledge of SSADM;

- the basic analysis and design skills.

Regardless of the nature of the role (team leader or manager), adequate time must be scheduled for the role activities. Otherwise some element of the work – managerial or technical – will suffer.

The responsibilities of the team leader include:

- activity control;
- change control;
- informal quality reviews to maintain a detailed view of the products of the team;
- formal quality control.

The team leader will report to the project manager.

PROJECT TEAMS

Introduction

The basic rule for size and composition of teams for the most efficient work at least cost is to have a small number of experienced people, and to give them the time they need. Attempting to work faster, with more people, or with less experience, is likely to cause costs and uncertainties to escalate. This is a topic that is discussed very readably by Brooks in *The Mythical Man-Month* – a book that should come high on any compulsory reading list for project managers.

User representation

If there is no user with the necessary skills to manage the project, or if it is decided that a developer should fill the role, then consideration must be given to user representation on the project team. This may be necessary anyhow. A project manager may not be aware of the detail of day-to-day operation of the system. There are many occasions during a system study when user knowledge and decisions are urgently required, and time should be allocated for this purpose. This will necessarily reduce the time that the nominated user has available for his normal responsibilities and arrangements must be made to cover these as necessary.

Team structure

Experience has shown that the ideal team structure for an SSADM development is as shown in Figure 25.1.

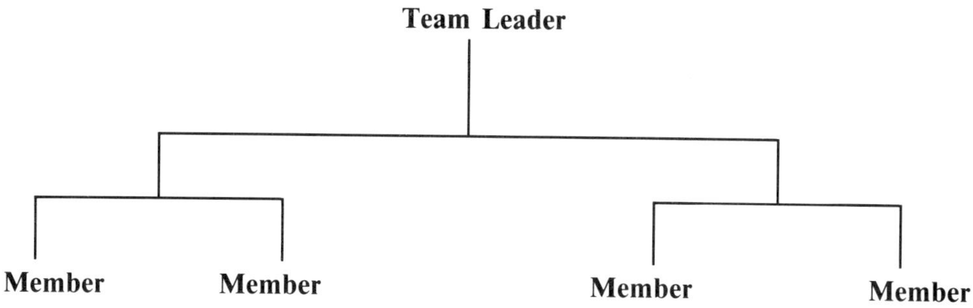

Figure 25.1 An SSADM team structure

This gives a team organisation capable of dealing with the three main types of work that occur under SSADM, ie:

- work which can be done individually, such as Relational Data Analysis (Step 340) and the preparation of Update and Enquiry Process Models (Steps 520 and 530);
- work best done in pairs; this applies mainly to the diagramming techniques, and particularly to DFDs and ELHs;
- team work, eg brainstorming sessions when options are being created.

However, such an organisation is not always possible, and many projects are developed with fewer people.

Multiple teams

Where work is beyond the capacity of a single small team, the requisite number of people can be built up from teams of five to give a structure of the kind depicted in Figure 25.2.

This is, of course, only one of many possible structures, but the small team concept should not be discarded lightly. It has much to offer, both in efficiency and effectiveness.

Work should be allocated to teams by business functional area, and not by SSADM tasks or techniques. The techniques gain their strength from their interaction with each other. To have them done in isolation is likely to give poorer individual products and more problems when they are brought together.

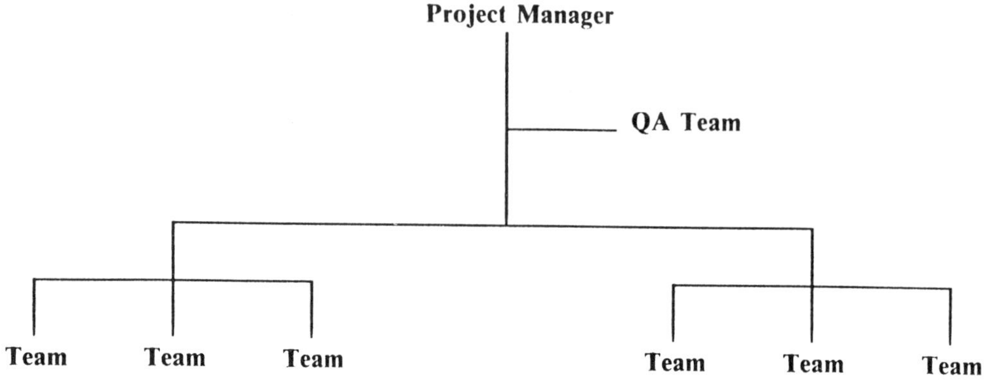

Figure 25.2 An SSADM team structure for a larger project

The products of the separate teams must be co-ordinated as the work proceeds. This may be the responsibility of the manager (or an intermediate level of management if project size requires layers of management). It could also be the responsibility of one of the teams, perhaps with other specialist roles, eg:

- monitoring standards;
- organising the quality reviews (but not carrying them out);
- providing expert assistance on SSADM.

INTRODUCING SSADM INTO YOUR ORGANISATION

If SSADM is to be accepted within your organisation, there can be no better start than to make a success of the first project. Steps to be taken are recommended in the following paragraphs.

Obtain corporate approval and commitment

The introduction of SSADM will cost money both in terms of the direct expenditure and the fact that computer staff will not be able to carry out other duties because of the need for training. There may be further expenses for experienced SSADM consultants and for CASE (Computer Aided Software Engineering) software.

It will involve many people at all levels in the company.

Senior management must be aware of the changes that will occur, be prepared for the costs, and be committed to its use. This applies particularly in ensuring co-operation from users and understanding that time will be lost in their normal work as a consequence.

SSADM will need corporate approval and commitment if it is to succeed.

Choose a pilot project

Projects which an organisation may wish to develop, possibly as a result of a detailed strategic analysis, should be considered with a view to selecting a project that would be suitable for pilot use of the method.

The characteristics of a project suitable for a pilot study should include some of the following:

- scheduled to start in a few weeks, to allow adequate time to organise suitable training;
- short in duration, for example capable of development by a small team with analysis and design measured in weeks rather than months, and with an elapsed time of no more than six to nine months with the resources that will be available;
- non-critical to the continued existence of the company;
- non-urgent, perhaps by bringing forward a project that had been scheduled for later development;
- require no technical experience beyond that already held by the development team;
- in a business area that is already familiar to the analysts;
- not require any pioneering work, and not be likely to need major hardware or software purchases;
- considered to be fairly restricted in its corporate impact, ie only one or two user departments will be involved;
- with user involvement readily available.

In other words, there should be no pressure, and the only new element in the development should be SSADM itself.

Maybe there really is no alternative other than to start with a development that is big, complex or innovatory. In those circumstances every effort should be made to identify a distinct part of the total system that would be suitable as the pilot. If this is not possible, then consideration should be given to obtaining the services of someone who is already an expert in the use of the method.

Choose a project team

This will usually be the responsibility of the computer department, but you may know some of the likely candidates and be in a position to influence the choice. The ideal team leader is one who is keen to use SSADM, and who will also be credible in the eyes of the rest of the team and in his department. As SSADM skills are much in demand, self interest should ensure that a suitable candidate will not prove too difficult to find.

When problems arise, as inevitably they will, an interested and enthusiastic team leader should be able to see them through.

If possible, at least two people should be involved in the pilot project. This permits some discussion and teamwork, provides some cover to a development that would otherwise be very vulnerable to staff absences, and permits practical experience of the method to be made available more quickly around the installation.

Arrange training

Computer people and business people involved in SSADM projects need different courses. These are available from many computer training organisations, and are regularly advertised in the computer press. It is worth checking that the courses have been officially recognised for teaching SSADM. Such courses are ISEB (Information Systems Examination Board) accredited. Trainers should hold the *Certificate of Proficiency in SSADM.*

SSADM courses for computer staff are not general systems analysis courses. SSADM assumes that its practitioners will have the basic skills such as interviewing, fact finding, proposal writing, presentations, form design, screen design, etc. These skills are needed as much in SSADM as with any other approach to system development. Some practical experience of analysis and design is highly desirable for computer people before starting out on SSADM.

While you may cope quite well with a practitioner course, such a course is not necessary for the usual degree of user involvement in a project, and special courses are available for your needs. In the jargon you may be described as an end user. In this context, end users include project board members, quality reviewers, those involved in the lower level fact finding and informal reviews, and future users of the system after implementation.

Project managers

Project managers are not necessarily involved in the detailed SSADM production work, but require more knowledge of the method than do the users. If you are to be a project manager, you will need to know both the structure of the method and the documentation that will be produced. The full training course will be advisable – again as and when needed. This will be earlier than the team members because of the initial planning that will be needed.

Use consultants

This will be more for the computer department than for you, but you should be aware of the possible need and reasons for the employment of consultants.

A team tackling its first project with the method may have trouble in all sorts of ways, for example in knowing:

- how to start;
- what level to go to;
- when to stop;
- why they are doing what they are doing;
- how the techniques and products fit together;
- how to customise the method for the particular project in hand (although for the first project it is advisable to omit nothing, and regard it as all part of the learning process).

An experienced consultant can be invaluable in resolving such uncertainties, and keeping the project on the road. This does not mean that he must be present throughout the life of the project. It means having a consultant in for a day or so at strategic times, perhaps:

- within a day or so of the start, to resolve the initial problems;
- a week or so later to check progress made and to put right anything that is going wrong, before too much time is wasted;
- at the end of the first step to assist with quality reviews on the products that then exist;
- at other quality control points.

A useful guide would be to arrange to have the services of a consultant for an average of one day every two weeks, subject to negotiation as to the actual day of visit, perhaps on occasions grouping two or three days together.

It would also be useful to have advice fairly readily available through telephone support.

Monitor progress

It is worth recording details of the work, for example:

- time taken for each separately identifiable element, ie below task level wherever possible;

- notes of problems encountered;
- anywhere where it has been considered necessary to diverge from or to augment the method;
- system statistics as mentioned in Chapter 24;
- lack of experience in any area of the work, other than the use of the method itself, such as the first system for a new business area, or a Technical Option selected that has not been used before.

Plan ahead

The estimates for future system developments, as featured in the strategic plan, should be reconsidered in the light of experience of the pilot project.

26

Practical systems development

INTRODUCTION

The traditional approach to systems development is essentially based on hope:

- hope that the system's users really know all that they want, and will be able to communicate it successfully to the developers (this is not a criticism – just an acceptance that in any but the most trivial of systems, some things will be assumed, some will be forgotten, and some will not be realised until people actually get their hands on the system);

- hope that 'seat of the pants' estimates will really prove to be correct;

- hope that nothing goes wrong;

- hope that users will be satisfied with what they are given;

- hope that the unspoken and unmeasurable qualities will somehow be satisfied by the system that happens to emerge.

The fact that systems continue to be developed in this way is yet another triumph of hope over experience.

Taking SSADM on board is a significant step in the right direction. It provides the basis on which success can be built. However, it does not guarantee success. SSADM alone will not deliver successful systems. Good organisation and effective management were considered in Chapters 24 and 25. This is not all that is necessary. Success also requires strategies appropriate to the situation. You should consider:

- development of the right projects;

- evolutionary development;

- prototyping;
- coping with change;
- avoiding complexity.

This chapter considers these aspects. They are not a part of SSADM and would apply equally to *any* approach to system development.

DEVELOPMENT OF THE RIGHT PROJECTS

Introduction

There are many examples in the computer world of systems being designed, or often in use, which totally fail to meet expectations. There can be many reasons for this – poor methods, lack of communication, inexperience, incompetence and more. One which is rarely mentioned is where the system itself is not the right one for the company. There is nothing to stop you from using SSADM (or any other approach to systems analysis and design) on a system that you should not be developing in that way, or at that time, or even at all.

There are two difficulties:

- realising that the requirements may not be the right ones, for example, going forward uncritically with a system because it happens to be there, or because someone with influence has made sufficient noise;
- knowing how to recognise at an early stage that the requirements, as initially specified, are going to cause problems.

Every computer system development is an attempt to take something that a user wants to do and to translate it into a system of which a computer forms some part. The conventionally-seen problems are those of finding what the user needs, and then of designing the system.

Unfortunately, what systems analysis often finds is what the user says he wants rather than what he needs. Sometimes it may indeed be what the user, in isolation, actually does need, but seen in the limited context of the user and not of the company. In either case the result is the same – the outcome of the technical exercise is a system that fails to make significant improvements in company performance. It tends to substitute a new way of doing something for an old way of doing more or less the same thing without any real consideration for the wider view of the company and its overall aims, objectives and information needs. It brings along all the trauma of change, but few of the benefits of which it is potentially capable.

The reason for the poor performance of a system from the corporate viewpoint is not lack of knowledge on the part of the user as to his present responsibilities, nor lack of technical expertise on the part of the development staff, nor even a lack of communication, but rather a failure to appreciate:

- the business objectives and priorities of the organisation;
- the real problems of the organisation;
- the basic objectives of the system;
- the difficulties inherent in the development process;
- the finite nature of the resources of time, cost, experience and equipment.

The net result is that systems often cause disappointment. They come as an anti-climax after long months, or sometimes years, of effort. The reason can very often be identified as lack of sufficient attention to the design objectives.

Effectiveness is a composite property of a system, its environment, and its development. For a system to be truly effective it needs to be the right one for the environment and the capabilities of its users, developed within the resource constraints. The factors involved are considered in this section.

Can It Be Done?

Virtually anything can be done given sufficient time and money. Unfortunately they are seldom available in limitless quantities and, in real life, restrictions exist. Among them are such considerations as:

- Are the requirements sufficiently precise and objective to allow a proper assessment of costs and benefits to be made?
- Are the users who are specifying the requirements a representative sample of all of the users, and do they have the vision to anticipate likely future needs?
- Do the user managers have the power and commitment to drive the project through the inevitable rough water?
- Is the equipment which is currently installed, capable of doing the work as suggested, and does it have sufficient spare capacity?
- Do the technical staff have the necessary expertise to develop the system – not the capability to do it given training, but the experience of actually having done something very similar before?
- Will the necessary people be available to do the work as and when required?

- Is the project timescale short enough so that users will not lose interest (or retire!) whilst waiting for it?

Negative answers to any of these questions do not necessarily indicate that the work cannot be done, but they do suggest that to go ahead is likely to entail extra expense and delay, and to introduce areas of risk. For instance:

- If the necessary equipment is not already held, then it must be found and procured, and performance does not always match expectations or the optimism of salesmen. Particular care should be taken with products that are said to be still under development. The vendor's priorities might change. They might run into unexpected difficulties. They might abandon the work. Building a system on something that does not currently exist and is not under the direct control of your own company has got to be regarded as high risk.

- Without experience in every development area the development team may hit problems of unknown magnitude. Training will be needed, and the ability to apply the new knowledge effectively almost invariably takes longer than expected.

- People with the required knowledge may be working on other projects and not be available for yours.

It is important to remember that too much pioneering work can very easily turn a development project into a research project in which both cost and time are indeterminable.

Should It Be Done?

Because a system is technically possible, it does not necessarily follow that development should go ahead. Computerisation introduces change to an organisation, and change carries with it risks (*Mumford and Pettigrew,* 1975) of:

- financial loss through the investment of capital in a system that will not necessarily give the expected return;

- industrial unrest through changes to work, skills required, and staffing levels;

- political consequences of changes to status, influence and power;

- operational problems where the system is innovatory in any way.

Additionally, the project may run counter to a wider strategy for computing and systems in the company as a whole.

Conclusions

Probably the greatest difficulty in attempting to assess costs and benefits at the analysis stage is trying to envisage how the system could be operating in five years time. Practical use will eventually show how accurate the predictions have been, but regrettably this is rather late in the life cycle to serve any useful purpose except to add to experience and hopefully to prevent the same mistakes from being made in the next system. Unfortunately this does not prevent a totally new set of mistakes from being made next time.

EVOLUTIONARY DEVELOPMENT

Introduction

There are two basic approaches to the task of developing computer systems – 'big bang' and evolutionary development. This section considers these approaches, and how they interface with each other and with SSADM.

The intended development strategy should be considered when initiating analysis at the start of SSADM.

'Big Bang'

'Big bang' is one of the more colourful phrases in data processing. It is used to describe the approach to systems development that starts with the Analysis Requirement and delivers the complete final system as an all-at-once implementable chunk. It has become well-known over the years for the regularity with which systems developed in this way have been found to overrun budgets of time and cost by amounts that would be almost unbelievable if they were not so common.

There may be occasions when the 'big bang' approach is viable, eg:

- where the project is in a well-understood area, using well-understood hardware and software;
- if there are many staff available, then many parts may be developed in parallel and be brought into use together;
- it may give fewer problems with interfaces;
- low staff turnover in the development team may give reasonable prospects of the same people carrying the project through to completion;
- it may really not be possible to break it down into anything smaller.

However, as an approach, 'big bang' is potentially fraught with problems. Among them are:

- a lengthy development time during which the needs of the users change, and even the users themselves may change;
- the near necessity for a 'freeze' date (ie a date after which no further requests for changes to the specification will be considered for the initial implementation), and the near impossibility of making such a date stick in practice;
- the likelihood of changes in the development staff, with the consequent additional costs of the familiarisation and training of replacements;
- the inability of the user to see all the possibilities and implications until he actually gets his hands on the system, especially if the project is innovative in its use of technology or the type and scope of the application;
- the likelihood that many changes will all be requested at once in the early days after implementation;
- people find it difficult to cope with change. They tend to like stability. The 'big bang' approach risks making too many changes too quickly.

Any headlong rush into system development without thought could lead to a 'big bang' implementation, but is absolutely *everything* really needed all at once? The 'big bang' is not a good idea. Sometimes it may seem to be the only way to proceed, but this is seldom the case on close examination:

- A careful study of high level DFDs should show whether a breakdown of the total development task is possible, and where boundaries can be drawn.
- A study of priorities in the Requirements Catalogue will show initial requirements and future enhancements.

The evolutionary approach should *always* be considered. This particularly applies to projects that are innovatory in any way.

The Evolutionary Approach

All systems, both manual and computer, evolve over a period. Statistics show that many organisations spend over half their resources on maintenance, and most of this is spent on enhancements. Evolutionary development accepts that there will be many versions of a system before the ultimate is achieved (if it ever is), and seeks to install systems in parts over a period rather than all at once (the 'big bang') at the end.

The evolutionary development of computer systems is similar to (and sometimes taken to be the same as) incremental development. The main difference is that a learning process is involved, each part implementation being modified where it fails to meet requirements, and influencing the design of what comes later.

The evolutionary concept consists of dividing a big project up into sub-projects, each of which is useful in its own right and can be developed over a short timescale. Each part:

- either adds to or improves on the earlier parts; or

- will eventually integrate with other parts.

As an approach it is advocated by many writers, and is embraced enthusiastically by those who have used it. The guidelines and advantages listed below have been derived from several sources. Probably the leading proponent of this approach is Tom Gilb (*Gilb* 1988).

Guidelines for Evolutionary Development

- A top-down approach is required, ie the complete project must be considered and broken down into sub-projects, each of which may be broken down further until separately useful and implementable parts have been identified.

- The final design must be clearly established in outline at an early stage, so that development of each part does not lead to a cul-de-sac.

- Ultimate hardware requirements must be assessed to ensure that later parts of the project can be physically installed without having to reprogram all of the earlier work on different hardware. If all of the hardware is not purchased initially, then an upgrade path and some guarantees about future availability of compatible equipment will be needed.

- Final result goals should be set in measured quantitative form, for control purposes throughout the project.

- It is important to use a simple approach in the first implementation.

- The cost of the first part should be in the region of 1 percent to 5 percent of the estimated total cost.

- The first step could be an improvement by logicalisation of the current clerical system. This could give a very quickly implemented improvement at minimal cost, and/or make eventual computerisation a much less traumatic experience.

- If possible, most of the real usefulness should be included in the earliest deliveries. Pareto's Law is worthy of consideration. Pareto was an Italian sociologist and economist who formulated the 20/80 Law. In principle it says, for example that 20 percent of the salesmen will bring in 80 percent of the business, 20 percent of the parts will represent 80 percent of the cost, and so on. Conversely the other 80 percent of the salesmen will account for only 20 percent of the work, etc. In computer system terms, this law suggests that 80 percent of requirements would be met by 20 percent of total effort, and that, conversely the remaining 20 percent of requirements would require 80 percent of the effort.

- Detailed planning is needed only of the next part to be developed.

Advantages of Evolutionary Development

- Estimates of time and cost, being for smaller pieces of work, are more likely to be reliable.

- Initial costs are comparatively low.

- As useful work is brought into production, the ultimate cost of the complete project can be seen with greater accuracy. If necessary, management can call a halt at any stage, before costs escalate to unacceptable levels.

- The user gets something usable, quickly.

- The user is involved throughout development, and is basing his requirements on actual experience in the earlier stages.

- As each part is implemented, the experience gained influences the future design of the rest of the system.

- It avoids overwhelming people with change. The system can be learned in small stages as it is implemented.

- Development is less complex, ie it is done a (relatively) simple step at a time.

- Each new step adds to and improves on the previous stage.

- It gets over the difficulties of trying to make a complete project design at the start.

- Scheduled completion date pressure from outside the computer department is lessened.

- People make mistakes. If a mistake is made in any phase it will not invalidate earlier work, which continues to be useful.

- Benefits are actual, not promised.
- The 'final' system is more likely to match the real requirements.
- Typically, the first thing implemented is the top and this is the most used. It is then thoroughly tested by the subsequent developments.
- It may be possible to bring data into the database gradually. This is only of value, of course, if:
  - it can be used from the start; or
  - updating it until it will be of real use requires negligible effort; or
  - it would be impractical to attempt to input it all at one time.

Possible Problems With Evolutionary Development

- the work may be more coherent if developed as a whole;
- interfaces between the evolutionary system elements will require care;
- later phases may be inhibited by earlier developments;
- it may be more difficult to justify the costs of hardware purchases that will be under-utilised in the early stages;
- if early design is sloppy there may be some dead ends and rework, although this should be minimal given proper use of SSADM;
- *final* completion may be later.

Basic Evolutionary System

The basic evolutionary system is the first one that is of real use to the user. It:

- must be robust;
- must in some way cope with (but not necessarily process) all that is thrown at it, without falling down or allowing invalid data to go through;
- may be lacking in some functions;
- may be producing lists rather than an on-line response;
- may perform below the *final* target levels of qualities (but should not be below the least acceptable level, and should meet its own target levels for this delivery);

- must be open-ended to accept further evolutionary implementations with minimal rework as they are made available.

It may be implemented as a pilot system, for example, at a single site before implementing at all sites in the UK. This could be a simplification of the final system, for example, by:

- removing the need for a communications network;
- simplifying the product line;
- omitting functions not required at that particular site.

PROTOTYPING

Introduction

Every new project is a research project to some extent, but for some projects the research element is such that there may be real fears about a clear mutual understanding of requirements or of making estimates with reasonable accuracy. Instances are where a new venture is being undertaken, eg:

- work not done by the company before;
- systems which will change the way that work is done;
- a venture into new technology, which may cause problems for the developers, eg their first:
  - project employing a database management system;
  - real-time system;
  - distributed data processing system;
- where performance is in doubt.

SSADM techniques, in experienced hands, are very effective in digging out the information needed to develop effective systems. But even so it remains an unfortunate fact that all people:

- have difficulty in envisaging the hypothetical;
- do not necessarily think of everything they need;

- do not always realise the consequences of their requests;

- sometimes fail to communicate their requirements.

Additionally, hardware, software and communications do not necessarily perform as expected/hoped, or even as specified/promised/in theory. This is especially true of new mixes of these system elements.

In such circumstances, where there is a significant element of doubt regarding any element of understanding, performance or quality, it is prudent for the computer department to attempt to show users what their understanding of the problem is, before investing too much effort in solving it. Prototyping can help with this. It may also help to dispel some of the fears and uncertainties that users often feel when venturing into the unknown, and the active co-operation between yourselves and the developers can be a considerable advantage to the project.

It should be very clearly understood that whilst prototyping offers developers the opportunity to lash together instant systems with minimal prior thought and unfounded optimism, prototypes are not to be regarded as operational. For operational systems there is no substitute for thorough analysis, considered design, detailed plans, and management control, and all of these should be visible to the users who are most closely involved.

Among the points to be considered are:

- Prototyping will be heavily dependent on the availability of suitable software. This may not be available in your installation, and so may require an additional early cost and some delay whilst the developers become acquainted with its use.

- Areas to be prototyped will need to be planned with the developers to decide where it will be done, who will be involved, and what is the aim of each prototype.

- Provision of hands-on experience should be made available to you wherever possible, to permit some feel for the system.

- Experience of each prototype should be subject to reviews in the same way as are all other products of SSADM.

- Tight control is essential to avoid endless prototyping. The number of prototypes should be agreed in advance, and what problems each is to address. This can, of course, be changed, but there should be an initial target rather than a 'see how it goes' approach.

There are many different forms of prototyping. The more usual ones are now discussed.

Prototype Screen Design

This is the simplest form of prototyping. It can be done in Stage 1 of SSADM for obtaining a quick overview of the system as it will be seen by you, and is also useful to the developers in giving an early idea of the system size.

In Stage 2 it can be used as an aid to the selection of a Business System Option.

In Stage 3 it provides a means of establishing and refining input and output requirements with users. It can then be done as part of the task of establishing menus, command structures and dialogues. This use is described in Step 350.

It should be noted that the screen formats in the operational system may differ in appearance from the prototypes because of restrictions/facilities in the software finally used. These differences should be discussed with you as they arise, before any software is purchased that would require basic changes from that shown in the prototypes.

Business Simulation

As with screen design, the business simulation is used to help clarify requirements. It shows how it is proposed (or understood) that you will interact with the system. It would typically be done as part of the process of selecting a Business System Option, and again at Step 350.

A demonstration system looks like a working system, but operates on data structures that are unlikely to be those that will form a part of the finished system. It may hold records in memory rather than access them from the disk files that will be used in the actual implementation. It may do no processing, but merely present screens with the information preset within them. There are many possibilities, depending on the information that is to be established and the software that is available.

You will need to be aware that the performance of a prototype may be very different from that of the actual system. Beware of making unrealistic performance assumptions about the final system. The instantaneous response possible on a business simulation is unlikely to be matched by an eventual multi-user system contending for resources with other systems running on the computer at the same time, and accessing a database that is nearing its capacity. Developers may build time delays into a prototype to avoid giving a false impression. You will need to check this point with them.

Technical Simulation

A technical simulation is used to verify the practical feasibility of proposed design solutions, for example, to check:

- the successful transmission and reception of messages over a communications link;

- response times during a preliminary saturation test, for example to ensure that the system can cope with simultaneous transmissions from all terminals;

- that recovery mechanisms work correctly;

- that operation of a new piece of software is fully understood.

Technical simulation is most likely to be of use after selection of the technical option. It will require use of the actual equipment and systems software for the item under test, but will probably require little of the application software. You may be involved in some aspects of the simulation, and would no doubt hear of the results, but this work is primarily of interest to the developers (unless it shows the solution to be inadequate, in which case you may well be involved in reconsideration of the technical option).

If the tests are for file or database access, they must have been preceded by Relational Data Analysis.

Minimal Functional Prototype

A minimal working system is one with some program logic but with restricted capabilities. It may:

- accept no complications in the data;

- have no validation;

- be lacking in functions;

- have no security or recovery routines.

Typically it can do some straightforward processing of valid input data and maintain some of the data files. Anything complex will be beyond its scope. Depending on its capabilities it could be the first implementation of an evolutionary development strategy. In practice it is unlikely to be usable for live work because of the number of short cuts that will have been taken. Its main purposes are:

- to help in establishing the requirements;

- to provide you with early experience in the use of the system.

Intermediate Functional Prototypes

Intermediate prototypes are developed when it is the intention to reach the final system via a number of prototypes. They are the alternative to throwing the prototypes away when they have served the purpose of helping to establish requirements, and continuing with the development of the system by other means. It can be a useful approach if the system is likely to be subject to an exceptionally high rate of change.

When using this approach, consideration should have been given to making the first (or an early) prototype into a framework on which the system can be built, so ideally it should contain full:

- security;
- backup and recovery;
- audit and control.

Greater functionality can then be gradually added in successive prototypes.

The distinction between prototyping and evolutionary development is rather blurred with intermediate prototypes. At some stage the final prototype will be the basic evolutionary system. Trying to draw a line between the two is an academic rather than a practical exercise.

COPING WITH CHANGE

Introduction

For too long, the modification of systems after implementation (maintenance) has been regarded as a frustrating add-on at the end of system development, diverting the technical staff from their 'real' task of developing new systems. In reality, maintenance is a necessary and unavoidable phase within the system life cycle, as every system must adapt to changes in perception and circumstance.

The effort in maintaining a transaction processing system with a 10 year life can easily be double the initial development effort. Systems that need high maintenance can engulf the staff with so much work that they have little time for anything else.

The real problem is one of attitude and approach. Accepting the inevitability of change, the requirement is to ensure that work expended on it is used effectively and not in thrashing about in an unstructured and incomprehensible mess. This being so, the entire development procedure should be geared to cope with the fact and to accept the inevitable change with the minimum of disruption. In other words, systems should be developed from the start with a view to changing them in the future.

SSADM helps to get the system as right as possible in the first place by:

- close user involvement;

- structured techniques of analysis and design;

- inspection of every deliverable.

The use of SSADM thus gives well-designed systems into which the inevitable changes can be built in the most effective way, but designing for change in itself is insufficient to solve the maintenance problem. To achieve low maintenance, the strategy should be to develop for change, ie to consider the problem of change throughout the whole of the development life cycle. Superb design will not rescue an inadequate specification and will be destroyed by badly constructed programs.

Strategy

- start with consideration of corporate objectives to ensure that the right systems are developed in the right sequence;

- start each project with a Feasibility Study;

- use the evolutionary approach: the speedy implementation of small increments, with relatively short development times for each sub system, cuts down the number of changes required during the development process;

- use prototyping where appropriate;

- take positive action to achieve simplicity (or face up to the problems inherent in complexity).

Anticipation

Many changes can be anticipated by making a critical examination of requirements to consider what may change within the system, why, and when. Demands may be imposed by legislation, or by replacement or enhancement of hardware or software.

Future changes may also be anticipated by consideration of:

- items in the Requirements Catalogue that may be deferred from the initial implementation;

- possible future variation of the computer system boundary as established in the DFDs of the Business System Option.

Questions to be asked that might help in anticipation of change are:

- Is any data outside the control of the company? (payroll is just one of the systems that regularly have to be changed because of new legislation).

- Is any data supplied to external organisations? (eg to the Inland Revenue, Customs and Excise, Department of Social Security, Bankers Automated Clearing Service, University Central Council for Admissions).

- Any of the data may change, but which is most vulnerable, and what could cause the most trouble? (Probably the greatest difficulty would be by any change to the format or length of a record key, and this should be considered in relation to the size of the system at the end of its planned life – perhaps ten or more years ahead).

- How could the information in the system be usefully combined with that in any other system?

- What is known of possible changes to systems with which this one will interface?

- How might the organisation and method of working of the users vary in future?

Any future requirements that can be anticipated, can be built into the high level logical design, but not carried forward into the detailed/physical design. This ensures that the developed system has ready built hooks for the future enhancements.

Control

Requests for change during the life of the system should be carefully controlled to ensure that:

- the benefits are worth the costs;

- the changes can be justified when compared with changes needed to other systems and other developments;

- the work is done in the best sequence.

This is a corporate rather than just a user or a computer department responsibility and should be controlled at the appropriate level. A senior manager in the user department could be appointed as owner of the system, with responsibility for assessing the costs and benefits of the proposed changes. At least one company requires such senior managers to make the case for changes at Board level.

The Payoff

A low maintenance policy has many advantages. Besides saving costs in the change process itself, a saving will also be made in time. As changes are implemented more quickly, they start to benefit the company at a much earlier date. The savings are thus twofold:

- the change process costs less;
- the benefits are realised earlier.

Clearly, design for change should be a fundamental aim. With maintenance levels that are often more than 50 percent of total effort, the rewards accruing from such a policy are potentially immense.

AVOIDING COMPLEXITY

The best way of dealing with complexity is to avoid it.

For all practical purposes, perfection is unattainable; simplicity is not. But people, in their search for perfection, often lose sight of simplicity – and they pay heavily for it. The all-singing, all-dancing system may be fine as a concept, but its costs are high. An unfortunate truth for you is that the more you want a system to do, the more it will cost and the longer it will take to develop.

Computers can do whatever is precisely defined for them, but the costs of ambitiously over-complex systems can be immense and take virtually forever to develop. Indefinite waits and escalating costs can drive companies to the verge of bankruptcy.

Complex systems are difficult to specify, difficult to design, difficult to program, well-nigh impossible to test exhaustively, and in consequence tend to be subject to much change as problems arise. Unfortunately they are then found to be difficult to understand and as a result difficult to maintain. This should not inhibit your first go at your 'wish list' as noted in the Requirements Catalogue (Chapter 13), but it will be something for you to keep in mind when you are deciding what the first implementation of the system is to do.

So I would like to encourage you to actively seek simplification. Does the system really have to cope with everything, no matter how obscure, or how seldom it happens? Pareto's Law (mentioned earlier in the chapter under *Guidelines for Evolutionary Development*), suggests that 20 per cent of the facilities provided by a system would take 80 percent of the effort to develop. Experience suggests that this law does indeed apply. Certainly much more effort normally goes into designing a system that attempts to cater for all eventualities than would be needed if the computer system was designed to identify for manual action say up to 20 percent of the 'funnies'.

Cost/benefit and system acceptability are obviously involved and would probably make a 20 percent rejection rate impractical. However, human involvement in the more complex areas of the system can save a great deal of effort, as well as leading to greater job satisfaction for users. The boundary where the line is drawn between the human and the computer elements of the system can be of critical importance to time, cost, and subsequent ease of change.

This is an area that requires negotiation. Some trade-offs will almost certainly be needed between facilities, qualities, costs and time.

SYSTEM TESTING

Quality control, applied during the use of SSADM, should continue throughout the ubsequent development procedures. Whilst this should have picked up most of the errors and misunderstandings, inevitably some will get through.

Before the system is implemented it should go through stringent testing. Testing is all too often skimped – it becomes an early casualty of over-optimistic estimates of time and cost. If your project has been running late, then you should keep as close an eye as you can manage on what testing is being done.

If you were conscientious and thorough with your involvement in the analysis of your system, the developers will have had a solid structure from which to work. You have sown the seeds of success. That doesn't mean that success will automatically follow without any further effort on your part. You have said what the system must do, and how well it must do it. You must now ensure that what you are being given does, in fact, match up with your specification. This requires your involvement in system testing.

Testing is done at several levels, mostly within the computer department, but one in which you are totally involved is Acceptance Testing. You should expect to be responsible for this, with suitable guidance from the developers. It will be as a result of your experience with these tests that you will decide whether to accept the system. The tests should be carried out on test data prepared to your requirements (and this must be the agreed requirements, not any ideas that may have occurred later).

You must define the testing that you require. This should include:

- a complete test of data entry and acceptance procedures;
- a test of all conceivable error conditions, including reporting in a clearly understandable way with precise identification of the error, and correction and resubmission procedures;
- tests of the security arrangements against illegal access, particularly where there could be any chance of someone outside the organisation obtaining access to the system over public telephone lines (hacking);
- forced failure of the system to test the recovery and/or rerun procedures;

- tests to ensure that the levels of performance that you have specified are being achieved; this must be done in a normal operating situation, with other systems running on the computer whilst the tests are in progress, as they will be when the system goes live, ie when it is handed over to you;
- saturation tests to check that performance is adequate with all on-line devices installed and sending data to the system at the same time;
- tests to ensure that the system can cope with the anticipated volume of data with a satisfactory response at times of peak pressure (peak pressure within your system, and also peak pressure of other systems which may be running concurrently on the same computer hardware);
- tests that all the controls built into the system are returning the correct results;
- tests to check every output that the system should provide;
- tests by the auditors that the agreed facilities are all present in the system and are operating as required.

In addition to specifying the data that you wish to input to the system, you will also need to specify the results you expect from each of the tests.

You must be realistic about the time that this work will cost you. It is a non-trivial task. It entails:

- Devoting time to thinking about all the things that you want to test. The Requirements Catalogue will form the basis for these.
- Preparing specifications for the test data.
- Entering the data yourself for on-line elements of the system.
- Checking the results.
- Repeating tests when you are not satisfied with the initial results.
- If the tests include parallel running, you will need the time and manpower for the input to your current system, input to the new system, comparison of results, resolution of queries, and re-input to one or both systems.

It is worth devoting time to consideration of problems and how and why they occurred. This is not with a view to apportioning blame, but to learn the lessons for future use.

SYSTEM IMPLEMENTATION

When the system has successfully passed the tests it will be implemented, ie it will be ready to go into operation. This can be a traumatic time for all concerned. Adequate planning will take much of the pain out of this process. Plans for the eventual implementation should be considered at an early stage in the development process. You must think about:

Data conversion planning

It is stating the obvious to say that data must be in the system before the system can operate. Nevertheless, the potential magnitude of the task could catch you unprepared. It may be necessary for you or your people to enter some, or even all, of the data yourselves. Your existing work may have to continue whilst this is being done. You will need to ensure that sufficient effort is available when needed, both to enter the data and to resolve the inevitable errors and queries thrown up by the system. It may be possible for you to spread the data entry over a fairly lengthy period whilst other parts of the system are still under development.

In many cases, data required by the system will already be available in machine-readable form, either in other systems or in an existing version of the system you have been redeveloping. Existing data may be converted by program to the format needed by the new system, and thus save much of the manual work that would otherwise be required (but it will require effort to prepare the conversion program). However, you must be prepared for the queries that will inevitably arise. The application of further validation to existing data will undoubtedly find discrepancies that may have lain hidden for years.

System implementation planning

An Implementation Plan should cover such considerations as:

- how the system will be implemented, eg:
  - phased versus all at once;
  - pilot running, perhaps in one department rather than in the whole organisation;
  - parallel running, ie alongside your existing system, and taking into account the extra work that will be involved (a time limit should be set for parallel running);
- when the system will be implemented, ie a schedule covering the tasks involved;
- identification of the people/departments involved, and their responsibilities;

human factors – people must be prepared for change and involved in planning, office layout, etc;

- provision of training, to cover computer familiarity as well as all the tasks for which users will be responsible.

Epilogue

This book did not set out to make you an expert in SSADM. Only a training course and practical experience can do that. But you should now be well on your way to being an expert in self defence against the experts. Hopefully, though, your experience will be one of co-operation rather than confrontation, and the systems you develop together should prove to be both better and more cost effective that ones developed in the 'traditional' environment.

SSADM, as you have seen, provides a framework on which facts can be hung as they are found during a system investigation, with cross-checks that will have given a coherent specification with no loose ends hanging around. If a need has been recognised and rated sufficiently highly, it will have been built into the system.

The close liaison between yourself and the developers throughout the project will ensure that there should be no nasty surprises for you when the system is implemented.

Quality control will have picked up most of the errors and misunderstandings.

The system will be well structured and documented so that future change is as easy as it can be to accommodate.

But SSADM will only help so far. It won't manage itself. For example, a project control system must be in place or costs will escalate.

Without effective management it is possible to continue interminably around the system investigation tasks. SSADM cannot prevent this from happening – only the manager can do that.

Senior management interest and commitment are needed, which doesn't mean their involvement in the detail, but it does need it in setting objectives, checking progress, and ensuring that objectives are being met.

A criticism sometimes levelled against SSADM is the amount of effort that goes into analysis and design. There are several points to be made:

- The things that are done in SSADM have to be done somewhere in the development process. If they are done later they are likely to cost a lot more.

- Taking three different viewpoints of the system takes more time initially, but elicits more information. There is a saving in testing, implementation and maintenance.

- Much time goes on quality checking. True, but you do want good quality, don't you? Again this is more than compensated for by more reliable systems, and by savings at implementation and on maintenance.

So the method helps to derive as complete a picture as the developers are likely to get of what is required from a system.

SSADM can be summed up as being a good method, arguably better than most, widely used, well supported, thoroughly documented in the publicly available *SSADM Manual,* taught by many organisations, under permanent review to ensure that it incorporates generally accepted best practices, and is well on the way to becoming a *de facto* standard. Should anyone expect more of a data processing analysis and design method?

With SSADM you don't tell the analysts what you want and then sit back optimistically, hopefully, expectantly, pessimistically or any other way, depending on your previous experience of systems development. You roll up your sleeves and accept that you are going to be deeply involved throughout. There is no other way that will make it *your* system rather than one that is imposed on you. So please be ready to be involved and regard this as a necessary part of your work – not an interruption of it. You will get the system you deserve. That is both a threat and a promise. You will have to take many decisions – subjective ones as well as the objective ones. You will inevitably have problems while you get on the right side of the learning curve, but no one said it it was going to be easy.

Good luck with your SSADM projects!

Appendix 1
References

Albrecht A J, Gaffney J E, Software function. source lines of code, and development effort predictions: a software science validation, *IEE Transactions on Software Engineering,* Vol SE–9, No.6, pp 639–648, November 1983.

Behrens C A, Measuring the productivity of computer systems development activites with function points, *IEE Transactions on Software Engineering,* Vol SE–9, No 6, pp 648–652, November 1983.

Boehm B, *Software Engineering, IEE Transactions on Computers,* Vol C–25 December 1976.

Boehm B W, *Software Engineering Economics,* Prentice Hall, 1981.

Brooks F P, *The Mythical Man–Month – Essays on Software Engineering,* Addison–Wesley Publishing Company, 1975.

Fagan M E, *Design and Code Inspections to Reduce Errors in Program Development,* IBM Systems Journal, Vol 15, No 3, 1976.

Gilb T, *Principles of Software Engineering Management,* Addison–Wesley Publishing Company, 1988.

Ingevaldsson L, *JSP – a Practical Method of Program Design,* Chartwell-Bratt, 1980.

Jackson M A, *Principles of Program Design,* Academic Press, 1975.

Longworth, G, *Getting the System You Want: A User's Guide to SSADM, (Version 3),* NCC Publications, 1989.

Longworth G, *Introducing SSADM Version 4,* NCC Blackwell Ltd, 1992.

Longworth G, Nicholls D P, *SSADM Manual, (Version 3),* NCC Publications, 1986.

Longworth G, Nicholls D P, Abbott J, *SSADM Developer's Handbook, (Version 3),* NCC Publications, 1988.

Miller G, *The Magical Number Seven, Plus or Minus Two: Some Limits on Our Capacity for Processing Information,* Psychology Rev, 63(2), 1956.

Mumford E, Pettigrew A, *Implementing Strategic Decisions,* Longman, 1975.

NCC, *SSADM Manual Version 4,* NCC Blackwell Ltd, 1990.

Nicholls D P, *Introducing SSADM, (Version 3),* NCC Publications, 1987.

PA Computers and Telecommunications, *Benefits of Software Engineering Methods and Tools: A Study for the Department of Trade and Industry,* Department of Trade and Industry, 1985.

Peters L J *Software Design: Methods and Techniques,* Yourdon Inc, 1981.

Proctor I M, *Project Management and Control Manual,* NCC Publications, 1988.

Putnam L H, Tutorial: *Software Cost – Estimating and Life Cycle Control,* IEEE, 1980.

Skidmore S, Farmer R, Mill G, *SSADM: Models and Methods, (Version 4),* NCC Blackwell Ltd, 1992.

Appendix 2
SSADM forms

Samples of the SSADM forms referred to in the test as involving you, have been included in this appendix in form number order. They are printed in bold in the list below. There are other forms which are used by the developers. These are also listed, but in lighter type, and they are not included. You will find that all of the forms are mentioned in the Stage diagrams in Chapters 15 to 21.

Packs of the forms are available from the National Computing Centre Limited.

	Form No
Attribute/Data Item Description	**1**
Command Structure	2
Context Diagram	**3**
Data Flow Diagram Level 1	**4**
Data Flow Diagram – Lower Level	**5**
DBMS Data Storage Classification	6
DBMS Performance Classification	7
Dialogue Control Table	8
Dialogue Element Descriptions	9
Dialogue Level Help	10

Attribute/Data Item Description

SSADM Version 4

Project/System	Author	Date	Version	Status	Page of

Attribute/data item name	Attribute/data item ID
Cross-reference name/ID	**Cross-reference type**

Synonym(s)

Description

Validation/derivation

Mandatory ☐ Default value	Optional ☐ Value for null
Logical format	Unit of Measure
Logical length	Length description

User role	Access rights

Owner

Standard messages

Notes

 SSADMv4 1

Context Diagram

VERSION 4

Project/System	Author	Date	Version	Status	Page of

Data Flow Diagram Level 1
Variant:

Project/System	Author	Date	Version	Status	Page of

Data Flow Diagram - Lower Level

Variant:

SSADM Version 4

Project/System	Author	Date	Version	Status	Page of

Document Flow Diagram

SSADM Version 4

Project/System	Author	Date	Version	Status	Page of

SSADMv4 12

Effect Correspondence Diagram

SSADM Version 4

Project/System	Author	Date	Version	Status	Page of

Elementary Process Description

Variant:

SSADM Version 4

Project/System	Author	Date	Version	Status	Page of

Process ID/common processing ref	

Process name

Common processing cross-reference	

Description

SSADMv4 14

Enquiry Access Path

SSADM Version 4

Project/System	Author	Date	Version	Status	Page of

Entity Description - Part 1
Variant:

SSADM Version 4

Project/System	Author	Date	Version	Status	Page of

Entity name	Entity ID

Location	Occurrences		Average		Max

Description

Synonym(s)

Attribute name/ID	Primary key	Foreign key

Rel no	'must be'/ 'may be'	'either'/ 'or'	Link phrase	'one and only one'/ 'one or more'	Object entity name

Notes

SSADMv4 17

Entity Description - Part 2 **Variant:**					SSADM Version 4
Project/System	**Author**	**Date**	**Version**	**Status**	**Page of**
Entity name				Entity ID	
User role			Access rights		
Owner					
Growth per period					
Additional relationships					
Archive and destruction					
Security measures					
State indicator values					
Notes					

 SSADMv4 18

Entity Life History					SSADM Version 4
Project/System	**Author**	**Date**	**Version**	**Status**	**Page of**

SSADMv4 19

Event/Entity Matrix

SSADM Version 4

Project/System	Author	Date	Version	Status	Page of

Entity / Event																	

 SSADMv4 20

External Entity Description

Variant:

SSADM Version 4

Project/System	Author	Date	Version	Status	Page of

ID	Name	Description

SSADMv4 21

Function Definition

SSADM Version 4

Project/System	Author	Date	Version	Status	Page of

Function name	Function ID
Type	
User roles	
Function description	
Error handling	
DFD processes	
Events	Event frequency
I/O descriptions	
I/O structures	
Requirements Catalogue ref.	
Volumes	
Related functions	
Enquiries	Enquiry frequency
Common processing	
Dialogue names	

Service level requirements

Description	Target value	Range	Comments

 SSADMv4 22

Grouped Domain Description

SSADM Version 4

Project/System	Author	Date	Version	Status	Page of

Grouped domain name	Grouped domain ID

Synonym(s)

Description

Validation/derivation

Default value	Value for null
Logical format	Unit of measure
Logical length	Length description

User role	Access rights

Owner

Notes

 SSADMv4 25

I/O Descriptions

Variant:

SSADM Version 4

Project/System	Author	Date	Version	Status	Page of

From	To	Data flow name	Data content	Comments

 SSADMv4 26

I/O Structure Description SSADM Version 4

Project/System	Author	Date	Version	Status	Page of

Data flows represented

I/O structure element	Data item	Comments

 SSADMv4 27

I/O Structure Diagram

SSADM VERSION 4

Project/System	Author	Date	Version	Status	Page of

Logical Data Store/Entity Cross-reference

SSADM Version 4

Project/System	Author	Date	Version	Status	Page of

Logical data store	Entities

SSADMv4 29

Logical Data Structure
Variant:

SSADM Version 4

Project/System	Author	Date	Version	Status	Page of

RDA Working Paper

SSADM Version 4

Project/System	Author	Date	Version	Status	Page of

Source name

UNF		1NF	2NF	3NF	Result	
Attributes	Level				Relation	Attributes

 SSADMv4 40

Relationship Description

Variant:

VERSION 4

Project/System	**Author**	**Date**	**Version**	**Status of**	**Page**

Entity name	Entity ID

Mandatory ☐ Optional ☐ %Optional ☐

Link phase

Description

Synonmyn(s)

Object entity name	Object entity ID

One (1:) ☐	Many (m:) ☐	Minimum	Average	Maximum

Cardinality description

Growth per period

Additional properties

User role	Access rights

Owner

Notes

 SSADMv4 41

Requirements Catalogue Entry

SSADM VERSION 4

Project/System	Author	Date	Version	Status	Page of

Source	Priority	Owner	Requirement ID

Functional requirement

Non-functional requirement(s)

Description	Target value	Acceptable range	Comments

Benefits

Comments/suggested solutions

Related documents

Related requirements

Resolution

SSADMv4 42

Resource Flow Diagram

SSADM Version 4

Project/System	Author	Date	Version	Status	Page of

User Catalogue					SSADM Version 4
Project/System	**Author**	**Date**	**Version**	**Status**	**Page of**

Job title	Job activities description

 SSADMv4 45

User Role/Function Matrix

SSADM Version 4

Project/System	Author	Date	Version	Status	Page of

Functions

User roles

SSADMv4 46

User Roles

SSADM VERSION 4

Project/System	Author	Date	Version	Status	Page of

User role	Job title	Activities

Index